TROPICAL FISHES

The PocketExpert™ Guide Series
for Aquarists and Underwater Naturalists

All cover photographs by Aaron Norman
FRONT: Lake Tebera Rainbowfish
(*Melanotaenia herbertaxelrodi*), page 302.
BACK: Oscar (*Astronotus ocellatus)*, page 321.
Betta (*Betta splendens*), page 397.
Corydoras paleatus (Hifin Paleatus), page 224.
SPINE: Angelfish
(*Pterophyllum scalare*), page 377.

Produced and distributed by:
T.F.H. Publications, Inc.
One TFH Plaza
Third and Union Avenues
Neptune City, NJ 07753
www.tfh.com

TROPICAL FISHES

500+ ESSENTIAL-TO-KNOW SPECIES

MARY E. SWEENEY
MARY BAILEY
AARON NORMAN

MICROCOSM

tfh

PROFESSIONAL SERIES™

T.F.H. Publications
One T.F.H. Plaza
Third and Union Avenues
Neptune City, NJ 07753
www.tfh.com

Library of Congress Cataloging-in-Publication Data

Sweeney, Mary Ellen.
Tropical fishes : 500+ essential-to-know species / Mary E. Sweeney, Mary Bailey, Aaron Norman.
     p. cm. -- (A pocketexpert guide)
Includes bibliographical references and index.
ISBN 0-9820262-0-X
1. Tropical fish. I. Bailey, Mary. II. Norman, Aaron, 1929- III. Title.
SH457.S85 2009
639.34--dc22

                    2009004497

Designed by Linda Provost
Color separations by Digital Engine, Burlington, Vermont

Co-published by

T.F.H. Publications, Inc.
Neptune City, NJ 07753
www.tfh.com

Microcosm, Ltd.
P.O. Box 550
Charlotte, VT 05445
www.MicrocosmAquariumExplorer.com

This book is dedicated to Ray "Kingfish" Lucas,
with big hugs.

ACKNOWLEDGMENTS

MARY SWEENEY WOULD LIKE TO THANK the readers of this book. All the best to you in your fishkeeping hobby—where the heart and science can meet. Many thanks to Martin Thoene, Ad Koning, and Alan Rollings. I am extremely appreciative of the work of the Microcosm team, especially Linda Provost, Janice Heilmann, Judith Billard, and James Lawrence. Thanks also to all the folks at T.F.H. Publications, especially Glen Axelrod, for helping this effort come to fruition.

—*Mary Sweeney, Monmouth Hills, New Jersey*

MARY BAILEY WOULD LIKE TO THANK Daphne Layley and Ian Fuller for invaluable advice on catfishes; all the aquarists and ichthyologists who have shared their knowledge and love of fishes with her for more years than she cares to admit; and her family, especially Henderson, for putting up with erratic mealtimes during the writing of this book.

—*Mary Bailey, East Village, Devon, England*

CONTENTS

FAMILY & SPECIES ACCOUNTS

THIS BOOK IS NOT INTENDED TO TELL THE READER HOW to keep fishes in general—there are plenty of excellent aquarium books on that subject, one or two of them listed in the bibliography at the end. There are also plenty of aquarium "picture-books" that show what a myriad of ornamental fishes look like, in glorious technicolor, but with little information on their care. Our objective is to bridge the gap, by providing specific information on individual species of fishes that are likely to be encountered in aquarium stores. Thus, armed with a basic knowledge of how to set up and maintain a basic aquarium, the aquarist can go one step further and either choose fishes suited to his particular tank size, water parameters, and so forth, or tailor the aquarium to suit the needs of the fishes that catch his particular interest.

It is perhaps appropriate to remind that every single fish is different, even if only slightly so. Some are very different and quite incompatible, either because they have specific environmental requirements and will not thrive, or maybe even die, if these are not met; or because other aspects such as size and behavior make combining them a disaster waiting to happen. Some fishes feed on other, smaller, fishes, and even a slow-moving, gentle giant of a herbivore represents a source of considerable fear (and stress) to a smaller fish whose every instinct is to stay out of the way of anything larger and possibly predatory. Some fishes have long graceful finnage, but others will snap at anything that drifts past their mouths, including long fins. Some fishes become alarmed at sudden rapid movement, and are best not housed with hyperactive species prone to sudden dashes across the tank. Some fishes routinely sold for aquaria are completely unsuitable as they grow far too large. But at the same time, some fishes often regarded as requiring highly specialized culture—and so reserved for experts—will do extremely well in a novice's community tank, some killifishes, for example.

Hence this book endeavors to point out not only the special needs of any particular fish, but also its compatibility with other species and which ones. It also provides the maximum size (Total

Leopold's Angel can be kept with Discus. It is one of many aquarium myths that Discus and Angelfish cannot be kept in the same aquarium.

Length = TL) for each species and any bad habits to be expected. Conveniently pocket-sized, it can be taken with you to the store, so you can check out any potential purchase before parting with your money, rather than finding out an expensive or disastrous mistake when you get home. Alternatively, you can use it to plan your aquarium population, or to dream of how you will one day fill a whole fish-room if your first aquarium spawns a host of others as your interest expands.

Hyphessobrycon eques. These small schooling fish make a splendid display because of their movement and color.

Trichogaster leeri. Pearl Gouramis are brilliantly colored and very elegant fish. They can be a little dominant, so they should be "top dog" in the tank.

Water Parameters

First and foremost, you need to be aware of the water parameters in your tank—temperature range, pH, and hardness. A remarkable number of aquarists stop at temperature and have no idea of their water chemistry, yet awareness of these details is the key to healthy fishes and successful breeding.

Temperature. The temperature ranges provided are those the fish in question is known to normally tolerate in the wild and/or in the aquarium. In most cases where the range is wide, the upper and lower extremes are best avoided, in the long term at least. They are what the fish can survive, not what it enjoys! Fishes kept too cool are

Because of their social habits, many cichlids may require more space than their size would seem to dictate.

likely to be sluggish, and sooner or later unhealthy, and are unlikely to breed. Fishes kept too warm will have to work their gills harder than nature intended to get enough oxygen, and may be uncomfortable and stressed.

Consider the temperature range in conjunction with the geographical range of the species, using an atlas if necessary. If the fish lives between the Tropic of Cancer and the Tropic of Capricorn, it will probably experience a relatively small annual temperature variation except when the cooling rains come and during the height of the dry season. But if it lives outside the tropics—as is the case in aquarium fishes from Paraguay and Argentina—it will experience seasons like those in the USA and Europe. Some "tropical" fishes experience frosts in the wild. Likewise fishes from mountain streams in the tropics usually prefer conditions cooler to their cousins at identical latitudes on the plains below. Whether the habitat is shaded or not, the water level at which the fish lives can make a difference. Many Amazonian catfishes need water a few degrees cooler than characins from the same river, simply because they live on the bottom where the sun doesn't penetrate. Many species experience a rise in temperature seasonally and this helps stimulate breeding, and an increase in temperature is often used as a trigger for breeding in the aquarium.

pH and hardness. These data should again be regarded as maximum ranges that the fish will tolerate, with the optimum being towards the middle of the range.

Hardness is measured in German degrees (°dGH) as these are the units now used by most aquarists and test kits. One "German degree" is equivalent to 17.9 parts per million (ppm) or milligrams per liter (mg/l) of calcium carbonate ($CaCO_3$). But it is important to be aware that there are different types of degrees of hardness—U.S., Clark (UK), and French—that represent different ppm measurements, and in the case of French it is calcium oxide (CaO) that is measured.

Generally speaking, pH is the more important parameter. Hardness measures only one element of the dissolved salts in the water, and is only a rough guideline. Most hardwater fishes will not react badly to soft water as long as the pH is appropriate. By contrast, however, many softwater fishes do not do well in hard water.

Salinity. We have not given any salinity figures for those species that require the addition of salt (sodium chloride, $NaCl$) as most such fishes are subject to tidal influences and hence the salinity varies continually.

Water quality. We have given indications of water quality requirements only where these are particularly critical and special measures may be required. It should go without saying that even if a fish lives in a putrid swamp in nature, the aquarist should always provide the best quality water that can be reasonably achieved.

Ancistrus sp. The bristlenose catfishes are aptly named as the snouts of males in particular are adorned with bizarre "tentacles."

Sizes

All measurements (fishes and tanks) are given in American and metric units.

Fish sizes. These are the Total Length (TL) of the fish, from tip of snout to tip of tail. It must be borne in mind that some fishes, e.g. stingrays, are more tail than fish, but even so it is total length rather than body or Standard Length (SL) that is most relevant when considering tank size, as the fish should be able to move around freely without its tail constantly contacting the glass. Note too that tank-bred fishes often grow larger than their wild counterparts because of a richer food supply. Our data are based on maximum known sizes, which may be for tank-bred or wild-caught fish depending on whether or not they have been bred regularly and reared. Thus an adult wild specimen may not grow as large as its tank-bred counterpart, but equally a species known only as wild may grow larger if bred and reared.

Fish lengths are given in both inches and centimeters. Unfortunately comparative measurements of this type rarely equate to whole numbers, so for larger fishes (and aquarium sizes) we have approximated to the nearest sensible whole number, as the difference isn't critical. For smaller fishes a greater degree of accuracy is desirable, so we have worked to the nearest quarter inch and half centimeter.

Betta splendens. Inexpensive, hardy, and personable, this is an ideal fish to start with in the aquarium hobby.

Colossoma macropomum (above) and *Pseudoplatystoma fasciatus* (right). Both of these fishes require huge aquaria and long-term commitment.

Tank sizes. There has always been some international variation in "standard" sizes depending on whether imperial (inches) or metric (centimeters) units are used. The advent of all-glass construction has meant that any size is feasible, and "standard" sizes may vary from country to country or even from manufacturer to manufacturer. Hence the sizes we quote are not writ in stone, they are guidelines. Length is the most important criterion, and if possible our lengths should be regarded as the minimum. The other dimensions are more flexible as long as the fish can turn around comfortably and doesn't protrude from the water!

We have also quoted tank volumes as some tanks are sold in this way rather than by dimensions, as water volume is the important criterion in the marine hobby. Often these standard volumes are round numbers (e.g. to the nearest 5 gallons or 10 liters) rather

The Oscar, *Astronotus ocellatus*, semi-albino form. These are personable and endearing cichlids. They are sold small, and grow big.

than exact figures and are greater than the dimensions of the tank permit! For freshwater fishes, however, surface or bottom area is more important, as for many community aquaria the optimum population density is calculated from combined total length of fishes relative to surface area, and for some fishes (notably cichlids) available territory (bottom area) is the deciding factor. We suggest taking a tape measure when purchasing a tank.

The gallons cited are US gallons. It may be useful to know that 1 US gallon = 0.8 Imperial gallons = 3.79 liters.

Systematics and taxonomy

SYSTEMATICS IS THE SCIENCE OF DETERMINING THE RELATION-SHIPS of living things, and taxonomy is the science of naming them. The two are closely linked, and are often confused and used interchangeably. Neither is static: As scientists learn more about relationships, errors are detected and corrected, which often involves changing the name of the plant or animal. The advent of the use of DNA study in systematics has meant that changes have become more frequent.

Systematics and taxonomy work largely on a consensus basis. If all the workers in a particular field are happy with a change, it is accepted. But sometimes there are disputes that may take years to resolve. Sometimes only part of a group of animals or plants can be reclassified at one time (because of the sheer volume of work involved), and this leaves some species in a sort of limbo, where their "old" name is known to be wrong but nobody has as yet given them a new one. There are even disagreements about the overall

Peckoltia sp. Often fishes are imported before they are named by science. Importers use a temporary numbering system to describe the fishes.

Rasboras are generally ideal for the community aquarium. Schooling fishes seldom cause trouble with tankmates.

structure of the "family tree" of living things. We have had to negotiate this minefield to produce something that is as correct as possible without getting involved in disputes.

The order in which fish families are presented is an area where authorities vary in their views. We have largely followed Nelson (1984), except where this would split up what aquarists have traditionally regarded as a unit (e.g. African killifishes). Likewise we have sometimes used familiar hobby terms, e.g. "characins" for a variety of tetras and piranhas, even though these are not strictly correct scientifically. While we have made extensive use of Fishbase for up-to-date taxonomy, we have tried to stay out of disputes as far as possible. And where a species is currently in limbo, we have unashamedly continued to use the "wrong" name that everyone knows.

For each species we cite the scientific name with author and date, and what we believe to be the most frequently used common name. If there are several we have listed them as well, though we do not claim such lists to be exhaustive. If a fish is well known to aquarists under a previous scientific name, now incorrect, we give that name as a common name, but without italics. We hope that our efforts will enable readers to match the fishes we are writing about to those to be found in shops, hobby magazines, and older literature.

Read around the subject

OFTEN THERE IS TOO MUCH INFORMATION ABOUT A SPECIES TO fit into the format used in this book. In such cases the most important points are given. Much more can be learned by reading the texts for other, similar, species, and in some cases we refer the reader to these. Where we discuss a series of similar fishes, for

Serrasalmus geryi. Holland's Piranha is one of the piranhas that can be kept in groups—with care, by experienced aquarists.

example, *Corydoras* catfishes and killifishes, you will find a thread running through the set, so instead of repeating the same information for each species, we have started with the basics and then added different additional data and tips for each species.

There is an important lesson to be learned here. Every time you read about a fish you will learn something, even if it isn't immediately relevant to those swimming in your tank at present. After a while you will realize that maybe what is known to apply to fish A could equally apply to fish B, which has features in common but is virtually unknown to hobbyists, or is uncommon so not often discussed in the literature. Even if you have no intention of ever

Microgeophagus ramirezi. The ram is a dwarf cichlid, and one of the most beloved of aquarium fishes.

Notobranchius kafuensis. There are many species of killifish. This makes them favorites with aquarists who specialize in one type of fish.

keeping a species of fish, if you read about it you may learn something useful about fishes in general. So, just because you are "into" African cichlids, for example, don't just ignore information on other fishes that comes your way.

This book covers only a handful of the tropical freshwater fishes that exist, there are thousands more. Some groups—cichlids, catfishes, and killifishes in particular—have attracted the attention of specialist aquarists, and this has in turn spawned specialist books. Some of the best of these are listed in the bibliography at the end of this book, and we recommend them to anyone who finds they are developing a taste for something more challenging than a community tank in the living room. We must stress: You can never read too much! At the same time a warning: books are usually written by experts, but the same is not true of everything you may read on the Internet. If in doubt, a good book by an expert is usually the more reliable source.

We hope you enjoy reading our little book and find it helpful. Happy fishkeeping!

Potamotrygon motoro (Müller & Henle, 1841)
Motoro Ray (Ocellate River Stingray, Black River Stingray)

Overview: Motoro Rays are timid bottom-dwellers. They have no swimbladders, so like sharks, they move constantly. The spikes of the tail fall out and regrow several times each year. The spikes are venomous and inflict a painful injury which requires a trip to the emergency room.

Native Range: Uruguay, Paraná-Paraguay, Orinoco, and Amazon river basins.

Maximum Length: 40 in (100 cm) TL.

Water: 75–78°F (24–26°C); pH: 6.0–6.8; hardness: 10°dGH.

Min. Tank Size: 1000 gal | 96x72x34 in (3785 L | 240x18x86 cm).

Feeding: Live fish, clams, mussels, bloodworms, shrimp, aquatic insects; can be trained to take frozen foods and even pellets.

Behavior & Care: Water quality must be perfect at all times with this very sensitive fish. A dark, fine substrate enhances color and is in keeping with the wild habitat, where the rays partially bury themselves in the sandy substrate. Use low light over the tank.

Breeding: Motoro Rays are livebearers whose breeding is stimulated by changes in the water. They breed at the end of the rainy season when food is plentiful, having 1–8 pups in a litter.

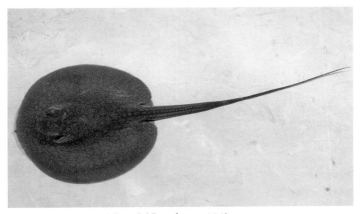

Potamotrygon orbignyi (Günther, 1880)
Reticulated Stingray (Teacup Stingray, Potamotrygon Reticulatus)

Overview: *P. orbignyi* is one of the more common rays in the hobby. Geographical variations produce an array of colors and patterns.

Native Range: Amazon and Orinoco river basins, Surinam, Guyana and Guiana.

Maximum Length: 12 in (30 cm) TL.

Water: 75–80°F (24–26°C); pH: 6.8–7.5; hardness: 0–10°dGH.

Min. Tank Size: 150 gal | 72x18x28 in (565 L | 180x45x70 cm).

Feeding: When it is small, this ray must be tempted to feed. Breeding small, clean feeder fish from quarantined parents produces great live food for rays. Gut-pack the live bait with vitamins and good food for extra nutrition for the ray. Supplement diet with other meaty fare such as ghost shrimp and blackworms. Remove uneaten foods. Do not underestimate nutritional requirements.

Behavior & Care: Though a small ray, it still must have significant amounts of meaty foods, which in turn, require highly efficient filtration as the animals are exquisitely sensitive to ammonia, nitrite, and even nitrate. Use a soft, sandy substrate where the ray will hide.

Breeding: Has been accomplished. Males are rough with females.

Protopterus dolloi Boulenger, 1900
Spotted African Lungfish (Slender Lungfish)

Overview: Eel-like in appearance, this lungfish is a powerful animal. It shows a brownish base color overlaid with dark splotches. The bases of the dorsal and anal fins are long, and the pectoral fins are threadlike. The blue eyes are very small. In nature, they aestivate, balling up and burying themselves in the mud until the rains return. This is not necessary in the aquarium.

Native Range: Ogowe, Kouilou-Niari, lower and middle Congo river basins.

Maximum Length: 51 in (130 cm) TL.

Water: 75–86°F (25–30°C); pH: 6.5–7.5; hardness: 6–16°dGH.

Min. Tank Size: 210 gal | 72x24x29 in (780 L | 180x60x72.5 cm).

Feeding: Highly carnivorous and predatory, this lungfish takes live foods: fishes, insects, worms. Can be trained to take beef heart.

Behavior & Care: This is an aggressive fish that will bite its keeper. Keep this fish in a large, heavily planted tank with a fine sand substrate. They are messy eaters and like to dig, so highly efficient filtration is required.

Breeding: Has not been bred in captivity. In the wild, the female lays large eggs in holes that the male guards with great attention.

Erpetoichthys calabaricus Smith, 1865
Reedfish (Ropefish)

Overview: The Reedfish is an olive to yellowish color with a yellow underside and dark spots at the base of the dorsal fin. It is snakelike in appearance, without ventral fins, and with serrated dorsal and anal fins. It is not a good community fish, and is recommended only for aquarists with a special affinity.

Native Range: Ogun River mouth in Nigeria to Chiloango River in Congo Brazzaville.

Maximum Length: 14 in (37 cm) TL.

Water: 72–82°F (22–28°C); pH: 6.0–8.0; hardness: 5–19°dGH.

Min. Tank Size: 65 gal | 48x18x18 in (240 L | 120x45x45 cm).

Feeding: This is a nocturnal carnivore feeding on an assortment of living foods: fishes, worms, insects, etc, and meaty items like beef heart.

Behavior & Care: Slow-moving, brackish waters are home to this fish that tolerates low oxygen levels and can temporarily live out of water. This accomplished escape artist requires a tight-fitting cover. Provide hiding places with rocks, wood, and pipes. Use a sandy substrate and tough plants. Leave open swimming space.

Breeding: Not reported in the aquarium.

Polypterus delhezi Boulenger, 1899
Delhezi Bichir (Barred Bichir, Armored Bichir)

Overview: This primitive, carnivorous fish lives in streams, lakes, and flood zones. Captive-bred specimens are commonly available, but lack the color quality of the wild-caught specimens. The upper body is light brown to olive in color with touches of green or yellow. There are 7–8 dark vertical bands and 10–13 dorsal finlets. The mouth is relatively small.

Native Range: Central basin of the Congo River.

Maximum Length: 18 in (45 cm) TL.

Water: 78–82°F (26–28°C); pH: 6.0–8.0; hardness: 6–16°dGH.

Min. Tank Size: 65 gal | 48x18x18 in (240 L | 120x45x45 cm).

Feeding: Delhezi will consume any fish that it can swallow as well as pellets, worms, and other meaty foods.

Behavior & Care: This fish is non-threatening to other large tankmates, but can be feisty with other bichirs. It's a jumper, so keep the aquarium well covered and the lid weighted down if possible. This is a very hardy fish if kept well fed and in excellent water quality.

Breeding: Commercial captive breeding programs are producing this bichir, but aquarium spawning has not been reported.

Polypterus ornatipinnis Boulenger, 1902
Ornate Bichir

Overview: A native of calm swamps and rivers, this is a solitary, noc-turnal, easy-going fish. The most attractive of the bichirs, the Ornate Bichir is commonly available, but pricey.

Native Range: Congo River basin, Lake Rukwa drainage, and Lake Tanganyika.

Maximum Length: 24 in (60 cm) TL.

Water: 78–82°F (26–28°C); pH: 7.0–8.0; hardness: 10–18°dGH.

Min. Tank Size: 90 gal | 48x18x24 in (320 L | 120x45x60 cm).

Feeding: Offer earthworms, shrimps, mussels, frozen meaty foods, and trout and catfish pellets. Feed every other evening.

Behavior & Care: External parasites, such as the fish leech, are a prob-lem for this species. Keep the Ornate Bichir in a clean tank with a sandy substrate and good hiding places and with a secure cover.

Breeding: The male wraps his body around the female, fertilizing the eggs that are held in their cupped fins. The eggs are adhesive and scatter through the tank. Two to three hundred eggs hatch in 3-4 days. The yolk sac is depleted in about a week, when the fry start to feed on small moving foods like brine shrimp nauplii.

Osteoglossum bicirrhosum Cuvier, 1829
Silver Arawana (Silver Aruana, Silver Bonytongue)

Overview: The Silver Arawana is a very large, very elegant fish that can be an incredible pet, but only for the aquarist prepared to house and feed it properly. This is the least expensive and easiest of the Arawana species to obtain, but it is also the largest.

Native Range: Amazon river basin, Rupununi and Oyapock rivers in South America, Guyana.

Maximum Length: 48 in (120 cm) TL.

Water: 75–82°F (24–28°C); pH: 6.0–7.0; hardness: 3-10°dGH.

Min. Tank Size: 1000 gal | 96x72x34 in (3785 L | 240x18x86 cm).

Feeding: They cruise the water's surface for insects and other floating foods, including pellets, shrimp, smaller fishes, beef heart and the like. There are excellent Arawana specialty prepared foods.

Behavior & Care: Never try to keep an Arawana in a small tank as this will cause deformities. These are large, powerful fish. They are accomplished jumpers and need firmly seated tank covers, as they are inclined to leap for food. No tankmates under 12 in (30 cm).

Breeding: Arawanas are paternal mouthbrooders that hold the eggs for about two months, by which time most of the yolk sac has been absorbed. The fry are 3–4 in (8–10 cm) at this time.

Osteoglossum ferreirai Kanasawa, 1966
Black Arawana (Black Aruana, Black Bonytongue)

Overview: Black Arawanas are often sold as young fry, black, with a broad silver or yellow stripe running from barbels to tail, the yolk sac still visible. The black turns to silver with age, and the scales and fins are bordered with pink and indigo.

Native Range: The Rio Branco, a tributary of the Rio Negro in South America.

Maximum Length: 39 in (100 cm) TL.

Water: 75–82°F (24–28°C); pH: 6.5–7.5; hardness: 8–18°dGH.

Min. Tank Size: 1000 gal | 96x72x34 in (3785 L | 240x18x86 cm).

Feeding: Prefers floating foods, including crickets and other insects, earthworms, shrimp, smaller fishes, beef heart, and floating pellet food. Overfeeding leads to "drop eye."

Behavior & Care: This is a shy, jumpy fish that is best kept by itself, or only with large, quiet bottom-dwellers when young. It gains confidence with size, and can become quite territorial with its own kind. Pristine and consistent water quality is paramount.

Breeding: Large ponds filled with very soft, acidic, peat-treated water are required. The fry are difficult to maintain, requiring very stringent attention to water quality.

Scleropages formosus (Müller & Schlegel, 1844)
Asian Arawana (Red Dragon, Asian Bonytongue)

Overview: The Asian Arawana is variable in color, with gold, red, and green morphs. This fish has been protected by CITES since 1975, but is farm-bred under very strict official regulation and supervision. Many modern Chinese and Japanese aquarists have an especially high regard for this ancient fish. Found in slow, blackwater forest rivers and swamps.

Native Range: Southern Burma to Malay Peninsula and Indonesia, eastern Thailand to Cardamon Range.

Maximum Length: 35 in (90 cm) TL.

Water: 75–86°F (24–30°C); pH: 6.5–7.5 hardness: 8–18°dGH.

Min. Tank Size: 1000 gal | 96x72x34 in (3785 L | 240x18x86 cm).

Feeding: Surface feeders with hinged jaws, these carnivores need a high quality diet of meaty foods.

Behavior & Care: Use a large tank with excellent filtration.

Breeding: This male mouthbrooder holds the fry for three months before they become free-swimming. Sexually mature at about five years. They do not readily breed in captivity and generally only spawn in large ponds. Even with perfect water conditions, the male often swallows the eggs for no apparent reason.

Scleropages jardinii (Saville-Kent, 1892)
Northern Barramundi (Australian Bonytongue, Saratoga)

Overview: Highly territorial and should be kept alone or with other large fishes unlike itself. Greenish brown dorsally and light brown or green-gray on its sides with silver scales, usually with a red or pink crescent-moon shape.

Native Range: Northern Australia from the Jardine River of the Cape York Peninsula to the Adelaide River near Darwin, as well as in the rivers that flow into the Timor Sea and the Gulf of Carpentaria; also found in Papua New Guinea.

Maximum Length: 40 in (100 cm) TL.

Water: 72–80°F (22–27°C); pH: 6.0–7.5; hardness: 5–12°dGH.

Min. Tank Size: 1000 gal | 72x24x29 in (780 L | 180x60x72.5 cm).

Feeding: Good eaters, but do not overfeed. Fatty deposits can result in "drop eye," where the eyes look down constantly.

Behavior & Care: This is a fish of clear streams and rivers, so keep the nitrite at 0 (which of course is best for all aquarium fishes!) and the water current strong. Cover the tank well.

Breeding: Maternal mouthbrooders that hold the eggs for about one or two weeks, and tend the brood for several weeks after release. When threatened, fry return to the safety of the mother's mouth.

Pantodon buchholzi Peters, 1876
Butterflyfish

Overview: This bizarre "flying fish" is found in still waters where it hovers just below the surface until it spies an insect and then it leaps out of the water with great power.

Native Range: West and Central Africa.

Maximum Length: 6 in (15 cm) TL.

Water: 75–86°F (24–30°C); pH: 6.0–7.5; hardness: 2–10°dGH.

Min. Tank Size: 20 gal | 30x12x12 in (65 L | 75x30x30 cm).

Feeding: Insects, crustaceans, and live foods that float.

Behavior & Care: Most important is a tight-fitting aquarium cover through which the fish cannot escape. Do not keep with other than bottom-dwellers such as loricariids or small mailed catfishes, as the long pelvic fins will be pecked by fishes swimming midwater. They do not welcome other fishes that inhabit the upper water column either, and will fight with competitors. Pristine water conditions are required. Use floating plants to help keep the fish from jumping.

Breeding: Low pH, plants, and peat filtration help to initiate spawning. About 3–7 floating eggs are produced with each spawning pass for a total of about 250. The fry hatch within 42 hours, but are very difficult to raise, requiring microscopic live foods.

Chitala ornata (Gray, 1831)
Clown Knifefish (Clown Featherback)

Overview: A very distinctive, flat, silvery fish with a long anal fin that gives the knifefish its common name. It has a tiny dorsal fin and several ocellated spots on the rear flanks. The long anal fin allows for forward and backward moves.

Native Range: Indo-China and Thailand.

Maximum Length: 40 in (100 cm) TL.

Water: 74–84°F (23–29°C); pH: 6.0–7.0 hardness: 8–10°dGH.

Min. Tank Size: 1000 gal | 96x72x34 in (3785 L | 240x18x86 cm).

Feeding: Feeds on a variety of prey including small fish, insects and crustaceans. It has sensors that detect the presence of prey. It drifts quietly behind potential prey, and with a quick snap, devours it.

Behavior & Care: This fish prefers slow-moving water and a well-planted aquarium, where it can hang in the shadows. They are best when kept without other knifefishes.

Breeding: Reportedly spawning takes place in spring when females each lay thousands of eggs on the substrate or a piece of wood. The male cares for the eggs by fanning them with his tail, keeping them aerated and silt-free; later the male reportedly protects the fry.

Chitala blanci, Indo-China Featherfin.

Chitala ornata, juvenile, Clown Knifefish.

The most commonly seen knifefish is *Chitala ornata*, which is often found in the hobby as very young fish, only about 3–4 in (8–10 cm) in length. They will need larger aquaria as they grow.

Notopterus notopterus (Pallas, 1769)
Ghost Knifefish (Bronze Featherback)

Overview: The Ghost Knifefish has an arched back and an elongated, laterally compressed body. Body coloring is brown to bronze with lighter colored fins. The dorsal is small. The mouth is very large.

Native Range: Southern India, Thailand, Malaysia, Sumatra, and Java. Clear, moving waters.

Maximum Length: 24 in (60 cm) TL.

Water: 75–82°F (24–28°C); pH: 6.0–6.5; hardness: 3–8°dGH.

Min. Tank Size: 210 gal | 72x24x29 in (780 L | 180x60x72.5 cm).

Feeding: Accepts most kinds of live and frozen food. Can be trained to take pellets. Try cucumber.

Behavior & Care: A large, well-planted aquarium is perfect for this easy-going, evening-active fish. Unless the aquarium is large enough for separate territories to be formed, keep only one of these fish per tank. This fish is peaceful with large fishes of other species but should not be kept with tankmates small enough to be eaten. Likes a shelter to call its own—driftwood is okay.

Breeding: Over 200 eggs are deposited on plants during the night. The male guards and fans the eggs for about two weeks until hatching. The fry take newly hatched brine shrimp.

Xenomystus nigri (Günther, 1868)
African Knifefish

Overview: Identified by its lack of a dorsal fin, the African Knifefish has an unsual hunchback shape and dusky coloration. It is a nocturnal species, but will appear during daylight hours if that is when it is fed. Can produce barking sounds. Detects prey with an electrical organ.

Native Range: Sierra Leone, Liberia, Togo, Benin and Cameroon.

Maximum Length: 12 in (30 cm) TL.

Water: 72–82°F (22–28°C); pH: 6.0–8.0; hardness: 5–19°dGH.

Min. Tank Size: 75 gal | 48x18x20 in (270 L | 120x45x50 cm).

Feeding: Live worms, crustaceans, insects, snails. Can be trained to accept pellets and even flake food.

Behavior & Care: Should be kept in a small group when young, but they become aggressive with their own kind when older. They are tolerant of other tankmates that they cannot consume. Provide plenty of hiding places and a quiet tank without too much turbulence. They are not particularly jumpy, but the aquarium should be well covered nonetheless.

Breeding: Not reported in the aquarium.

Campylomormyrus tamandua (Günther, 1864)
Congo Elephantnose (Blunt-jawed, or Worm-nosed, Elephantfish)

Overview: This is a delicate, specialized fish best reserved for experienced aquarists. It has an electric organ at the base of its tail that discharges when the fish is searching for food and which is used to communicate with others of its kind.

Native Range: West Africa.

Maximum Length: 17 in (43 cm) TL.

Water: 72–75°F (22–24°C); pH: 5.0–7.0; hardness: 3–7°dGH.

Min. Tank Size: 120 gal | 48x24x24 in (430 L | 120x60x60 cm).

Feeding: Live tubificids, small earthworms, and small crustaceans are ideal, but the addition of quality protein in the form of frozen meaty foods will help maintain nutritional balance.

Behavior & Care: Use a planted, pristine aquarium with a soft sand substrate. This fish is best kept alone or with other large, non-aggressive, slow-feeding fishes, as the weak electromagnetic field can lead to violent confrontations between mormyrids. As with other mormyrids water quality needs to be excellent at all times. Keep the substrate well vacuumed to prevent infections of the "nose."

Breeding: Not reported in the aquarium.

Gnathonemus petersii (Günther, 1862)
Peters's Elephantnose

Overview: Peters's Elephantnose is a quiet fish. It has a small, round mouth opening on the trunk-like proboscis that is used to root for food in a soft, sandy substrate.

Native Range: West and Central Africa.

Maximum Length: 14 in (35 cm) TL.

Water: 72–82°F (22–28°C); pH: 6.0–8.0; hardness: 5–19°dGH.

Min. Tank Size: 50 gal | 48x16x16 in (190 L | 120x40x40 cm).

Feeding: These fish have tiny mouths and need to feed from the bottom. This makes small, live foods the first choice, with frozen meaty foods next. If they will take prepared foods, use sparingly.

Behavior & Care: This fish generally keeps to the bottom levels of the tank and appreciates abundant hiding places in the form of halved flowerpots, driftwood, and low-light plants like Anubias. The electrical activity in mormyrids increases with stress, so it is inadvisable to keep more than one in the average community. They are territorial and at the same time companionable, as they will swim together in little "pods," but to keep them together requires a very large tank.

Breeding: Not reported in the aquarium.

Petrocephalus bane (Lacepède, 1803)
Baby Whale

Overview: This fish has a glossy grayish to brown body with a blunt profile. The dorsal and anal fins are set far back. It produces a mild electrical current that aids in the search for prey and is sometimes used aggressively toward other mormyrids, necessitating larger aquaria than usual to keep multiple specimens.

Native Range: Africa: Nile Basin.

Maximum Length: 8 in (20 cm) TL.

Water: 75–82°F (24–28°C); pH: 6.5–7.5; hardness: 5–7°dGH.

Min. Tank Size: 30 gal | 36x18x12 in (120 L | 90x45x30 cm).

Feeding: Requires small live foods: worms, larvae, crustaceans. Can be trained to accept frozen foods. Feed in the evening.

Behavior & Care: They are territorial toward other Baby Whales, but can be kept together as long as the tank is large enough that each fish has a tank footprint of about 240 sq in (1550 sq cm). Use a fine, sand substrate, and provide plants and hiding places. Mormyrids do not tolerate less than excellent water quality, so maintenance is very important. Baby Whales are nocturnal, so keep the tank dim.

Breeding: Not reported in the aquarium.

Pollimyrus isidori isidori (Valenciennes, 1847)
Elephant Fish (Baby Whale)

Overview: Gray to grayish brown, sometimes with small spots, and with a distinctive bullet-like shape.
Native Range: West and Central Africa.
Maximum Length: 6 in (15 cm) TL.
Water: 77–84°F (25–29°C); pH: 6.0–8.0; hardness: 5–7°dGH.
Min. Tank Size: 30 gal | 36x12x16 in (105 L | 90x30x40 cm).
Feeding: Filters substrate detritus for insect and plant matter. In the aquarium, feed live tubificids, brine shrimp, bloodworms, mosquito larvae, etc, and occasional prepared foods after the lights are turned off.
Behavior & Care: The Elephant Fish is kept in the same manner as the other mormyrids. It tends to stay near the bottom of the aquarium, favors the evening hours, and is peaceful in the community except where territories and other Elephant Fish are involved.
Breeding: Not reported in the aquarium. In the wild, the males build nests and both the males and females produce electrical organ discharges. They are also quite vocal, making an assortment of moans, grunts, and growls while patrolling the nest site.

Barbonymus schwanenfeldii (Bleeker, 1853)
Tinfoil Barb

Overview: The Tinfoil Barb has a bright, silvery body with a red dorsal fin with a black tip at maturity. All other fins are red, and the red caudal fin shows a white margin with a black inner stripe.
Native Range: Malay Peninsula, Sumatra, and Borneo.
Maximum Length: 14 in (35 cm) TL.
Water: 72–77°F (22–25°C); pH: 6.0–7.0; hardness: 0–10°dGH.
Min. Tank Size: 150 gal | 72x18x28 in (568 L | 180x45x70 cm).
Feeding: The Tinfoil Barb is an omnivore with a penchant for greenery and will consume most plants within range. Feed vegetable foods as well as small worms and crustaceans; also takes flakes, pellets, or freeze-dried foods. Eats filamentous algae, but not Java Moss, Java Fern, or Anubias, etc.
Behavior & Care: This showy schooling species does best in a group, where they will play in strong water currents that mimic their native waters. Beware of the growth potential of this species. They are very active and adults require a lot of space. That said, they are wonderful tankmates for large cichlids and catfishes. Tinfoils will jump, so be sure to cover the tank very securely.
Breeding: Unreported in the aquarium. They are egg-scatterers.

Barbus jae Boulenger, 1903
Jae Barb

Overview: This dwarf barb deserves to be far more popular than it is. A small school of these colorful little gems will grace any community, and they are also an excellent alternative to small characins as dither fish for dwarf cichlids. Alternatively can be kept in a small species aquarium.

Native Range: West Central Africa: south Cameroon and north Gabon.

Maximum Length: 1.5 in (4 cm) TL.

Water: 75-80°F (24–27°C); pH 6.0–7.5; hardness 2–10°dGH.

Min. Tank Size: 15 gal | 24x12x12 in (50 L | 60x30x30 cm).

Feeding: Small live and frozen foods. Acclimated fish will also take flake and small granules, Cod roe, and other small foods.

Behavior & Care: Keep in a school of at least six in a planted tank with dark substrate. Dislikes bright light and shows its best colors under muted lighting, so select plants that do not mind low light or species with surface vegetation (e.g. *Nymphaea*) to provide shade.

Breeding: Males are more colorful. Breed in a group of several males and females for best results. Soft, acid water with peat filtration. Will eat the eggs, so use marbles or mesh on the tank bottom.

Puntius conchonius (Hamilton, 1822)
Rosy Barb

Overview: This a good beginner's fish, hardy and durable, easy to feed, and brings nice action to the aquarium when kept in a school. During spawning the male becomes deep red. Long-finned varieties have been developed and are often available.

Native Range: Afghanistan, Pakistan, India, Nepal, and Bangladesh.

Maximum Length: 6 in (15 cm) TL.

Water: 72–79°F (22–26°C); pH: 6.0–8.0; hardness: 5–19°dGH.

Min. Tank Size: 40 gal | 36x18x16 in (160 L | 90x45x40 cm).

Feeding: The omnivorous Rosy Barb accepts most commercial meaty and vegetable-based aquarium fare, including good-quality *Spirulina* flakes, algae wafers, and color-enhancing rations.

Behavior & Care: Plants are good, and they can be restricted to the sides and back of the tank, leaving plenty of open swimming space. This is easier to provide in a long, rather than tall, aquarium. Because the Rosy Barb may root around in the gravel, a fine-grade substrate is best. Darker colors (substrate and background) accentuate color and provide a sense of security for the Rosy Barb.

Breeding: Egg-scatterers. Easy to breed. Provide protection for the eggs in a separate spawning tank.

Puntius denisonii (Day, 1865)
Denison's Barb (Red Line Torpedo Barb)

Overview: Golden above and silvery below a black line that runs the length of the body, and with a red line from head to midbody, this torpedo-shaped fish is a real aquarium stunner.

Native Range: Kerala, southern India. Endangered in the wild.

Maximum Length: 6 in (15 cm) TL.

Water: 72–79°F (22–26°C); pH: 6.8–7.8; hardness: 5–25°dGH.

Min. Tank Size: 40 gal | 36x18x16 in (160 L | 90x45x40 cm).

Feeding: Omnivores with good appetites that will accept all regular aquarium fare, especially small worms and crustaceans. Add vegetable matter to the diet. They can be especially tough on tender-leaved aquarium plants if they do not receive adequate greens.

Behavior & Care: These are peaceful schooling fish, but at times their adult size and activity level can be a bit overwhelming to more sedate species. Keep water well oxygenated and moving. Use tough plants like Anubias, Crinum, Java Fern, etc. These fish need open space, but will use ornamentation well, swimming in and out and through obstacles.

Breeding: There are reports of accidental spawns in groups at 4 in (10 cm) in size in large aquaria with dense vegetation.

Puntius lateristriga (Valenciennes, 1842)
T-Barb (Spanner Barb)

Overview: This is a high-energy fish that sports an unusual configuration of dark and light coloration. It is an ideal beginner's fish, but kept by experienced aquarists as well for its good aquarium comportment and ready availability.

Native Range: Malay Peninsula to Borneo.

Maximum Length: 7 in (18 cm) TL.

Water: 70–82°F (21–28°C); pH: 6.0–6.5; hardness: 2–10°dGH.

Min. Tank Size: 40 gal | 36x18x16 in (160 L | 90x45x40 cm).

Feeding: This is a true omnivore that will eat virtually any kind of fish food. It is partial to vegetable foods and will destroy plants if not well supplied with greens. Java Moss is impervious to the barb's nipping.

Behavior & Care: This active fish needs a lot of open space and strong currents in clean water. It has a quirky habit of burying itself in the substrate when in danger. Will school when young, not as much in adulthood.

Breeding: Egg-scatterers that will consume unprotected eggs. Condition adults separately. Use a large aquarium with shallow water for the spawning which will occur early in the morning. Employ protection for eggs and remove parents after spawning.

Puntius nigrofasciatus (Günther, 1868)
Black Ruby Barb

Overview: The head is deep red and the sides are marked with three to four dark transverse bars. The back is usually dark brown. The other fins are black. In the spawning season, males sport a bright crimson red body and a red caudal fin. Females are shades of peach. It is a hardy schooling species that can be kept in a community tank.

Native Range: Sri Lanka.

Maximum Length: 2.3 in (6.0 cm) TL.

Water: 70–82°F (21–28°C); pH: 6.0–6.5; hardness: 2–10°dGH.

Min. Tank Size: 25 gal | 24x12x20 in (90 L | 60x30x50 cm).

Feeding: Omnivore that appreciates good quality aquarium fare.

Behavior & Care: This barb is sensitive to poor water quality so good maintenance is required. When stressed, it is particularly inclined to White Spot (Ich). The tank should have ample open swimming space, but should also be well planted and decorated to create hiding spaces. Use dark, fine substrate and a dark background. Use a slow filter that does not create excessive turbulence.

Breeding: Egg-scatterer. Condition parents separately. Use shallow water. Protect eggs. Keep eggs in darkness until hatching. Feed fry on infusoria, or keep with dense Java Moss when free-swimming.

Puntius oligolepis (Bleeker, 1853)
Checker Barb

Overview: Here's a fish with a classic barb shape, a tricolored dorsal, red fins, and a strong, interesting pattern. The male is more highly colored and has black edging on the dorsal and anal fins. These are active, schooling fish that can be territorial. Best kept in groups of at least three. Males display toward one another, but it rarely results in injury.

Native Range: Indonesia: Sumatra.

Maximum Length: 2 in (5 cm) TL.

Water: 70–82°F (21–28°C); pH: 6.0–6.5; hardness: 2–10°dGH.

Min. Tank Size: 20 gal | 30x12x12 in (65 L | 75x30x30 cm).

Feeding: Omnivore that requires small food items and appreciates small worms, crustaceans, larvae, and vegetable matter.

Behavior & Care: Use a planted tank with a dark substrate and background for this lively fish. The water should be well filtered and aerated and clean. Use a fitted tank cover to prevent fish losses from leaping.

Breeding: Egg-scatterer that spawns at sunrise. The males have territories. The spawning tank should be long and low and well equipped with spawning mops, Java Moss, or other egg-saving devices. Remove parents immediately to save fry. Java Moss used as a spawning medium supplies first food in form of resident rotifers and infusoria.

Puntius padamya Kullander & Britz, 2008
Odessa Barb (Scarlet Barb, Ticto Barb)

Overview: Moscow street vendors used to sell the Odessa Barb from flasks that they carried under their shirts to keep the fish warm. Until recently, though, this lovely barb didn't have a valid scientific name. The species name, *padamya*, is the Burmese word for "ruby" and it is so named because of the rich red of the males.

Native Range: Nepal, India, Pakistan, Burma, Bangladesh, Thailand, and Sri Lanka.

Maximum Length: 4 in (10 cm) TL.

Water: 70–82°F (21–28°C); pH: 6.0–6.5; hardness: 2–10°dGH.

Min. Tank Size: 20 gal | 30x12x12 in (65 L | 75x30x30 cm).

Feeding: Flake foods, live and frozen worms, crustaceans, insects, vegetable portion necessary.

Behavior & Care: The Odessa Barb is an active schooling fish, and while it may get a little rough with other Odessas, it is generally a good community fish. Keep a group of six-plus in a tank with a dark substrate and background with plants and plenty of open swimming space.

Breeding: Typical egg-scatterers with high fertility. Use a separate spawning tank and remove the parents after the eggs are laid.

Puntius pentazona (Boulenger, 1894)
Fiveband Barb

Overview: The Fiveband Barb may be the shyest of the barbs. It can tolerate other barbs, but boisterous tankmates should be avoided.

Native Range: Pakistan, India, and Sri Lanka.

Maximum Length: 3 in (7.5 cm) TL.

Water: 70–82°F (21–28°C); pH: 6.0–6.5; hardness: 2–10°dGH.

Min. Tank Size: 20 gal | 30x12x12 in (65 L | 75x30x30 cm).

Feeding: Flake foods, live and frozen worms, larvae, crustaceans, insects; vegetable portion necessary.

Behavior & Care: They prefer a well-planted aquarium with rocks and driftwood, and dark substrate and background. Maintain open space, though, because they still need plenty of room to school.

Breeding: Use peat-filtered water in the spawning tank, which is equipped with marbles, Java Moss, or a spawning mop. The pair can be conditioned in this tank. Feed them well with meaty, preferably live, foods until the female is visibly swollen with roe. The male will be his brightest shades of color just before spawning. Remove the pair as soon as possible after spawning. They lay 150–250 adhesive eggs that will hatch in about 30 hours. The fry are free-swimming in about five days. Start feeding with infusoria and liquid fry foods.

Puntius sachsii (Ahl, 1923)
Gold Barb (Sachsii, Goldfinned Barb)

Overview: Here is a hardy fish that is colorful and generally peaceful, perfect for a community aquarium. The gold body sports small dark blotches from behind the gills to the caudal peduncle.

Native Range: Asia.

Maximum Length: 3 in (8 cm) TL.

Water: 72–82°F (22–28°C); pH: 6.0–8.0; hardness: 5–15°dGH.

Min. Tank Size: 20 gal | 30x12x12 in (65 L | 75x30x30 cm).

Feeding: Omnivore. Will take all prepared and frozen aquarium foods. Small, live foods are also taken with gusto.

Behavior & Care: In a school of six or more, the Gold Barb is generally a good citizen, for the most part only squabbling amongst themselves. Do not tempt them, though, with long-finned tankmates. In the well-planted aquarium their treatment of the plants is more along the lines of gentle pruning than destruction.

Breeding: The males drive the females through plants, ideally Java Moss. The eggs are fertilized and cling to the strands of the moss. Remove the parents after spawning. The eggs hatch in 48 hours (more quickly in higher water temperature), and the fry will find first foods in the form of microorganisms that reside on the moss.

Puntius semifasciolatus (Günther, 1868)
Half-banded Barb (Green Barb, Chinese Barb)

Overview: The Golden Barb is an active, outgoing fish. Decades of selective breeding have transformed the rather plain wild fish into glittering aquarium beauties. This fish is unusual among freshwater fishes in showing some green coloration. Males tend to be smaller and more intensely colored.

Native Range: Southeastern China.

Maximum Length: 3 in (8 cm) TL.

Water: 72–79°F (22–26°C); pH: 6.0–8.0; hardness: 5–19°dGH.

Min. Tank Size: 20 gal | 30x12x12 in (65 L | 75x30x30 cm).

Feeding: The Golden Barb is a hearty eater that will accept just about any aquarium fare, including flake and freeze-dried foods. Some vegetable matter is a must, so include *Spirulina*-based foods as well. Occasional treats of frozen or live foods, including brine shrimp, are also appreciated.

Behavior & Care: The Golden Barb does best in a long aquarium, well-planted at the sides and back with plenty of open room in the center for swimming. Because they may root around in the substrate, use only fine-grade or rounded gravel.

Breeding: Willing spawner; egg-scatterer.

Puntius tetrazona (Bleeker, 1855)
Tiger Barb (Sumatra Barb)

Overview: The Tiger Barb is a wonderful little fish with four distinctive stripes and a spirited personality. A large school makes an impressive display. The Tiger Barb today is mostly commercially bred and comes in a variety of color forms, including albino and the moss green, which is a very impressive-looking fish.

Native Range: Sumatra and Borneo.

Maximum Length: 2.7 in (7cm) TL.

Water: 72–79°F (22–26°C); pH: 6.0–8.0; hardness: 5–19°dGH.

Min. Tank Size: 20 gal | 30x12x12 in (65 L | 75x30x30 cm).

Feeding: Omnivore. Tiger Barbs are good eaters that will accept any appropriately sized aquarium fare, including flakes and pellets. Supplement their diets with frozen and live foods; include vegetable matter like *Spirulina*-based foods.

Behavior & Care: Unless kept in a school of six or more fish, the Tiger Barb is an unrepentant fin-nipper. Looks best against a background of aquatic plants. It makes little difference if the plants are live or plastic, as the Tiger Barb is not known to be tough on greenery. What is important is to leave plenty of open areas for swimming.

Breeding: Egg-scatterers that will eat any unprotected eggs.

Puntius titteya Deraniyagala, 1929
Cherry Barb

Overview: A classic aquarium species, this small, slender barb is torpedo-shaped with chameleon-like color variations in different conditions and different strains. An albino form is now being propagated. The Cherry Barb is probably near extinction in the wild, but it is widely propagated for the aquarium hobby.

Native Range: Sri Lanka.

Maximum Length: 2 in (5 cm) TL.

Water: 72–79°F (22–26°C); pH: 6.0–8.0; hardness: 5–15°dGH.

Min. Tank Size: 20 gal | 30x12x12 in (65 L | 75x30x30 cm).

Feeding: Omnivore. Cherry Barbs feed mostly on vegetable matter in nature, but they will accept a wide variety of prepared aquarium fare, including good-quality flakes. Their diets must include algae and plant matter, maybe include _Spirulina_-based foods. Treat occasionally with frozen or live brine shrimp or bloodworms.

Behavior & Care: Provide lots of open swimming room with plants. Use a fine gravel or sandy substrate. They do peck a bit at algae.

Breeding: Extremely easy to breed, Cherry Barbs scatter their adhesive eggs among plants, and should be immediately removed or they will eat the spawn.

Puntius conchonius, Golden Rosy Barb.

Puntius conchonius, Neon Rosy Barb.

Rosy Barbs are commonly found in pet stores. They are inexpensive and hardy. Genetically malleable, they are available in several appealing forms.

Puntius conchonius, Long-finned Rosy Barb.

Puntius filamentosus, Blackspot Barb.

Barbs are highly active schooling fish. Their busy natures should be assessed before purchase. If a quiet, sedate aquarium is your goal, these fishes may not be for you.

Danio albolineatus (Blyth, 1860)
Pearl Danio

Overview: Danios are active schooling fishes. The Pearl Danio is a peaceful, hardy species with a pink-blue coloration overlain with mother-of-pearl. There is also a yellow form.

Native Range: Burma to Laos, and Sumatra, Indonesia.

Maximum Length: 2.5 in (6.5 cm) TL.

Water: 70–77°F (21–25°C); pH: 6.0–8.0; hardness: 5–19°dGH.

Min. Tank Size: 20 gal | 30x12x12 in (65 L | 75x30x30 cm).

Feeding: They are small carnivores. In the wild their diet consists primarily of insects and insect larvae, and in the aquarium they will accept most commercial aquarium foods, including good-quality tropical flake or granular food, as well as frozen and live foods such as Tubifex, mosquito larvae, brine shrimp and Daphnia.

Behavior & Care: *D. albolineatus* does best in a well-lit aquarium, planted at the sides and back with lots of room in the center to swim. Acquire a group of five-plus, and house them with other mild-mannered fishes. These are jumpers, so a tight-fitting cover is a must.

Breeding: They scatter non-adhesive eggs that fall to the bottom and must be protected to acquire young.

Danio feegradei Hora, 1937
Yoma Danio

Overview: This fish only arrived in the hobby in 2005, despite its having been described in 1937. Its colors are compelling: sky-blue sides with two bands of gold, a short dark line on the caudal, and areas of orange of variable intensity—perhaps dependent on social status— in the males. Both sexes have an orange spot just behind the gills. This delightful danio is an esteemed jumper, able to leap repeatedly to heights of over a foot (30 cm).

Native Range: Burma.

Maximum Length: 3 in (8 cm) TL.

Water: 70–77°F (21–25°C); pH: 6.0–8.0; hardness: 5–19°dGH.

Min. Tank Size: 20 gal | 30x12x12 in (65 L | 75x30x30 cm).

Feeding: Omnivore accepting prepared foods; include live and frozen insects, worms, etc; vegetable foods.

Behavior & Care: This is not a difficult fish to keep, but do make sure to use a fitted aquarium cover. Use plants around the sides and back, and a soft, dark substrate. An airstone will add movement to the water, which is appreciated by this fish. Keep in schools of six or more fish.

Breeding: Egg-scatterers. Use standard methods for breeding danios.

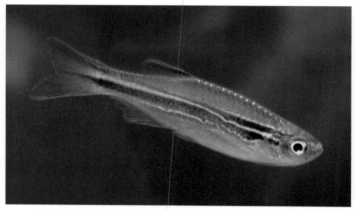

Danio kerri Smith, 1931
Blue Danio (Turquoise Danio)

Overview: The Blue Danio does well with other danios and other peaceful fishes of similar size. Kept with others in a school, this fish will be very active. The deep blue midline stripe, bordered in yellow, makes this a very attractive and unusual community-tank fish.

Native Range: Malay Peninsula.

Maximum Length: 2.5 in (6 cm) TL.

Water: 73–77°F (23-25°C); pH: 6.5-7.0; hardness: 3-10°dGH.

Min. Tank Size: 20 gal | 30x12x12 in (65 L | 75x30x30 cm).

Feeding: This fish is omnivorous, and will accept most aquarium fare. Be sure to include abundant greens as well as some meaty frozen foods to keep them in the best possible condition.

Behavior & Care: The Blue Danio prefers a planted aquarium with plenty of open swimming space.

Breeding: Blue Danios are egg-scatterers that spawn best in shallow water over marbles or a mesh to protect the eggs. The eggs hatch within 36 hours. The fry will take egglayer fry food and advance to newly hatched brine shrimp. A mature sponge filter harbors microscopic organisms that are nutritious food for fry.

Danio margaritatus Hamilton, 1822
Celestial Pearl Danio (Galaxy Danio)

Overview: This is a new star in the aquarium, only coming into the hobby in 2006. The currently accepted scientific name is used above, but it was formerly found in the genus *Celestichthys*. Enthusiastic collection has already endangered it in the wild, but it is easily bred in captivity.

Native Range: Burma.

Maximum Length: 1 in (2.5 cm) TL.

Water: 70–77°F (21–25°C); pH: 6.5–7.5; hardness: 3–12°dGH.

Min. Tank Size: 15 gal | 24x12x12 in (50 L | 60x30x30 cm).

Feeding: This fish can only handle very small foods. Even flake foods should be crumbled first. Small live foods are greatly appreciated.

Behavior & Care: The Celestial favors shallow, clean water with plenty of plants, but it is quite adaptable to varying conditions. This is a schooling fish that is initially quite timid. They will acquire courage as the new school (of six or more) forms in the tank. The males can be a little bossy, but basically they are a peaceful species.

Breeding: These fish are bred using conditioned adults in a 2:1 male to female ratio. Use Java Moss or spawning mops and remove breeders after one or two days; fry follow shortly. Start fry on infusoria.

Danio rerio (Hamilton, 1822)
Zebra Danio (Brachydanio Rerio)

Overview: Zebra Danios have been in the hobby for more than a century and are still top of the "bread and butter" species. When kept in schools, as it should be, it puts on a constant show of flashing stripes without threatening other peaceful fishes. A variety of color forms and long-fin varieties have been commercially developed, including albino, veiltail and leopard varieties. Zebras are extensively used in scientific genome research.

Native Range: Pakistan, India, Bangladesh, Nepal, and Burma.

Maximum Length: 2 in (5 cm) TL.

Water: 72–81°F (22–27°C); pH: 6.0–8.0; hardness: 6–19°dGH.

Min. Tank Size: 20 gal | 30x12x12 in (65 L | 75x30x30 cm).

Feeding: Omnivore. Will accept most aquarium foods, including flakes, freeze-dried, and frozen. Supplement their diet with *Spirulina*-based foods. Treat occasionally with live foods like brine shrimp and bloodworms.

Behavior & Care: The Zebra Danio is a schooling species that needs at least six fish in their group. Cover the tank well as they are jumpers.

Breeding: Easy. Scatters eggs that hatch in about 36 hours. Remove the parents after spawning to prevent the eggs from being eaten.

Devario aequipinnatus (McClelland, 1839)
Giant Danio

Overview: One of the largest of the danios, *D. aequipinnatus* has a blue and yellow torpedo-shaped body with gray and clear fins. It's peaceful with its own kind and with others, making it a wonderful community fish. There is also a Golden Giant Danio, which is a xanthic form.

Native Range: Sri Lanka, Nepal, and the west coast of India.

Maximum Length: 6 in (15 cm) TL.

Water: 72–81°F (22–27°C); pH: 6.0–8.0; hardness: 6–19°dGH.

Min. Tank Size: 30 gal | 36x12x16 in (105 L | 90x30x40 cm).

Feeding: Omnivore. Accepts most aquarium foods, and it is especially fond of small worms and crustaceans.

Behavior & Care: Use a fine, dark gravel and provide extra aeration with airstones or powerheads. Keep the water clean with good filtration and water changes. These fish will school when there are six or more in the aquarium.

Breeding: Egg-scatterers, danios produce about 300 eggs at a time, scattering them in plant thickets. Remove the parent fish if you intend to raise any fry. When the fry hatch, they will live off the yolk sac for several days. When it's gone, start egglayer fry foods.

Devario devario (Hamilton, 1822)
Bengal Danio

Overview: Fishes in the genus *Devario* have small barbels and have a vertical pattern on the flanks. The Bengal Danio is ideal for an active community aquarium and bears no animosity toward either its own or other species of similar size.

Native Range: Pakistan, India, Nepal, Bangladesh, and Afghanistan.

Maximum Length: 4 in (10 cm) TL.

Water: 70–77°F (21–25°C); pH: 6.0–8.0; hardness: 5–19°dGH.

Min. Tank Size: 20 gal | 30x12x12 in (65 L | 75x30x30 cm).

Feeding: Omnivore that feeds on worms, crustaceans, plant matter, and insects. Will take prepared and live and frozen meaty foods.

Behavior & Care: Keep this fish in an aquarium with open space, as it is an active swimmer. Plants help make the fish feel secure, and it will look better with dark substrate and background. It is very sensitive about water quality and requires pristine water conditions. It is a lively jumper, so be sure to cover the tank well

Breeding: Separate the sexes, and condition them with live foods. When reunited, they generally spawn within 24 hours. Use Java Moss or a mesh to protect eggs. Remove the parent fish after spawning. Raise fry on increasingly large foods, starting with infusoria.

Devario malabaricus (Jerdon, 1849)
Malabar Danio

Overview: The Malabar Danio is widely available in the hobby. It's an active fish that needs to be kept in a school of six or more. With the typical danio shape and a pattern of gold and blue, this is a nice addition to the community aquarium.

Native Range: West coast of India, Sri Lanka.

Maximum Length: 6 in (15 cm) TL.

Water: 70–77°F (21–25°C); pH: 6.0–8.0; hardness: 5–19°dGH.

Min. Tank Size: 30 gal | 36x12x16 in (105 L | 90x30x40 cm).

Feeding: Omnivore that feeds on worms, crustaceans, plant matter, and insects. Will take prepared and live and frozen meaty foods.

Behavior & Care: Fine, dark gravel and dark background will help keep this fish calm. Keep the water clean with good filtration and water changes. Use a fitted aquarium cover to prevent the loss of leaping fish.

Breeding: A water change will induce spawning in conditioned fish that are in a long, shallow, well-planted aquarium. Around 200 adhesive eggs are produced. Remove adults after spawning. Incubation lasts 1–2 days, and the fry are free-swimming in five days.

Danio choprai, Glowlight Danio.

Danio dangila, Moustached Danio.

The Glowlight Danio is one of the smallest, at 1.5 in (3.75 cm), while the Moustached Danio is the largest of the true danios at 5 in (13 cm).

Danio rerio var. *frankei*, Leopard Danio.

Danio roseus, Rose Danio.

The Rose Danio is a peaceful danio, good in a community aquarium. Its two pairs of long barbels distinguish it from other danios.

Rasbora borapetensis Smith, 1934
Red-tailed Rasbora (Bora Bora Rasbora)

Overview: The Red-tailed Rasbora is one of the prettiest of the rasboras, a group of small fishes generally found in large schools in nature. Often, they are found in the same biotope as *Cryptocoryne.*

Native Range: Thailand and Malaysia.

Maximum Length: 2 in (5 cm) TL.

Water: 72–79°F (22–26°C); pH: 6.5–7.0; hardness: 0–10°dGH.

Min. Tank Size: 20 gal | 24x12x16 in (70 L | 60x30x40 cm).

Feeding: Will take flakes, small pellets, and frozen foods.

Behavior & Care: The Red-tailed Rasbora hails from shallow, still waters where it occupies the mid-to-upper levels of the water. It is peaceful and should be kept in schools with other small, peaceful fishes. The tank should be well planted with an open area for swimming. Use floating plants to diffuse light and reduce jumpiness.

Breeding: The females are only slightly larger than the males, and there is little difference in coloration. The water in the spawning tank should be shallow, soft, and acidic, with a temperature about 79°F (26°C). Adhesive eggs are laid a few at a time, deposited in the plants, and will be eaten promptly unless the parents are removed. The fry appear in about 36 hours. Use infusorians as first food.

Rasbora pauciperforata Weber & de Beaufort, 1916
Red-striped Rasbora

Overview: This is an excellent dither fish for dwarf cichlids and other small, nervous bottom-dwellers with similar water requirements. The bright stripe is especially appealing when this lively fish is kept properly in a school of six or more individuals.

Native Range: Western Malaysia, Sumatra.

Maximum Length: 3 in (7 cm) TL.

Water: 73–77°F (23–25°C); pH: 5.8–6.5; hardness: 0–5°dGH.

Min. Tank Size: 20 gal | 24x12x16 in (70 L | 60x30x40 cm).

Feeding: Will take flakes, small pellets, and frozen foods.

Behavior & Care: This is a great community fish when kept with other small, peaceful species. It is sensitive about water quality, so regular water changes are critical. Use peat in the filter or use peat extract to mimic the natural water conditions. Plant the tank, but leave some open swimming areas.

Breeding: Ripe females are plump, and the ventral profile is curved. Condition the entire school of fish in a well-planted spawning tank. They will choose their own partners. The eggs are scattered among the plants; remove the adults. Expect hatching in about 24 hours.

Rasbora trilineata Weber & de Beaufort, 1916
Scissortail

Overview: While the silvery Scissortail is not particularly colorful, its caudal fin is quite eye-catching and gives rise to the fish's common name. As the fish opens and closes its tail during swimming, the black dots on the ends of the lobes of the fin move up and down, giving the appearance that the tail is "slicing" through the water like a pair of scissors cutting fabric.

Native Range: Sumatra, Borneo, and western Malaysia.

Maximum Length: 6 in (15 cm) TL.

Water: 72–79°F (22–26°C); pH: 6.0–6.5; hardness: 1–8°dGH.

Min. Tank Size: 65 gal | 48x18x18 in (240 L | 120x45x45 cm).

Feeding: Flake, pelleted, and freeze-dried foods. Treat occasionally with frozen and live foods such as brine shrimp and bloodworms.

Behavior & Care: These schooling fish need room to move. The ideal is a long tank densely planted at the back with lots of open water in the center and a dark substrate to show off their striking color pattern.

Breeding: Not easy to spawn. Increase water temperature to 82°F (28°C). Use dark substrate and plants. Remove parents after spawning. Eggs are prone to bacterial and protozoal attack.

Rasbora kalochroma, Clown Rasbora.

Rasbora vulcanus, Reticulated Rasbora.

The small rasboras such as *R. vulcanus* are peaceful, agile community fishes. Some are territorial in that they will stake out a small space, but the damage they can inflict is minimal.

Trigonostigma heteromorpha (Duncker, 1904)
Harlequin (Rasbora Heteromorpha, Ras)

Overview: One of the classic aquarium fishes, the Harlequin is an ideal choice for the peaceful community. The distinctive black triangle on its side is a hallmark of the species, but a second species, *T. espei*, has similar markings and is often sold as the Harlequin, though it is much slimmer.

Native Range: Malaysia, Singapore, Sumatra, and Thailand.

Maximum Length: 2 in (5 cm) TL.

Water: 72–77°F (22–25°C); pH: 5.0–7.5; hardness: 0–10°dGH.

Min. Tank Size: 20 gal | 24x12x16 in (70 L | 60x30x40 cm).

Feeding: Flake, granular, and freeze-dried foods. Treat occasionally with frozen and live foods such as brine shrimp and bloodworms.

Behavior & Care: Dense vegetation and driftwood, lots of open space for swimming, a dark substrate, and a cover of floating plants to produce subdued lighting will make this active, schooling species feel right at home. Keep them with other small, peaceful species in a community aquarium. Excellent as dither fish.

Breeding: Harlequins are egglayers that deposit their adhesive spawn better on the undersides of leaves. Remove the parents and darken the tank. The fry hatch in 24 hours.

Tanichthys albonubes Lin, 1932
White Cloud Mountain Minnow (Tan's Fish, Meteor Minnow)

Overview: White Clouds are the delight of minimalist aquarists. Colorful and very peaceful, these charming little minnows are ideal schooling fish. They have simple needs. The long-finned form is generally called the Meteor Minnow.

Native Range: China and Vietnam.

Maximum Length: 1.5 in. (4 cm) TL.

Water: 64–72°F (18–22°C); pH: 6.0–8.0; hardness: 5–19°dGH.

Min. Tank Size: 15 gal | 24x12x12 in (50 L | 60x30x30 cm).

Feeding: A small-mouthed omnivore that eats zooplankton and detritus in the wild, the White Cloud does well on fine prepared foods, and brine shrimp, bloodworms, mosquito larvae, etc.

Behavior & Care: This is a versatile fish, able to be kept in a variety of water conditions, but it does better in cooler temperatures with good oxygen levels. Maintenance requirements of tankmates must be taken into consideration in a community setting. Any changes in temperature, water chemistry, etc., must still be gradual, or the White Cloud, like any other fish, will not survive.

Breeding: It is a prolific egg-scatterer that will eat the eggs if given the chance. The fry hatch after 36 hours and will take liquid fry food.

Balantocheilos melanopterus Bleeker, 1851
Bala Shark (Tricolor Shark, Silver Shark, Shark Minnow)

Overview: Bala Sharks are big for aquarium fishes, but slow-growing, and specimens of modest size are widely sold in fish shops. They are relatively peaceful—unless you happen to be a smaller fish, which makes you prey—but they are often kept with cichlids. Balas are rare in the wild. Those in the trade are captive-bred.

Native Range: Malay Peninsula, Thailand, Sumatra, and Borneo.

Maximum Length: 15 in (38 cm) TL.

Water: 72–82°F (22–28°C); pH: 6.0–8.0; hardness: 5–19°dGH.

Min. Tank Size: 50 gal | 48x16x16 in (190 L | 120x40x40 cm).

Feeding: Bala Sharks accept standard aquarium fare, and their diets should be enhanced with live or frozen crustaceans and worms.

Behavior & Care: These large fish prefer to be in a group, although single specimens also do well as long as there are no tankmates that harass them. Regardless, a large tank is still required even for a single Bala, as they are fast swimmers that need room to maneuver, so avoid using decorations that could impair their movement. They are adept jumpers, so a fitted aquarium cover is essential.

Breeding: Not reported in the aquarium, but it is an egglayer that is bred in ponds.

Crossocheilus siamensis (Smith, 1931)
Siamese Algae Eater (SAE, Flying Fox)

Overview: The Siamese Algae Eater is the only known fish that eats red and black algae. This is the "true" SAE of aquarium fame. Distinguising features from other types of algae-eating cyprinids are: dark band at upper edge of body is uneven; horizontal bar through the middle of the caudal fin; scales on dorsal surface have dark margins; clear fins except for caudal barring; surface appears cross-hatched due to the dark margins around each scale. The fins are almost colorless except for the aforementioned caudal bar. Though herbivorous, it does not eat live plants in the aquarium.

Native Range: Thailand, Malay Peninsula.

Maximum Length: 6 in (15 cm) TL.

Water: 75–78°F (24–26°C); pH: 6.5–8.0; hardness: 5–20°dGH.

Min. Tank Size: 25 gal | 24x12x20 in (90 L | 60x30x50 cm).

Feeding: General aquarium fare with a concentration of greens.

Behavior & Care: Use a fine, sandy substrate for this fish that "mouths" every element of its environment for algae. Requires clean, well-oxygenated water.

Breeding: The Siamese Algae Eater has not been bred in the aquarium, and this is largely responsible for its being difficult to find.

Epalzeorhynchos bicolor (Smith, 1931)
Red-tailed Black Shark (Red-tailed Labeo, Labeo Bicolor)

Overview: This is a beautiful fish, but it is often a bad actor in the community setting, where its relentless activity and intolerance of even its own kind can turn it into a tyrant.

Native Range: Thailand. It may be extinct in the wild.

Maximum Length: 4.7 in (12 cm) TL.

Water: 72–78°F (22–26°C); pH: 6.5–7.5; hardness: 6–15°dGH.

Min. Tank Size: 55 gal | 48x13x20 in (195 L | 120x32.5x50 cm).

Feeding: Omnivore. Feeds from the bottom and will take all manner of sinking foods for herbivores, omnivores, and carnivores. In the wild it feeds on vegetable matter, small crustaceans, worms, and other small bottom-dwelling prey.

Behavior & Care: They can be kept singly in community tanks as long as they are the dominant fish and tankmates are benign. In a very large aquarium outfitted with ample hiding places, and if all are introduced when young, small groups can live in relative harmony. These are very active fish that require clean, well-oxygenated water.

Breeding: Not reported in the aquarium. Widely bred in ponds in southeast Asia for the aquarium trade.

Epalzeorhynchos frenatum (Fowler, 1934)
Rainbow Shark (Ruby Shark, Labeo Frenatus)

Overview: The Rainbow Shark is an interesting fish related to the barbs and danios. It tends to be a territorial species that may be aggressive, particularly toward its own kind and should not be housed with small, passive species. An albino form has been established. Do not purchase dyed fish sold by some stores. Body gray or black.

Native Range: Thailand, Cambodia.

Maximum Length: 6 in (15 cm) TL.

Water: 75–80°F (24–27°C); pH: 6.0–8.0; hardness: 5–12°dGH.

Min. Tank Size: 55 gal | 48x13x20 in (195 L | 120x32.5x50 cm).

Feeding: Omnivore. Feeds from the bottom and will take all manner of sinking foods for herbivores, omnivores, and carnivores.

Behavior & Care: Swims at all levels of the aquarium, and is a loner that prefers a densely planted aquarium decorated with rocks and driftwood, allowing the fish to avoid other tankmates and thereby avoiding confrontations. They are useful in that they will clear away detritus from the surfaces of the aquarium. They love hollow ornaments and caves.

Breeding: Although it has been bred in the aquarium, spawnings are rare because of its aggressive nature toward its own kind.

Epalzeorhynchos kalopterus (Bleeker, 1851)
Flying Fox

Overview: Often confused with *Crossocheilus siamensis*, the Flying Fox is not the most efficient of the algae-eaters, and it will eat aquarium plants. Its dorsal area is brownish. The lower half of its body is dirty white. There is a dark line through the mouth and eye to the tail. Above the dark line is a gold-colored stripe. The dorsal, anal and ventral fins are yellow- or red-tipped with white edges.

Native Range: Malaysia, Thailand, Indonesia, Borneo, Java, Sumatra.

Maximum Length: 6 in (15 cm) TL.

Water: 73–81°F (23–27°C); pH: 6.5–7.5; hardness: 5–8°dGH.

Min. Tank Size: 33 gal | 48x13x12 in (115 L | 120x32.5x30 cm).

Feeding: Omnivore. Feed a good variety of prepared foods. Green matter should be a regular part of the diet.

Behavior & Care: Although peaceful when young, the Flying Fox is a solitary, territorial species that becomes more aggressive with age. Keep only one per tank. The aquarium should have a fine substrate, and hiding places in the form of plants, hollows, and driftwood.

Breeding: Not reported in the aquarium.

Garra cambodgiensis (Tirant, 1883)
False Siamese Algae Eater (Stone-lapping Minnow, False SAE)

Overview: The False SAE has a broad midlateral stripe that stops at the caudal peduncle with a gold stripe above. The yellow or red fins are not tipped with white. There are two black bands on the dorsal fin, and the caudal fin is plain or with dark margins. There are no visible barbels.

Native Range: Southeast Asia: Mekong and Chao Phraya basins, Malay Peninsula.

Maximum Length: 6 in (15 cm) TL.

Water: 68–77°F (20–25°C); pH: 6.5–7.5; hardness: 5–8°dGH.

Min. Tank Size: 30 gal | 36x12x18 in (120 L | 90x30x45 cm).

Feeding: This fish is more of an omnivore than an herbivore, and should be offered small, meaty items as well as flake, granular, and freeze-dried foods.

Behavior & Care: This is a bottom-dweller that is best kept as the single one of its kind in the aquarium. The aquarium should be well planted with a dark substrate and good water movement. It needs very clean and well-oxygenated water.

Breeding: Not reported in the aquarium.

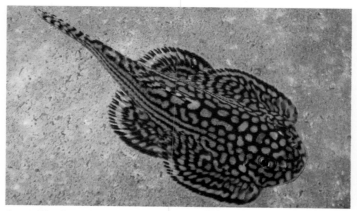

Sewellia lineolata (Valenciennes, 1849)
Gold Ring Butterfly Sucker (Tiger Hillstream Loach)

Overview: Arguably the most beautiful of all of the loaches, this hillstream loach is well worth the challenges presented by its specialized needs. Please, if you are not prepared to keep this fish properly, leave it to those who will.

Native Range: Vietnam.

Maximum Length: 2.5 in (6 cm) TL.

Water: 68–75°F (20–24°C); pH: 6.5–7.5; hardness: 5–15°dGH.

Min. Tank Size: 20 gal | 30x12x12 in (65 L | 75x30x30 cm).

Feeding: These fish have small mouths and require appropriately sized foods. Include algae, blanched greens, and *Spirulina* in the diet. Small live and frozen meaty foods are also appreciated.

Behavior & Care: Fast, well-aerated water is the order of the day with all hillstream loaches as they cling to rocks with suction from modified ventral fins. Use fine sand and small pebbles for the substrate. Plants not required, but help improve water quality, which must be pristine. Bright light promotes desirable algae growth.

Breeding: They are egglayers that produce about 20 eggs at a time over several days. The fry are tiny, and are sometimes found in the filter. Offer liquid fry food and use Java Moss in the tank.

Acantopsis choirorhynchos (Bleeker, 1854)
Horseface Loach

Overview: This fish is a burrower that will dive into the substrate, leaving only the eyes and top of its head exposed. It has an elongated, flattened body, and the eyes are protected by a transparent covering. It is diurnal as a youngster, but becomes crepuscular with age.

Native Range: Borneo, Burma, Java, Malaysia, Sumatra, Thailand, and Vietnam.

Maximum Length: 8 in (20 cm) TL. Smaller in the aquarium.

Water: 77–84°F (25–29°C); pH: 6.0–7.5; hardness: 1–15°dGH.

Min. Tank Size: 40 gal | 48x13x16 in (155 L | 120x32.5x40 cm).

Feeding: It is called a "sand sifter" because it filters sand through its gills to extract small morsels of food. Use sinking foods. Small worms and frozen meaty foods appreciated, but will take prepared foods as well.

Behavior & Care: This fish requires a deep sandy substrate so that it can bury itself. Avoid bright lights. They can be territorial with conspecifics.

Breeding: Has not been reported in the aquarium. Sexually dimorphic with the female being larger and broader than the male.

Botia almorhae Gray, 1831
Yoyo Loach (Pakistani Loach, Botia Lohachata)

Overview: The Yoyo Loach is a social animal that can be kept with other loaches and other small, peaceful fishes. Body markings are variable in this species, and there is a marked difference between juveniles and adults. Adults develop a more reticulated pattern than the juveniles. When stressed, this fish will "gray-out," darkening overall.

Native Range: India and Pakistan.

Maximum Length: 5 in (13 cm) TL.

Water: 74–82°F (23–28°C); pH: 6.0–7.5; hardness: 5–15°dGH.

Min. Tank Size: 40 gal | 48x13x16 in (155 L | 120x32.5x40 cm).

Feeding: Omnivore. New acquisitions may need live worms to get them feeding properly, after which they will accept prepared foods as well as live and frozen meaty foods, especially snails.

Behavior & Care: This is an active, generally peaceful fish that is best kept in a school of six or more individuals. It does best in a quiet, well-decorated and planted aquarium without strong water movement. Use a sandy substrate to protect the sensitive barbels.

Breeding: Not reported in the aquarium.

Botia kubotai Kottelat, 2004
Polka-dot Loach (Marble Loach)

Overview: The pattern on this fish is highly variable and its black, gray, and gold colors change with age. Dark areas increase over time, and in some fish blue shows up in the tan areas.

Native Range: Burma and Thailand.

Maximum Length: 5 in (13 cm) TL.

Water: 75–82°F (24–28°C); pH: 6.5–7.5; hardness: 5–15°dGH.

Min. Tank Size: 25 gal | 24x12x20 in (90 L | 60x30x50 cm).

Feeding: Omnivore. Start new fish on live worms to initiate feeding. Then they will accept prepared foods as well as live and frozen meaty foods which they take from the bottom of the aquarium.

Behavior & Care: Use a fine substrate to protect their tender mouth-parts. Provide numerous caves and shelters to give the Polka-dot Loach greater confidence. This is a gregarious fish that should be kept in schools of about six fish. Without scales, White Spot (Ich) is a concern, and medications should be chosen and used—usually at half-strength—with its scalelessness in mind.

Breeding: Not reported in the aquarium.

Botia striata Narayan Rao, 1920
Zebra Loach (Striped Loach)

Overview: The variable golden vertical stripes on the brown body of the Zebra Loach make quite a fashion statement on this most attractive loach. This is a smallish, peaceful fish with a reputation for becoming agitated prior to changes in the weather.

Native Range: India. Endangered in parts of its range.

Maximum Length: 4 in (10 cm) TL.

Water: 73–77°F (23–25°C); pH: 6.0–7.5; hardness: 5–12°dGH.

Min. Tank Size: 30 gal | 36x12x16 in (105 L | 90x30x40 cm).

Feeding: Omnivore. Readily accepts all standard aquarium fare. Small live snails are greedily eaten.

Behavior & Care: The Zebra Loach is sometimes found in still waters with low levels of oxygen and surprisingly poor quality, but in the aquarium should be provided with clean, well-aerated water, plenty of hiding places, and low-light plants. Leave open space for swimming. A fine-textured substrate will prevent damage to their four barbels as they continually sift about for food. Zebra Loaches are happiest in small groups, but can be a little aggressive with conspecifics.

Breeding: Not reported in the aquarium.

Botia histrionica, Burmese Loach, Max. Length: 4.6 in (11.5 cm).

Botia dario, Bengal Loach, Max. Length: 6 in (15 cm).

When kept in groups of three or more, loaches will often gather to perform "loach dances," making figure-8 patterns as they swim up and down in the water column.

Chromobotia macracanthus (Bleeker, 1852)
Clown Loach (Botia macracantha)

Overview: The Clown Loach is well named. When small, they are endearing comics that roll over, play dead, make amusing clicking noises, and even seem dressed for the circus with broad bands of orange and black. When grown, their size just makes them unmanageable in smaller aquaria.

Native Range: Borneo, Sumatra, and Kalimantan.

Maximum Length: 12 in (30 cm) TL.

Water: 77–83°F (25–30°C); pH: 6.0–7.5; hardness: 5–12°dGH.

Min. Tank Size: 65 gal | 48x18x18 in (240 L | 120x45x45 cm).

Feeding: Small Clowns often need live worms, like _Tubifex_, to start feeding, but once they start, they are omnivores that have a decided taste for live snails, sucking them right out of their shells.

Behavior & Care: These fish need room to grow, and since they are better in groups, require a very large aquarium when they are adults. They should have plenty of hiding places and subdued lighting. Use sturdy live plants, like Anubias or Java Fern. The water should be well aerated and very clean. There is a sharp spine under each eye that can inflict damage.

Breeding: Not reported in the aquarium.

Pangio kuhlii (Valenciennes, 1846)
Kuhli Loach (Coolie Loach, Acanthophthalmus Kuhlii)

Overview: This small, eel-like fish is peaceful and hardy. It has the sharp cheek spines common to other loaches, so beware when handling and bagging.

Native Range: Thailand, Malaysia, Indonesia.

Maximum Length: 4 in (10 cm) TL.

Water: 72–79°F (22–26°C); pH: 6.5–7.5; hardness: 5–15°dGH.

Min. Tank Size: 15 gal | 24x12x12 in (50 L | 60x30x30 cm).

Feeding: Kuhli Loaches "work" the substrate for tiny bits of food. They are very fond of small worms, but will take standard aquarium fare without reservation. Feed first thing in the morning and after turning off the lights at night.

Behavior & Care: Often groups of Kuhlis will tangle themselves into tight balls and secrete themselves under an object in the aquarium. Other times they will swim freely in the open. They do very well in established aquaria—they are sensitive to questionable water quality—and have a real affinity for planted aquaria. Use a fine sand substrate.

Breeding: May occasionally spawn in the aquarium, but few reports have been made to date.

Yasuhikotakia morleti Tirant, 1885
Skunk Loach (Hora's Loach, Botia Morleti, Botia Horei)

Overview: The Skunk Loach is a real beauty with a black stripe from the top of its head to its spotted tail and a gleaming brownish gold body.

Native Range: Cambodia, Laos, Thailand.

Maximum Length: 4 in (10 cm) TL.

Water: 79–82°F (26–28°C); pH: 6.0–7.5; hardness: 5–12°dGH.

Min. Tank Size: 30 gal | 36x18x12 in (120 L | 90x45x30 cm).

Feeding: Omnivore. Accepts most small foods: flake, algae wafers, and small live, and frozen meaty foods. It will eat any dead fish in the aquarium, but it is not a good practice to leave corpses in the tank, as this could lead to the spread of diseases.

Behavior & Care: A fine, sandy substrate protects the delicate barbels of this digging fish. Caves, plants, and driftwood all contribute to its sense of well-being. The water should be well aerated, and water quality should be tip-top at all times. This is a small, but lively loach that is best kept in groups of six or more to diffuse aggression. It is not suitable for any but the largest community aquarium, and then the other fishes must be fast and able to look out for themselves.

Breeding: Not reported in the aquarium.

Yasuhikotakia sidthimunki (Klausewitz, 1959)
Dwarf Loach (Sid, Dwarf Chain Loach, Botia Sidthimunki)

Overview: Peaceful and a little shy, the Dwarf Loach is great for a community aquarium. The chain pattern is quite distinctive on this attractive silver and black fish with a touch of gold above the eye.
Native Range: Cambodia, Laos, and Thailand. Critically endangered.
Maximum Length: 2.5 in (6 cm) TL.
Water: 75–82°F (24–28°C); pH: 6.0–7.5; hardness: 12°dGH.
Min. Tank Size: 30 gal | 36x18x12 in (120 L | 90x45x30 cm).
Feeding: Accepts most small foods: flake, algae wafers; and small live and frozen meaty foods.
Behavior & Care: They need to be kept in a school of five or more to thrive, and dither fish will make them less shy. Use a mature aquarium with a fine, sandy substrate. The tank should be furnished with plants, driftwood, and caves.
Breeding: It has been reported that this species has been spawned in the aquarium, which is good news, as it had previously only been spawned commercially through the use of hormones. Frequent water changes, a varied diet, and Indian Almond (*Catappa* sp.) leaves, which lower the pH, were thought to have stimulated the spawning.

Gyrinocheilus aymonieri (Tirant, 1883)
Chinese Algae-eater (Sucking Loach)

Overview: Although the Chinese Algae-eater has been in the hobby for decades, these loners can grow to about a foot (30 cm) in length and aren't particularly good at eating algae. They get more belligerent and unattractive with age and are a species to avoid. The Chinese Algae-eater will rasp the mucus off flat-sided tankmates, such as Angelfishes, *Pterophyllum* spp. and Discus, *Symphysodon* spp.

Native Range: India, Thailand.

Maximum Length: 12 in (30 cm) TL. (Usually smaller.)

Water: 75–82°F (24–28°C); pH: 6.0–8.0; hardness: 5–20°dGH.

Min. Tank Size: 30 gal | 36x18x12 in (120 L | 90x45x30 cm).

Feeding: Algae is required for young fish, but they become more carnivorous as they mature, when they will eat prepared foods in preference to foraging for algae.

Behavior & Care: Adults are highly territorial. They inhabit streams and river bottoms, and in swift currents cling to hard substrates with their suckermouths. They appreciate an aquarium equipped with hollows for hiding.

Breeding: Not reported in the aquarium, but they are mass-produced in the Far East, purportedly by hormone treatment.

Distichodus lusosso Schilthuis, 1891
Lusosso (Long-nosed Distichodus)

Overview: This impressive fish has an extended tubular shape with a longish snout, a high back, bright red fins, and six dark bars on an orange body. It grows slowly and the head stays smallish while the body expands in size—significantly. Colors fade with age.
Native Range: Africa: Congo basin including Malebo Pool (formerly Stanley Pool), Angola.
Maximum Length: 15 in (38 cm) TL.
Water: 72–78°F (22–26°C); pH: 6.0–7.5; hardness: 2–15°dGH.
Min. Tank Size: 75 gal | 48x18x20 in (270 L | 120x45x50 cm).
Feeding: Worms, invertebrates, and soft vegetation. It will take prepared aquarium foods, with algae-based pellets recommended.
Behavior & Care: This is a large, active fish that keeps to the lower region of the aquarium. Bearing in mind that open swimming space is important, add some driftwood or other cover to give Lusosso more confidence. It will eat any fish it can swallow and any live plants other than perhaps very tough-leaved ones like _Anubias_, _Crinum_, etc. Though a relatively peaceful fish, it can hold its own in large tanks with other big fishes.
Breeding: Not reported in the aquarium.

Distichodus engycephalus, Niger Distichodus.

Distichodus sexfasciatus, Six-lined Distichodus

Distochodus play well with larger West African cichlids. With their small mouths, they don't seem well equipped to look out for themselves, but their speed and courage allow them to live with other formidable—though not outright homicidal—fishes.

Hemiodus gracilis Günther, 1864
Red-tailed Hemiodus (Slender Hemiodus, Hemiodopsis Gracilis)

Overview: This sleek schooling fish has a lively manner and characteristic tail-down position. The red streak on the bottom edge of the lower tail lobe is the distinguishing feature of this elegant, agile, and peaceful community fish, ideally in a mixed tetra tank.

Native Range: Brazil and Venezuela in the Amazon and Orinoco river systems.

Maximum Length: 6.5 in (16.5 cm) SL.

Water: 75–82°F (24–28°C); pH: 6.0–6.8; hardness: 0–5°dGH.

Min. Tank Size: 38 gal | 48x12x16 in (140 L | 120x30x40 cm).

Feeding: Omnivore. Accepts standard aquarium fare, but needs some vegetable matter. Bloodworms and Daphnia are favorite foods.

Behavior & Care: Best kept in schools of ten or more fish, the Red-tailed Hemiodus will bring action to the middle range of a peaceful community aquarium. Keep the tank well covered, as these fish are a little nervous and will jump, especially if the tank is not long enough. They do best if they have cover in the form of floating plants like *Riccia*.

Breeding: Egglayers. Not reported.

Abramites hypselonotus Günther, 1868
Marbled Headstander (Leporinus Hypselonotus)

Overview: The Marbled Headstander is easy to keep and will hold its own with moderately sized cichlids. It generally swims in a head-down position, but this doesn't stop it from ravaging the tempting fins of long-finned fishes like Angelfishes (*Pterophyllum* spp.), etc. It will eat all but the toughest of aquarium plants.

Native Range: Amazon, Orinoco, and Paraguay-Paraná basins.

Maximum Length: 5.5 in (14 cm) TL.

Water: 72–83° F (18–28°C); pH: 6.5–7.5; hardness: 0–10°dGH.

Min. Tank Size: 30 gal | 36x18x12 in (120 L | 90x45x30 cm).

Feeding: Primarily herbivorous. Takes prepared foods such as algae tablets and pellets and live and frozen meaty foods as well. Fresh blanched greens are also appreciated.

Behavior & Care: They are relatively peaceful when young, but may take exception to conspecifics when grown unless they are in a fairly large group of six or more. They will jump when startled, so cover the aquarium. They should have a soft, sand substrate and hiding places formed from driftwood, rocks, and other aquarium decorations. Use bright light to promote algae growth.

Breeding: Has not been reported in the aquarium.

Anostomus anostomus (Linnaeus, 1758)
Striped Headstander (Leporinus Anostomus)

Overview: The Striped Headstander is a favorite of advanced aquarists, as there is still much to be learned about it. The upturned mouth suggests a top-feeder, but it can be seen pecking at algae from vertical surfaces, including the stalks of plants. It works the rocky edges of fast-flowing shallow waters, where the algae is most abundant.

Native Range: Guyana.

Maximum Length: 8 in (20 cm) TL.

Water: 75–82°F (24–28°C); pH: 6.5–7.5; hardness: 0–10°dGH.

Min. Tank Size: 40 gal | 36x18x16 in (160 L | 90x45x40 cm).

Feeding: Omnivore with herbivorous tendencies. Chopped, boiled spinach is useful as an occasional treat, but should not be fed daily.

Behavior & Care: This fish does well if it is the single specimen in a community of similarly sized, peaceful fishes or kept in a group of six or more to diffuse aggression. Use a dark substrate of soft sand or fine gravel and tough plants like *Anubias*. Provide hiding spaces, and use a fitted cover as the fish is a jumper. The water should be well aerated. Strong lighting will encourage algae growth for grazing.

Breeding: It is commonly bred in commercial hatcheries, and may have been bred in the aquarium.

Leporinus fasciatus (Bloch, 1794)
Black-banded Leporinus

Overview: This is an elongate fish with a small mouth and big eyes. The males sometimes have an orange or red throat. There are a number of subspecies as this fish is widely distributed across its range.

Native Range: South America: Amazon river basin.

Maximum Length: 12 in (30 cm) TL.

Water: 75–82°F (24–28°C); pH: 6.5–7.5; hardness: 2–15°dGH.

Min. Tank Size: 65 gal | 36x18x24 in (240 L | 90x45x60 cm).

Feeding: Omnivore with herbivorous tendencies. Green foods, either fresh (blanched or microwaved to soften tissue), or in the form of algae or _Spirulina_ wafers, are suggested.

Behavior & Care: Use a dark-colored substrate of soft sand or fine gravel. There should be a number of hiding places of driftwood, rocks, etc. Use an efficient filter that provides good water current. These fish jump, so a fitted cover is necessary. It is a peaceful fish that won't molest tankmates other than an occasional nibbled fin. It will, however, eat all but the toughest aquarium plants, ie, _Anubias_, Java Moss, and Java Ferns of all descriptions.

Breeding: Has not been reported in the aquarium.

Leporinus arcus, Lipstick Leporinus.

Leporinus friderici, Three-spot Leporinus.

Headstanders shelter and feed in crevices. They will lean into vertical fissures in rocks and cork-bark backgrounds where they feed off algae and detritus wedged in the nooks and crannies.

Hoplias malabaricus (Bloch, 1794)
Wolf Fish (Wolf Characin, Common Trahira, Tiger Tetra)

Overview: This is a formidable fish that is not to be kept without a full appreciation of its strength and sharp teeth. It cannot be kept with other fishes in the aquarium. It is a mottled brown or gray. In the wild, it can travel long distances overland when it rains.

Native Range: South America from Costa Rica to Argentina, Trinidad.

Maximum Length: 20 in (50 cm) TL.

Water: 75–78°F (24–26°C); pH: 6.0–8.0; hardness: 0–25°dGH.

Min. Tank Size: 120 gal | 48x24x24 in (430 L | 120x60x60 cm).

Feeding: It will eat any fish that it can hunt down. It also eats crustaceans, insects, earthworms, and other meaty foods.

Behavior & Care: This fish is not particularly choosy about its conditions, as it is found in clear, moving water as well as slow, turbid ditches, but the aquarium must be well filtered. It is a nocturnal predator that likes to hide under an overhang during the day. Use a weighted cover, as they will escape otherwise. Keep aquarium lights subdued. Live plants will be demolished.

Breeding: The female deposits between 2,000 and 3,000 eggs in a large nest that is guarded by the male.

Copella arnoldi (Regan, 1912)
Splash Tetra (Copeina Arnoldi, Pyrrhulina Filamentosa)

Overview: The Splash Tetra is well known for its unusual breeding behavior, where the pair actually leaps out of the water to lay eggs on overhanging plants where egg predators can't reach them. Other members of the genus spawn normally.

Native Range: South America from the mouth of the Orinoco to the lower Amazon.

Maximum Length: 3.5 in (9 cm) TL.

Water: 77–84°F (25–29°C); pH: 6.0–8.0; hardness: 0–20°dGH.

Min. Tank Size: 20 gal | 30x12x12 in (65 L | 75x30x30 cm).

Feeding: Small live foods, commercial aquarium foods.

Behavior & Care: Use floating plants, like Indian Fern. It is helpful to lower the water level, and use a roughened glass cover which will also be used as a spawning site. Peaceful and easy to keep.

Breeding: The pair leaps out of the water together to deposit about six eggs at a time on a plant leaf or roughened glass cover. There is a total of about 200 eggs. The male guards the site, splashing the eggs with water to keep them moist. When the eggs hatch, the larvae drop to the bottom and hover for about a week, after which they will start to feed on micro foods.

Nannostomus beckfordi Günther, 1872
Golden Pencilfish (Beckford's Pencilfish)

Overview: This is a fish with many color variations depending upon where it was collected. It is distinguished by a wide band of black from the snout to the caudal peduncle and touches of red on a gold body.

Native Range: Central Amazon and lower Rio Negro; coastal rivers in the Guianas and northeastern Brazil.

Maximum Length: 2.5 in (6.5 cm) TL.

Water: 75–78°F (24–26°C); pH: 6.0–7.5; hardness: 0–10°dGH.

Min. Tank Size: 20 gal | 30x12x12 in (65 L | 75x30x30 cm).

Feeding: Omnivore that takes tiny live and prepared foods.

Behavior & Care: This is a peaceful, timid fish that does well in a group of five or more. Provide plenty of hiding places and use live plants, including floating plants. Maintain superior water quality at all times. Use a dark-colored substrate. Use peat in the filter or peat extract to add tannins and humins to the water.

Breeding: Egglayers that will eat the eggs unless they are protected by fine-leaved plants or a spawning mop. Use dim light and peat-filtered water. The eggs hatch in 24–36 hours and the fry are free-swimming six days post hatching. Start the fry on liquid fry food added to the water near the fry and keep Java Moss in the tank.

Nannostomus marginatus Eigenmann, 1909
Dwarf Pencilfish

Overview: This tiny fish, one of the smallest members of its genus, is very peaceful and timid. It has been a staple in the hobby for some 80 years. It is an ideal fish for aquarists with small tanks, but it can also thrive in a community of small, peaceful tankmates. It has a wide range and exists in different geographical color forms.

Native Range: Northern South America, east of the Andes.

Maximum Length: 1.4 in (3.5cm) TL.

Water: 75–78°F (24–26°C); pH: 6.5–7.5; hardness: 0–10°dGH.

Min. Tank Size: 10 gal | 20x10x12 in (35 L | 50x25x30 cm).

Feeding: Small live foods are preferred, but will take prepared aquarium foods as well.

Behavior & Care: Above all, do not put this fish in a tank with larger, threatening fishes or it will spend all of its time hiding. Use fine-leaved plants like Java Moss and floating plants to diffuse light (Indian Fern, *Riccia*), a dark substrate, and a dark background. Then this little jewel will show its true colors.

Breeding: These egglayers should produce viable young in a single-species tank under the conditions described above.

Nannostomus mortenthaleri Paepke & Arendt, 2001
Coral Red Pencilfish (Mortenthaler's Pencilfish, Peru Red Pencilfish)

Overview: A recent discovery that became an instant hit in the hobby. The stunning coral red is more intense in the males.

Native Range: To date only from a limited area in Peru.

Maximum Length: 1.5 in (4 cm) TL.

Water: 75–78°F (24–26°C); pH: 6.5–7.0; hardness: 0–10°dGH.

Min. Tank Size: 10 gal | 20x10x12 in (35 L | 50x25x30 cm).

Feeding: Tiny live foods; prepared aquarium foods.

Behavior & Care: The tank should be well planted and the fish should be kept in larger groups to reduce intraspecific aggression and fin-nipping. They will get along with other small, peaceful fishes. They should have a well-planted tank with a dark substrate and background. Maintain excellent water quality at all times. The males can be very aggressive with one another, and this could lead to losses in this expensive, but desirable fish.

Breeding: They are inveterate egg-eaters, and the spawning tank should be filled with Java Moss *and* mesh on the bottom *and* the parents removed after spawning. The fry should be fed infusoria first, and after a week, they will accept brine shrimp nauplii.

Nannostomus trifasciatus Steindachner, 1876
Three-striped Pencilfish (Three-banded Pencilfish)

Overview: As with most pencilfishes, the Three-striped Pencilfish has a different color pattern between night and day. It has three black stripes that run the length of the body during the day, and at night there are three dark spots on its sides. *N. trifasciatus* is a greenish-gold color on its back and sides and silver on the belly.

Native Range: Amazon drainage, upper Orinoco system.

Maximum Length: 2.5 in (6.5 cm) TL.

Water: 75–80°F (24–27°C); pH: 5.5–7.0; hardness: 0–10°dGH.

Min. Tank Size: 20 gal | 30x12x12 in (65 L | 75x30x30 cm).

Feeding: Small live and prepared aquarium foods.

Behavior & Care: This is a good fish for a peaceful community aquarium. The males defend small territories. Keep them in a well-planted aquarium with some natural sunlight to see their colors pop. Maintain pristine water quality.

Breeding: They spawn among the leaves of plants. The eggs are adhesive; 30–70 eggs are produced at a time and hatch in 18–72 hours, depending upon the water temperature. First foods could consist of liquid egglayer fry food, infusoria, and later newly hatched brine shrimp.

Nannostomus eques, Brown Pencilfish.

Nannostomus unifasciatus, Oneline Pencilfish.

If a small group of pencilfishes is kept in a well-planted aquarium with the recommended water parameters, most species will spawn, and some fry will survive, to be discovered among the plants.

Carnegiella marthae Myers, 1927
Black-winged Hatchetfish

Overview: This is a delicate little fish with its share of endearing peculiarities—like leaping and flying. It is usually silver with black appearing to outline the body, but the color can show up as iridescent green or violet depending upon the light.

Native Range: South America: Rio Negro, Orinoco.

Maximum Length: 1.5 in (4 cm) TL.

Water: 75–84°F (24–29°C); pH: 5.5–6.5; hardness: 1–8°dGH.

Min. Tank Size: 20 gal | 30x12x12 in (65 L | 75x30x30 cm).

Feeding: Carnivore. Use small live, frozen meaty, and prepared aquarium foods that float. Wingless fruitflies are favorites.

Behavior & Care: This is a peaceful, top-dwelling community fish that should be kept only with other small, peaceful fishes, preferably ones that occupy the lower levels of the aquarium. Like all hatchetfishes, the Black-winged Hatchetfish may jump when chased or chasing food, so a secure aquarium cover is required. Use floating plants and filter the water over peat for best success with this fish.

Breeding: Egglayers that require intensive conditioning on live foods and peaty, soft water to produce fry. Remove the parents after spawning. The eggs hatch in 30–36 hours. Fine fry foods.

Carnegiella strigata (Günther, 1864)
Marbled Hatchetfish

Overview: Hatchetfishes really do "fly," unlike other flying fishes (who only jump and sail); they flap their largish pectorals while in midair.

Native Range: Entire Amazon basin, Rio Caqueta in Colombia, and rivers in the Guianas.

Maximum Length: 1.5 in (4 cm) TL.

Water: 75–84°F (24–29°C); pH: 5.5–6.5; hardness: 1–8°dGH.

Min. Tank Size: 20 gal | 30x12x12 in (65 L | 75x30x30 cm).

Feeding: Carnivore. It will take small frozen foods (like mosquito larvae) and prepared foods as long as they float, like frozen mosquito larvae. Use a worm feeder for sinking worms like bloodworms. This will keep the food up near the surface where the fish can access it.

Behavior & Care: Does best in groups in a community of small, peaceful fishes. Use floating plants, like Indian Fern, and plant the substrate as well. They are somewhat timid (with good reason, as many so-called community fishes will come up under them and try to eat them) and flighty. Blackwater extract is useful for these fish.

Breeding: Eggs are scattered to drop among plants or gravel. They hatch within 36 hours. Females have larger abdomens than males.

Gasteropelecus sternicla (Linnaeus, 1758)
Silver Hatchetfish (Common Hatchetfish, River Hatchetfish)

Overview: This is probably the hardiest of the hatchetfishes and the best for beginners, who may be unable to provide specialized water conditions.

Native Range: South America: the Peruvian and middle Amazon, the Guianas and Venezuela.

Maximum Length: 2 in (5 cm) TL.

Water: 73–81°F (23–27°C); pH: 6.0–7.5; hardness: 0–10°dGH.

Min. Tank Size: 29 gal | 30x12x18 in (100 L | 75x30x45 cm).

Feeding: Carnivore. They will take live and frozen meaty foods as well as small prepared aquarium foods, provided they float.

Behavior & Care: This is a schooling species best kept in groups of five or more. It spends most of its time in the upper level of the water. Peaceful toward other fishes, they frequently bicker among themselves. They are jumpers, so the tank must be well covered. Floating plants help prevent losses and provide security for the fish as well as keeping them from bouncing off the cover or light fittings during flying practices. Some keepers use deep tanks with lowered water levels and floating plants to help protect the little leapers.

Breeding: Egglayer. Breeding not reported in the aquarium.

Thoracocharax securis (De Filippi, 1853)
Platinum Hatchetfish (Giant Hatchetfish)

Overview: The largest known hatchetfish, easily confused with *Gasteropelecus sternicla*, but grows larger. It is found in fast-flowing streams, especially in the shallows on bends. We tend to think of "hatchets" as stillwater fishes from vegetated biotopes, but this is not usually the case, and most need well-oxygenated water, especially at higher temperatures.

Native Range: South America: Amazon river basin.

Maximum Length: 3.5 in (9 cm) TL.

Water: 73–86°F (23–30°C); pH: 6.0–7.5; hardness: 0–10°dGH.

Min. Tank Size: 30 gal | 36x12x16 in (105 L | 90x30x40 cm).

Feeding: Carnivore. A worm feeder is ideal for this fish. Fill with bloodworms or tubificids.

Behavior & Care: The Platinum Hatchetfish is a scaredy-cat that will hide or jump or be badly stressed if kept singly. A school of at least five Hatchets is ideal. The jumping is built in, and a response to flying insects above or predators below, so keep the tank covered. They are totally peaceful towards other fishes, and can be kept with non-aggressive middle- and bottom-dwellers.

Breeding: Not reported in the aquarium.

Ctenolucius hujeta (Valenciennes, 1850)
Freshwater Barracuda (Hujeta, Slant-nosed Gar)

Overview: The Freshwater Barracuda has lip membranes that extend posteriorly, enabling it to gather air from the surface of poorly oxygenated waters. This species and the rather similar *Ctenolucius beani* are calm-water predators that school when juveniles, but become solitary hunters when adult.

Native Range: Lowland rivers of Colombia and Venezuela.

Maximum Length: 28 in (70 cm) TL. Usually smaller.

Water: 75–82°F (24–28°C); pH: 6.5–7.5; hardness: 0–10°dGH.

Min. Tank Size: 180 gal | 72x24x24 in (650 L | 180x60x60 cm).

Feeding: Carnivore. Live feeder fish are taken with great gusto. It will also take live worms and other soft live foods like mealworms. Non-live foods are not accepted initially, but may be over time.

Behavior & Care: This is a predator that can only be kept with fishes it cannot eat or with others of its own kind. Plant well, but leave ample open swimming space. Cover the tank as it is a jumper.

Breeding: The male is smaller than the female with a larger anal fin with a "frayed" edge; it is straight in females. The fry are cannibalistic unless fed adequately. Otherwise, they are easy to rear.

Hepsetus odoe (Bloch, 1794)
African Pike Characin

Overview: Aquarists do not always realize that some of their charges are regarded as food in their native lands. This one is and is also a great angling fish that gives a good fight. Despite being a predator, it can be timid and panics easily, and can seriously injure itself against any sharp-edged decorations.

Native Range: West and Central Africa.

Maximum Length: 24 in (60 cm) TL. Usually smaller in aquaria.

Water: 76–79°F (25–27°C); pH: 7.0–7.5; hardness: 2–10°dGH.

Min. Tank Size: 65 gal | 48x18x18 in (240 L | 120x45x45 cm).

Feeding: Carnivore. This lightning-fast predator hides on the edges of dense areas of plant growth waiting for smaller fishes. It must be supplied with live foods until it will accept thawed frozen fish, or it will starve.

Behavior & Care: Tankmates should be large but peaceful. Heavy planting and efficient filtration are required. A heavy, full tank cover will prevent accidental losses. Be sure the fish sees you before putting your fingers in the water, or it might mistake you for food!

Breeding: These fish build free-floating bubblenests that are guarded by one or both parents. Breeding not reported in the aquarium.

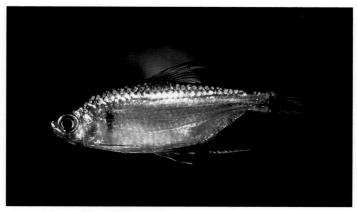

Alestopetersius caudalis (Boulenger, 1899)
Yellowtail Tetra (Yellow-tailed Congo Tetra)

Overview: This and most of the other African tetras (family Alestidae) that follow are peaceful but active schooling fishes that will grace any community. A common error is to keep them in too small a tank, as most are larger than the more familiar South American tetras.
Native Range: West Africa: lower Congo drainage.
Maximum Length: 3 in (7 cm) TL.
Water: 72–79°F (22–26°C); pH: 6.5–7.5; hardness: 0–15°dGH.
Min. Tank Size: 38 gal | 36x16x16 in (140 L | 90x40x40 cm).
Feeding: Small carnivore foods—live, frozen, and prepared.
Behavior & Care: A real gem of a fish, excellent for a reasonably-sized community tank. Keep in a school of six or more and ensure there is plenty of open swimming space against a backdrop of plants. A dark substrate will help encourage color and discourage shyness.
Breeding: Males have white tips to the pelvic fins, clear in females. Egg-scatterer that lays several hundred eggs. Use a breeding tank with Java Moss and a spawning mesh to prevent egg cannibalism. Bright (sun)light is thought to trigger spawning. Fry free-swimming after 6–7 days. Feed on infusorias or liquid food initially.

Arnoldichthys spilopterus (Boulenger, 1909)
Niger Tetra (African Red-eyed Characin)

Overview: A peaceful schooling fish that will grace any reasonably large general community with plenty of swimming space.

Native Range: Nigeria: coastal rivers from Lagos to the Niger Delta.

Maximum Length: 4 in (10 cm) TL.

Water: 75–82°F (24–28°C); pH: 6.0–7.5; hardness: 0–15°dGH.

Min. Tank Size: 38 gal | 36x16x16 in (140 L | 90x40x40 cm).

Feeding: Live and frozen foods; will also take flake.

Behavior & Care: Soft, slightly acid water is best, though higher hardness and pH are tolerated. Keep in a school of at least six. Will look its best with dark substrate and slightly peaty water. Plant the back of the tank but leave adequate open swimming space.

Breeding: In males the anal fin is curved and striped, in females straight with a black tip. Egg-scatterer that may lay more than 1000 eggs. Use a breeding tank with soft, slightly acid water and a substrate of fine sand or peat, then a layer of Java Moss. Remove adults after spawning. Hatching in about 36 hours, free-swimming on day 6–8. The soft substrate is required as the fry are nervous and will dive to the bottom if alarmed. Feed infusoria and other micro-foods initially; later *Artemia* nauplii, etc. Fast-growing.

Brycinus longipinnis (Günther, 1864)
Longfin Tetra (Long-finned Characin)

Overview: A sizeable African tetra and a long-time favorite in the hobby. The colors are subtle rather than gaudy, but given the right light—ideally indirect sunlight—and a dark substrate, these fishes are truly splendid.

Native Range: Lowland rivers in West and Central Africa, from Sierra Leone south to the DR Congo, and including the Niger Delta.

Maximum Length: 5 in (13 cm) TL.

Water: 72–79°F (22–26°C); pH: 6.5–7.5; hardness: 0–15°dGH.

Min. Tank Size: 50 gal | 48x16x16 in (190 L | 120x40x40 cm).

Feeding: Live, frozen, and prepared foods are all taken readily.

Behavior & Care: This species really does require a 4-foot (120 cm) tank as an absolute minimum. It is reported as being rather nitrate-sensitive, so monitor levels regularly, and perform extra partial water changes if required to keep the reading below 20 ppm. Planting the length of the rear glass will also help keep nitrate down, but do leave plenty of swimming space. Minimum school size: six.

Breeding: Adult males have elongated dorsal fin rays. Remarkably there are no reports of breeding even though this fish has been in the hobby for 80 years. It is probably an egg-scatterer.

Brycinus nurse (Rüppel, 1832)
Nurse Tetra

Overview: A large tank with large fishes needs a really large tetra—
and this is the one for the African community. But don't forget, like
most tetras it is a schooling fish, so "large tank" means just that.
For a big fish it is remarkably elegant in its deportment.

Native Range: Tropical Africa: widespread from Senegal to the Nile
drainage, in a wide variety of habitats.

Maximum Length: 10 in (25 cm) TL.

Water: 72-82°F (22-28°C); pH 6.0-8.0; hardness 0-25°dGH.

Min. Tank Size: 180 gal | 72x24x24 in (650 L | 180x60x60 cm).
Will need a larger tank for a school when fully grown.

Feeding: An omnivore that will eat any standard aquarium foods.

Behavior & Care: The school can be limited to 3–4 for practical reasons.
Hardy and totally peaceful. Does not harm plants, which should line
the rear and ends of the tank. Efficient filtration is essential.

Breeding: Easily sexed by the shape of the anal fin—the rear edge is
concave in males, straight in females. Because of its size, probably not
bred in captivity, but in today's large all-glass tanks all things are possible. In the wild it spawns in flooded grassland along river margins
during the rains. _Vallisneria_ might be a suitable alternative.

Ladigesia roloffi Géry, 1968
Jellybean Tetra (Sierra Leone Dwarf Characin)

Overview: This delightful little tetra shares some parts of its natural habitat with the tiny Chocolate Killie (*Pseudepiplatys annulatus*, qv), and there is no reason not to simulate nature in the aquarium as long as your skills and water chemistry are adequate to the rather tricky and delicate killifish.

Native Range: Africa: Liberia, Sierra Leone, Ivory Coast, Ghana.

Maximum Length: 1.5 in (4 cm) TL.

Water: 72–79°F (22–26°C); pH: 6.0–7.0; hardness: 0–10°dGH.

Min. Tank Size: 25 gal | 24x16x16 in (95 L | 60x40x40 cm).

Feeding: Any small live, frozen, and/or prepared foods.

Behavior & Care: Keep in a school of at least six, with peaceful tank-mates of similar size. These tetras jump if startled, so fit a tight lid; floating vegetation will help deter leaping. Dwarf tropical waterlilies are particularly effective as the fishes can then swim among the leaf stems, below the pads. Dark substrate and peat filtration advised.

Breeding: The male has a longer anal fin. Use a breeding tank with a loose peat substrate and very soft, somewhat acid (pH 6) water; remove the parent fish when spawning is over. The fry are extremely small and require infusorians or liquid food initially.

Lepidarchus adonis Roberts, 1966
Adonis Tetra

Overview: Unlike most African tetras, this one is tiny—in fact one of the smallest fishes kept in the aquarium. A miniature jewel!

Native Range: Lowland drainages in Ghana and Ivory Coast.

Maximum Length: 1 in (2.5 cm) TL.

Water: 72–79°F (22–26°C); pH: 5.5–6.5; hardness: 0–5°dGH.

Min. Tank Size: 10 gal | 18x12x12 in (40 L | 45x30x30 cm).

Feeding: Tiny carnivore foods—*Artemia* nauplii, Grindal Worms, sifted Daphnia, Cyclops, Cod roe, small, frozen and dried foods.

Behavior & Care: This fish can be kept in a very small tank, but remember, it is delicate and sensitive to poor water quality, and small volumes of water are difficult to keep healthy. A bigger tank is better. Keep in a school, with plants, and peat filtration to keep the pH low. House only with very small tankmates, eg pencilfishes.

Breeding: Males have purple spots on the tail and posterior body. Easy to breed. Use a breeding tank with Java Moss or feathery plants such as *Cabomba*, on which the 25–30 eggs will be laid. They hatch after 1–2 days and the fry swim free after about a week. They can take *Artemia* nauplii. They prefer dark conditions so put the tank in a dark spot and illuminate only a small feeding area in one corner.

Micralestes stormsi (Peters, 1852)
Red Congo Tetra

Overview: This fish and its cousins *M. acutidens* and *M. humilis*, the Sharp-toothed Tetra and the African Red-fin Tetra from Ghana, are among the hardiest members of the African tetras, with no special demands as regards water chemistry. All are good beginner's fishes for a community aquarium.

Native Range: Widespread in tropical Africa, in the Congo Basin, Chad and Ituri; also reported from Tanzania. Occurs in still, slow-moving, and fast-flowing waters.

Maximum Length: 4 in (10 cm) TL.

Water: 72–82°F (22–28°C); pH: 6.0–8.0; hardness: 0–20°dGH.

Min. Tank Size: 38 gal | 36x16x16 in (140 L | 90x40x40 cm).

Feeding: Any small foods, including live, frozen, and flake, are eagerly taken.

Behavior & Care: Peaceful. Keep in a school of six plus, in a tank planted along the back but with plenty of swimming space.

Breeding: Although this fish is easy to keep, so far breeding is unreported. The male is more slender than the female, and the sexes have differently-shaped anal fins. In the wild it migrates when the rains come, to spawn during the summer.

Phenacogrammus interruptus (Boulenger, 1899)
Congo Tetra

Overview: Probably the most popular African tetra in the hobby, this fish is often a victim of the perception that all tetras are little fishes for small tanks or a lack of understanding that it is a schooling fish—nothing is more miserable than a solitary Congo Tetra! But kept properly, in a school in a large tank, it is quite magnificent.

Native Range: West central Africa: Congo drainage.

Maximum Length: 3 in (8 cm) TL.

Water: 75–82°F (24–28°C); pH: 6.0–8.0; hardness: 0–15°dGH.

Min. Tank Size: 50 gal | 48x16x16 in (190 L | 120x40x40 cm).

Feeding: Will take almost any small carnivore foods.

Behavior & Care: Keep in a school of six or more in a large tank. Hardy as regards water chemistry, but ideally use very soft and slightly acid to neutral water. Plant the back of the tank with tall plants, but leave plenty of open swimming space for this active swimmer. Do not keep with fin-nippers that may attack its flowing finnage.

Breeding: Males larger, with longer fins. Egg-scatterer. Use a breeding tank with Java Moss over a spawning mesh. Bright (sun)light is thought to trigger spawning. Fry are free-swimming after 6–7 days. Feed them on infusorians or liquid food initially.

Alestopetersius smykalai, Smykalai.

Brycinus affinis, Redfin Robber.

Tetras are usually found in near-shore open water where they live and feed. They are active, but not overwrought as some busy fishes seem to be.

Alestopetersius nigropterus, Orange Flash Tetra.

Phenacogrammus altus, Altus Tetra.

The reflectiveness of the scales on many African Tetras is incredible when viewed in natural light. A little bit of indirect sunlight shows the special beauty of these fishes and should not overheat the water.

Aphyocharax anisitsi Eigenmann & Kennedy, 1903
Bloodfin Tetra (Glass Bloodfin, Red-finned Characin)

Overview: A school of six or more of these bright, colorful tetras is quite at home in a peaceful community or a species tank. These are ideal beginner's fish, hardy, long-lived, and easy to breed.

Native Range: Rio Paraná drainage, in southern Brazil, Paraguay, and northern Argentina.

Maximum Length: 2 in (5 cm) TL.

Water: 68–82°F (20–28°C); pH: 6.0–8.0; hardness: 2–20°dGH.

Min. Tank Size: 15 gal | 24x12x12 in (50 L | 60x30x30 cm).

Feeding: Omnivore. Brine shrimp and bloodworms are preferred, but standard aquarium fare is well accepted.

Behavior & Care: Use a dark substrate, a clear swimming area, and rooted and floating aquatic plants. *Ambulia* is as undemanding as this fish, and will help to purify the water and provide a sense of security and a spawning site for the Bloodfins.

Breeding: Mature males are brightest and have a hook-shaped anal fin. These fishes prefer a planted tank for spawning and must be removed if the eggs are to be saved. A few fry are likely to survive in a well-planted species tank where the adults are kept well fed.

Aphyocharax rathbuni Eigenmann, 1907
Green Fire Tetra (Rathbun's Bloodfin, Redflank Bloodfin)

Overview: A school of this Bloodfin would be at home with a school of White Clouds, *Tanichthys albonubes*, in terms of temperament, temperature, and water chemistry.

Native Range: South America: Rio Paraguay drainage in Paraguay. The species has a southerly distribution with seasonal climate variations.

Maximum Length: 2 in (5 cm) TL.

Water: 68–78°F (20–26°C); pH: 6.0–7.5; hardness: 0–12°dGH.

Min. Tank Size: 15 gal | 24x12x12 in (50 L | 60x30x30 cm).

Feeding: Omnivore. Will accept most small live, frozen, and prepared aquarium foods.

Behavior & Care: This is a relatively hardy tetra that should be kept in schools of at least six—the more the merrier. Because of their southerly, sub-tropical distribution, these tetras do well at the lower end of their temperature range, except for breeding, when the temperature should be raised.

Breeding: The males have white tips on the dorsal, pelvic, and pectoral fins. Each female scatters a few eggs in plants. Java Moss is ideal for protecting the eggs, which hatch in about 24 hours. Remove adults as they eat the eggs. Fry feed on infusoria.

Astyanax jordani (Hubbs & Innes, 1936)
Blind Cave Tetra (Blind Cavefish, Anophthichthys Jordani)

Overview: This popular fish is a curiosity rather than a beauty queen. It is one of a number of "blind cavefishes" that live in total darkness and hence have lost their pigment and their eyes, as both are redundant. Instead they use their lateral line systems to navigate and find food by scent. Note that this species is found in limestone caves and is a strictly hard-water fish, unlike most tetras. Some scientists regard it as simply a form of *A. fasciatus,* and it may also be found, in both shops and literature, under that name.

Native Range: Mexico: cave systems near San Luis Potosi.

Maximum Length: 3.5 in (9 cm) TL.

Water: 68–77°F (20–25°C); pH 7.5–9.0; hardness 10–25°dGH.

Min. Tank Size: 38 gal | 36x16x16 in (140 L | 90x40x40 cm).

Feeding: Any small aquarium foods are accepted readily.

Behavior & Care: A hardy, peaceful, schooling fish, ideal for any general community. Unfussy about décor though water-worn rocks are most natural. Best kept in a group of six or more.

Breeding: Males are slimmer. Breeding tank with marbles to save the eggs; temperature around 68°F (20°C). Remove adults after spawning. The fry have eyes initially; first food *Artemia* nauplii.

Axelrodia riesei Géry, 1966
Ruby Tetra

Overview: The common name tells the truth. This is a rare gem. They used to be very common, but retailers soon realized that they are fragile shippers that require careful acclimatization and are highly sensitive to poor water quality. That said, they are well worth the effort for experienced fishkeepers who like a challenge.

Native Range: Colombia: upper Rio Meta basin.

Maximum Length: 1.5 in (4 cm) TL.

Water: 68–78°F (20–26°C); pH: 6.5–7.0; hardness: 0–8°dGH.

Min. Tank Size: 15 gal | 24x12x12 in (50 L | 60x30x30 cm).

Feeding: Omnivore. Will accept most small live, frozen, and prepared aquarium foods. As color loss in captivity is an issue with these animals, color-enhancing foods rich in carotenoids will help retain color, as will careful attention to water chemistry and quality.

Behavior & Care: Keep the Ruby Tetra in the largest school practicable in a mature aquarium. Plants, a dark substrate, and frequent small water changes are advised.

Breeding: Difficult. The female is more rounded than the male. The best thing is to put six fish in a species tank with a densely planted substrate, using plants like Java Moss and Marimo, or Moss Balls, etc.

Boehlkea fredcochui Géry, 1966
Blue Tetra (Cochu's Blue Tetra, Microbrycon Cochui)

Overview: The bright colors on this active, streamlined fish make it a perfect candidate for the planted aquarium where the focus is on having a low fish population to favor the plant life. In such a setting, you want a lot of piscine intensity without big appetites.
Native Range: South America: upper Amazon river basin in the Peru/Colombia/Brazil border area.
Maximum Length: 2 in (5 cm) TL.
Water: 72–81°F (22–27°C); pH: 5.5–7.5; hardness: 0–10°dGH.
Feeding: Omnivore. Will accept most small live, frozen, and prepared aquarium foods. Will peck at aquarium plants, but generally doesn't do too much damage; supplement diet with vegetable foods.
Behavior & Care: This fish looks best in a shady aquarium with a dark substrate, so low-light plants are preferred. The fish need a spacious, well-oxygenated aquarium with ample swimming space. They do tend to be nippy, so avoid keeping them with long-finned fishes. In fact, they'd do best in a planted species tank with 10 or more fish.
Breeding: Rarely spawns in captivity. Males are slimmer than females. Eggs are deposited under leaves.

Chalceus macrolepidotus Cuvier, 1818
Pinktailed Chalceus

Overview: This very active fish is ideal for the large cichlid community. It is predatory, and moves through the water slowly, paying attention to happenings inside and outside the aquarium. Has been confused in the hobby with its relative, _C. erythurus_, from the Amazon.

Native Range: Rio Negro and Orinoco drainages and coastal rivers in the Guianas.

Maximum Length: 10 in (25 cm) TL.

Water: 72–78°F (22–26°C); pH: 6.8–7.5; hardness: 0–10°dGH.

Min. Tank Size: 50 gal | 48x16x16 in (190 L | 120x40x40 cm).

Feeding: Omnivore: live small fishes, crustaceans, worms, etc.; chopped meat; prepared foods.

Behavior & Care: This skittish fish is very jumpy, so a weighted tank cover is needed. Use tall plants along the back and sides to create a dimmed space in the upper reaches with an open area midwater. The water should be well-oxygenated, but not turbulent. They are a little touchy when newly imported, but acclimate well with care.

Breeding: Rarely bred in aquaria, and there are few details available, except that it happens only in very large tanks. Egg-eating parents.

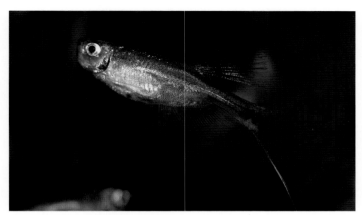

Corynopoma riisei Gill, 1858
Swordtail Characin

Overview: This is one of the glandulocaudines, fishes that practice "safer procreation." The females are inseminated internally, and later lay the eggs when the conditions are best for hatching.

Native Range: Northern Venezuela, eastern Colombia, Trinidad.

Maximum Length: 2.5 in (6.5 cm) TL.

Water: 72–82°F (22–28°C); pH: 6.0–7.0; hardness: 0–10°dGH.

Min. Tank Size: 20 gal | 30x12x12 in (65 L | 75x30x30 cm).

Feeding: Omnivore. Takes live and frozen foods such as Daphnia, bloodworms, etc., from the surface; will sometimes accept small prepared foods.

Behavior & Care: This is a gentle, delicate fish that should be kept in a group of at least six; more is better. Keep open space for swimming, and floating plants like Indian Fern are appreciated. A little driftwood and a dark substrate add to the ambiance. They should be quarantined carefully, as they tend to pick up diseases easily.

Breeding: The gill cover of the male is elongated into a thin, light-colored stalk with a small black tip that the male waves during courtship. After a few days of sexual activity females should be removed to a separate, planted tank. When fry are seen, remove the females.

Crenuchus spilurus Günther, 1863
Sailfin Tetra

Overview: This species is unusual: most characins school, but the Sailfin does not. Keep in groups of one male to three females. They get along well with small tetras, dwarf cichlids, and *Corydoras* spp., but they are territorial.

Native Range: Lower and middle Amazon, Orinoco, and coastal drainages in the Guianas.

Maximum Length: 2.5 in (6 cm) TL.

Water: 74–86°F (23–30°C); pH: 5.0–6.5; hardness: 1–5°dGH.

Min. Tank Size: 20 gal | 24x12x16 in (70 L | 60x30x40 cm).

Feeding: Small live and frozen meaty foods like Daphnia, flake, etc. It is called a micropredator; it tracks its food before striking.

Behavior & Care: The Sailfin is timid, and benefits from a "cozy" tank, with a dark substrate, plants, bogwood, caves, and a bit of peat extract. Dappled light is best, as when floating plants are used.

Breeding: The male is colorful and the dorsal and lower lobe of the tail are prolonged. The male guards the eggs, which are laid on the ceiling of a cave, for the 48 hours until hatching, and then the wrigglers for a week more until the wrigglers become free-swimming.

Exodon paradoxus Müller & Troschel, 1845
Bucktooth Tetra

Overview: The Bucktooth is not for sissies. Even when kept in schools of a dozen or more, they are still quite aggressive with other silvery fishes and will nip their scales and fins. Most catfishes are safe.

Native Range: Brazilian Amazon drainage and Guyana.

Maximum Length: 6 in (15 cm) TL. Smaller in captivity.

Water: 73–82°F (23–28°C); pH: 5.5–7.5; hardness: 0–12°dGH.

Min. Tank Size: 65 gal | 48x18x18 in (240 L | 120x45x45 cm).

Feeding: These are good eaters that will take virtually any food, dead or alive, as well as prepared aquarium foods.

Behavior & Care: This species is not suggested for the typical community tank as it is highly predatory. Use a sandy substrate and a few bits of bogwood, and a variety of plants. Pay special attention to filtration, as these fish produce a significant amount of waste.

Breeding: Condition a pair, and remove to a planted tank with soft, acidic water. The eggs are scattered among plants, and the parents should be removed. The young are cannibalistic and must be sized and culled often. Start the fry on brine shrimp nauplii and increase the food size frequently.

Gymnocorymbus ternetzi (Boulenger, 1895)
Black Widow Tetra (Black Tetra)

Overview: Black Widows are great community fish, and any little nippiness on their part is diffused in a school of six or more of these fish. They belong in a tropical rainforest setting with dappled light and shadowy corners, along with dwarf cichlids, other tetras, rasboras, and peaceful bottom-dwellers.

Native Range: Guaporé and Paraguay basins, south to Argentina. In the mid and upper zones of quiet waters.

Maximum Length: 2.5 in (6 cm) TL.

Water: 68–78°F (20–26°C); pH: 6.0–8.0; hardness: 0–20°dGH.

Min. Tank Size: 20 gal | 24x12x16 in (70 L | 60x30x40 cm).

Feeding: Omnivore. Takes most prepared aquarium foods.

Behavior & Care: Use a dark substrate and plants around the sides and back of the tank. The tank should not be too bright.

Breeding: The male is slimmer and more colorful than the rounded female. Add a pair or a group to an aquarium prepared as above, but use a spawning mesh and fine-leaved plants to help protect the adhesive eggs from the parents. Keep the tank lights dim. Remove the adults after spawning. Start the fry on liquid egglayer food, offering larger foods as the fry grow.

Hasemania nana (Lütken, 1875)
Silvertip Tetra (Copper Tetra)

Overview: These schooling tetras are fond of quiet, light-dappled waters. Like most tetras, they do well in a peaceful community, and proof that they are thriving is when you spy small silver slivers hovering over the substrate detritus. Yes, they will spawn in a community setting, and provided there is a good diet for all and plenty of cover, some fry will survive to keep the population steady. This is one of the few characins that does not have the characteristic adipose fin.

Native Range: Brazil: Rio São Francisco basin.

Maximum Length: 2 in (5 cm) TL.

Water: 74–82°F (23–28°C); pH: 6.0–8.0; hardness: 5–20°dGH.

Min. Tank Size: 20 gal | 24x12x16 in (70 L | 60x30x40 cm).

Feeding: Omnivore. Accepts small prepared aquarium foods supplemented with small live or frozen foods, e.g. brine shrimp, Daphnia.

Behavior & Care: The Silvertip is comfortable with fine substrate with some driftwood and fine-leaved plants, especially Java Moss. Add dried oak leaves to simulate "leaf litter" and to acidify the water.

Breeding: The male is the slimmer and more colorful fish. Females get fat when gravid. Soft, acidic water, dim lights, and protection for the adhesive eggs will generally result in at least some fry.

Hemigrammus bleheri Géry & Mahnert, 1986
Firehead Tetra

Overview: The Firehead is often confused with the Rummynose Tetra, *H. rhodostomus,* and the False Rummynose, *Petitella georgiae.*
Native Range: Brazil and Colombia: Rio Negro, Rio Meta basins.
Maximum Length: 2 in (5 cm) TL.
Water: 74–79°F (23–26°C); pH: 5.5–7.0; hardness: 2–15°dGH.
Min. Tank Size: 20 gal | 24x12x16 in (70 L | 60x30x40 cm).
Feeding: Omnivore. Accepts small prepared aquarium foods supplemented with small live or frozen foods, e.g. brine shrimp, Daphnia.
Behavior & Care: Must be kept in schools! It does best in a blackwater biotope with a sandy substrate and driftwood roots. Dim lighting and peat extract to stain the water a weak-tea color accentuates the coloration of the fish. If the red nose loses color, it is an indication of deteriorating aquarium conditions.
Breeding: The males are slimmer than the females. They will spawn in groups or pairs, either way, there must be an "egg safe" if you want to rear fry. An egg safe is anything that keeps the adults from eating the eggs: Java Moss, spawning mops, marbles, mesh, etc. To trigger spawning in ripe females, raise the temperature slightly and perform a water change. Eggs hatch in about 24 hours. The fry are tiny.

Hemigrammus erythrozonus Durbin, 1909
Glowlight Tetra

Overview: This is a fish native to quiet jungle streams with tannin-stained water and lazy water currents. This is a very popular community fish because a school gives great color and action without nippiness. Most aquarium stock is mass-produced, so it is an excellent beginner's fish. It is also available in an albino form.

Native Range: Guyana: Essequibo River.

Maximum Length: 1.5 in (4 cm) TL.

Water: 75–82°F (24–28°C); pH: 5.5–7.5; hardness: 0–12°dGH.

Min. Tank Size: 20 gal | 24x12x16 in (70 L | 60x30x40 cm).

Feeding: Omnivore. Accepts small prepared aquarium foods supplemented with small live or frozen foods and greens.

Behavior & Care: Six or more Glowlights will illuminate a dappled blackwater biotope. Use blackwater extract, a sandy substrate, and driftwood for an authentic feel. Plants are optional, but rarely would plants not be welcome in an aquarium—except when there are fishes that destroy them—and Glowlights do not molest plants.

Breeding: The females are larger; males are more colorful. Dim the lights, and perform water change with slightly warmer, soft, acidic, and peat-filtered water. Use Java Moss or mesh to protect the fry.

Hemigrammus ocellifer (Steindachner, 1882)
Head- and Tail-light Tetra

Overview: This is a schooling tetra that is perfect in a peaceful community tank with other tetra species, dwarf cichlids, corys, and other non-aggressive fishes with similar care requirements. Most tetras, however, will nip at fins that are long and/or flowing, so do not try to keep them with fish like bettas or gouramis, for example.

Native Range: Brazil, Peru, Guyana, Surinam, Guiana.

Maximum Length: 2 in (5 cm) TL.

Water: 75–82°F (24–28°C); pH: 5.5–7.5; hardness: 0–12°dGH.

Min. Tank Size: 20 gal | 24x12x16 in (70 L | 60x30x40 cm).

Feeding: Will accept all food types, suitably sized.

Behavior & Care: A calm, planted tank with open swimming space is preferred. Peat filtration or blackwater extract helps to bring out the colors and stimulates spawning.

Breeding: The pointed swimbladder of the male is discernible through the skin. Condition a group of fish with small live and/or frozen foods. When the females are gravid with eggs, remove them to the prepared spawning tank. They will spawn within 24–48 hours, usually in the evening. Remove the parents after spawning. The eggs will hatch in 24 hours depending on temperature.

Hemigrammus pulcher Ladiges, 1938
Pretty Tetra (Garnet Tetra, Black Wedge Tetra)

Overview: A native of slow-moving, rainforest streams and small rivers, this is an excellent peaceful-community fish, expecially for beginners.

Native Range: Peru: tributaries of the upper Amazon.

Maximum Length: 2 in (5 cm) TL.

Water: 74–80°F (23–27°C); pH: 5.5–7.0; hardness: 1–10°dGH.

Min. Tank Size: 20 gal | 24x12x16 in (70 L | 60x30x40 cm).

Feeding: Omnivore. Accepts small prepared and live/frozen foods.

Behavior & Care: Set up for this fish as you would other tetras. The addition of peat greatly enhances the well-being of this fish. Use a sandy substrate with plenty of plants, and these fish will do well, especially if the lighting is not too bright.

Breeding: The swimbladder is pointed in males and rounded in females. Ideally the spawning tank should be a mature aquarium with its own sponge filter and a substrate of marbles or mesh, and a spawning mop or Java Moss or other fine-leaved plants. The temperature should be raised to 82°F (28°C). The addition of aquarium-safe peat moss or blackwater extract to soft water is known to stimulate spawning in many rainforest fishes.

Hemigrammus rhodostomus Ahl, 1924
Rummynose Tetra

Overview: This tetra is famous for its use as a companion to Discus (*Symphysodon* spp.) They are especially effective in a group of a dozen fish, as they are tight schoolers—unlike some other schooling fishes that barely seem to know one another. The snout is pale first thing in the morning, but soon brightens up. If the red snout is washed out at other times, check the water quality immediately. They are like canaries in the coal mine as far as water quality is concerned.

Native Range: South America: Rio Orinoco and Amazon basins.

Maximum Length: 2 in (5 cm) TL.

Water: 76–80°F (24–27°C); pH: 5.5–7.0; hardness: 0–10°dGH.

Min. Tank Size: 20 gal | 24x12x16 in (70 L | 60x30x40 cm).

Feeding: Omnivore. Accepts small prepared and live/frozen foods.

Behavior & Care: The school will compulsively swim into the outflow of a powerhead; remove the powerhead, and they settle into a quiet area midwater and feed and swim normally. Use a dark substrate and background, and plants if possible. Leave open swimming room.

Breeding: Use a mature aquarium with soft, acidic water at 82°F (28°C) with fine-leaved plants and a mesh/marble substrate. The fry are tiny and start on infusoria.

Hyphessobrycon anisitsi (Eigenmann, 1907)
Buenos Aires Tetra

Overview: This long-time aquarium fish isn't welcome in most peaceful communities. It's a bit of a bully, and even when it's kept properly in a school, aggression is reduced but not eliminated. It also has quite an appetite for aquarium plants; not a fish for an avid aquatic gardener. Most aquarium stock is commercially produced.

Native Range: Brazil, Paraguay, and Argentina.

Maximum Length: 3 in (7 cm) TL.

Water: 64–82°F (18–28°C); pH: 6.0–8.0; hardness: 5–20°dGH.

Min. Tank Size: 30 gal | 36x12x16 in (105 L | 90x30x40 cm).

Feeding: Omnivore. Takes a variety of small prepared aquarium foods plus small live and frozen aquarium foods. Supplement the diet with a good vegetable flake, crushed peas with the skins slipped off, soft *Spirulina* pellets, etc.

Behavior & Care: Though it accepts a wide range of conditions, changes in water chemistry and temperature should be gradual to avoid shock. Use the dark substrate, driftwood, and peat extract commonly advised for tetras. To get around the plant-eating, use unpalatable plants, such as *Anubias*, Java Fern, and Java Moss.

Breeding: Typical egg-scatterer.

Hyphessobrycon eques (Steindachner, 1882)
Serpae Tetra (Callistus Tetra, Jewel Tetra)

Overview: This species is native to still rainforest backwaters. They are feisty little fish that really need the companionship of at least six, and preferably ten, conspecifics or they will abuse tankmates. The white "flag" on the anal fin is variable—sometimes bigger and brighter on one fish than on the others. It does well in a community as long as there are no flowing fins to tempt it, and it makes a good dither fish for timid cichlids.

Native Range: Rio Guaporé and Rio Paraguay, in Brazil, Paraguay, and Argentina.

Maximum Length: 1.5 in (4 cm) TL.

Water: 72–82°F (22–28°C); pH: 5.5–7.5; hardness: 0–12°dGH.

Min. Tank Size: 25 gal | 24x12x20 in (90 L | 60x30x50 cm).

Feeding: Omnivore. Takes a variety of small prepared aquarium foods, plus small live and frozen aquarium foods, from midwater.

Behavior & Care: This fish looks best in subdued light with a dark substrate and low-light plants. They usually stay in the same area of the tank—a place with calm water and plants—and dance around each other constantly, performing mock battles with no losers.

Breeding: Breeds in typical tetra fashion; eggs are light-sensitive.

Hyphessobrycon erythrostigma (Fowler, 1943)
Bleeding-heart Tetra

Overview: A school of Bleeding Hearts makes a real statement in the aquarium because they are deep-bodied with an erect dorsal that gives them presence. Keep them in a school of at least five conspecifics to minimize bad habits like nipping and chasing other fishes, especially those with long fins.

Native Range: South America: upper Amazon basin.

Maximum Length: 3 in (7.5 cm) TL.

Water: 73–82°F (23–28°C); pH: 5.5–7.0; hardness: 0–10°dGH.

Min. Tank Size: 30 gal | 36x12x16 in (105 L | 90x30x40 cm.

Feeding: Omnivore. Requires a varied diet of small aquarium foods.

Behavior & Care: Leave a little swimming room open in the center of the tank, and use plants and driftwood to create the nooks and crannies that will make these fish feel safe. Use dark materials for the substrate and background. Add peat to the water to bring out the intense colors of this fish. Avoid keeping them in alkaline water.

Breeding: The dorsal and anal fins of the males are longer and more colorful than those of the females. Egg-scatterers. They are considered difficult to breed, but will do so under ideal conditions. The eggs and fry are light-sensitive. The eggs hatch in about 30 hours.

Hyphessobrycon flammeus Myers, 1924
Flame Tetra (Fire Tetra, Red Tetra)

Overview: This fish does best in a school of at least six fish in a species tank or a community aquarium with other peaceful fishes.
Native Range: Coastal rivers near Rio de Janeiro, Brazil.
Maximum Length: 1.5 in (4 cm) TL.
Water: 72–82°F (22–28°C); pH: 5.5–7.5; hardness: 0–12°dGH.
Min. Tank Size: 15 gal | 20x10x18 in (55 L | 50x25x45 cm).
Feeding: Omnivore. Accepts small prepared, frozen, and live foods. Condition for breeding with live brine shrimp, Daphnia, etc.
Behavior & Care: A well-planted tank with a dark substrate and treatment with peat is the best way to see the spectacular colors of this fish. Can be kept in slightly alkaline water, but may fade in color.
Breeding: The male is distinguished by his deep red anal fin. Use a mature aquarium, with protection for the eggs as the parents will eat them as soon as they are laid. The eggs will not hatch if exposed to light, and the fry are sensitive to light, so keep the tank dim. The eggs will hatch in 24+ hours. The fry are tiny, and when they are seen to peck at the sponge filter and Java Moss in the aquarium, it is time to start adding liquid fry food or infusoria. When they are large enough to take them, add newly hatched brine shrimp to the diet.

Hyphessobrycon herbertaxelrodi Géry, 1961
Black Neon Tetra

Overview: These are slightly touchy tetras that do not fare well without a school of at least six fish. If there are only two, the dominant fish will assume a head-up posture and stalk the lesser until it kills it, but when there are six or more, relative peace reigns in the aquarium. The gold and black lines are prominent and distinct.

Native Range: South America: Paraguay basin.

Maximum Length: 1.5 in (4 cm) TL.

Water: 74–82°F (23–28°C); pH: 5.5–7.5; hardness: 0–12°dGH.

Min. Tank Size: 20 gal | 24x12x16 in (70 L | 60x30x40 cm).

Feeding: Omnivore. Requires a varied diet of small aquarium foods.

Behavior & Care: Give this fish a well-planted tank with dark substrate and background and an open swimming area. Peat extract or a mesh bag filled with aquarium-safe peat in the filter brings out the best color and condition in this fish.

Breeding: Use a separate breeding tank with fine-leaved plants and marbles and/or mesh to protect the eggs. The adults should be well conditioned with a variety of live foods before introduction to the spawning tank. The hugely distended abdomens of the females are an indication of their readiness to spawn.

Hyphessobrycon loretoensis Ladiges, 1938
Loreto Tetra (Hyphessobrycon Metae)

Overview: This little tetra has been known to the hobby and science for some 80 years, and is thus one of the evergreen species, though unfortunately it is not to be found in every store. It is very similar to the Peruvian Tetra, *H. peruvianus* (qv) in appearance. Well worth trying as a change from the bread-and-butter species.

Native Range: The upper Amazon drainage in Peru; described from the Loreto region, hence the common name.

Maximum Length: 1.5 in (4 cm) TL.

Water: 72–80°F (22–27°C); pH: 5.5–7.5; hardness: 0–12°dGH.

Min. Tank Size: 25 gal | 24x16x16 in (95 L | 60x40x40 cm).

Feeding: Small live, frozen, and prepared foods are relished.

Behavior & Care: Keep in a school of at least five or six in a well-planted aquarium. Peaceful and an excellent community fish. A little trickier than some of the commoner, mass-produced tetras, so pay attention to water chemistry and quality.

Breeding: Females are more rounded than males. Not often bred successfully. Use a breeding tank with soft, acid, peaty water, fine-leaved plants, plus spawning mesh or marbles to protect the eggs. Remove the parents after spawning. Infusoria as first food.

Hyphessobrycon peruvianus Ladiges, 1938
Peruvian Tetra (Blue Loreto Tetra)

Overview: This tetra is a close cousin of the Loreto Tetra (*H. loretoensis*) but has much less red in the tail. Like its cousin it has been in the hobby for some 80 years, but is one of the less commonplace species in stores.

Native Range: Upper Amazon drainage in Peru, in the area of Iquitos and Tabatinga.

Maximum Length: 1.75 in (4.5 cm) TL.

Water: 72–80°F (22–27°C); pH: 5.5–7.5; hardness: 0–12°dGH.

Min. Tank Size: 25 gal | 24x16x16 in (95 L | 60x40x40 cm).

Feeding: This tetra will do well on any small foods, live, frozen or prepared, but newly imported stocks may require live food initially.

Behavior & Care: This species tends to be rather nervous if kept under bright light, so a cover of floating vegetation is advised as well as the usual substrate planting. Keep in a school of six or more, with small, peaceful tankmates—not boisterous or much larger fishes. Dark substrate may also increase confidence.

Breeding: Males are slimmer-bodied than females. Reports of breeding apparently relate to the Loreto Tetra, but as they are closely related the procedure and requirements are almost certainly similar.

Hyphessobrycon pulchripinnis Ahl, 1937
Lemon Tetra

Overview: The Lemon Tetra is a gentle, curious fish with a bright yellow aura further enhanced by a snazzy black edge to the anal fin in the male. Often passed by as it rarely shows its best colors in the store tanks, it is a real jewel for those who prefer subtle loveliness.

Native Range: Brazil: Rio Tapajós basin, which empties into the Amazon just above Santarém. Vegetated habitat.

Maximum Length: 1.5 in (4 cm) TL.

Water: 72–82°F (22–28°C); pH: 5.5–7.5; hardness: 0–12°dGH.

Min. Tank Size: 25 gal | 24x16x16 in (95 L | 60x40x40 cm).

Feeding: Omnivore. Color-enhancing foods rich in carotene, e.g. shrimp, bring out the red and yellow pigments in this fish.

Behavior & Care: Use a dark substrate and background for a sublime contrast with a school (keep six or more) of bright gems who will play in the gentle current of an internal power filter. Adjust the directional flow occasionally to sweep up detritus in the tank. Surface vegetation—floating plants, dwarf waterlilies (*Nymphaea*), or long-leaved trailing growths. Loses color in hard alkaline water. Regular small water changes. Peat filtration (or peat extract) are beneficial.

Breeding: Keep six very well in a species tank and look for fry.

Hyphessobrycon socolofi Weitzman, 1977
Spotfin Tetra (Cherry-spot Tetra, Lesser Bleeding Heart Tetra)

Overview: This fish is often confused with the Bleeding Heart Tetra, _H. erythrostigma_, and is probably more frequent in the trade than the latter. Both are excellent tetras for the general community. However, this one is noted for being susceptible to bacterial infections, perhaps as it is mistakenly kept in the "easier" water conditions that suit its cousin. Acid water is anti-bacterial!

Native Range: South America: Rio Negro drainage in Brazil.
Maximum Length: 2 in (5 cm) TL.
Water: 75–82°F (24–28°C); pH: 4.5–7.0; hardness: 0–8°dGH.
Min. Tank Size: 25 gal | 24x16x16 in (95 L | 60x40x40 cm).
Feeding: Small live, frozen, and prepared foods, in variety.
Behavior & Care: A peaceful community fish for soft, acid, peaty water aquaria only. Keep a school of at least six. Plants (including floating), dark substrate, muted lighting.
Breeding: When adult, males are larger with a bluer dorsal fin; the female's dorsal fin is tipped with red and she is plumper. Use a breeding tank with fine-leaved plants or Java Moss, marbles or spawning mesh to protect the eggs, and water with a pH of 6.0 or less and a temperature at the top end of the range given above.

Hyphessobrycon sweglesi (Géry, 1961)
Red Phantom Tetra (Megalamphodus Sweglesi)

Overview: Like its cousin *H. megalopterus*, the Black Phantom Tetra, this tetra is better known in its old genus *Megalamphodus*. Be warned, it is much fussier in its requirements than its relative, and while it is an equally good community fish, the water must be to its liking, with tankmates chosen to match

Native Range: Upper Orinoco drainage in Colombia.

Maximum Length: 1.5 in (4 cm) TL.

Water: 68–73°F (20–23°C); pH: 5.5–7.5; hardness: 0–12°dGH.

Min. Tank Size: 25 gal | 24x16x16 in (95 L | 60x40x40 cm).

Feeding: Small live, frozen, prepared foods. Frequent small feeds.

Behavior & Care: This fish should not be kept too warm (including for breeding), and prefers soft acid water and subdued lighting. Frequent small water changes are beneficial. Floating plants and dark substrate will encourage its best colors. A good fish to keep with dwarf cichlid and catfish species with similar water requirements.

Breeding: The female has a red, white, and black dorsal fin, the male's is larger and red. Condition with live foods. Use a breeding tank with very soft water at pH 5.5–6.0, fine-leaved plants, spawning mesh, and dim light. The fry can take *Artemia* nauplii as first food.

Inpaichthys kerri Géry & Junk, 1977
Royal Tetra (Blue Emperor Tetra)

Overview: This fish is one of many brought back by the explorer and collector Heiko Bleher from the remote areas of South America to which he ventures in search of new fishes. It is the only member of its genus, a unique jewel of a tetra. Only the males are blue. It is rather delicate and best left to experienced aquarists.

Native Range: South America: the Rio Aripuanã in the Madeira drainage; Mato Grosso, Brazil.

Maximum Length: 1.5 in (4 cm) TL.

Water: 75–82°F (24–28°C); pH: 6.0–7.0; hardness: 0–8°dGH.

Min. Tank Size: 25 gal | 24x16x16 in (95 L | 60x40x40 cm).

Feeding: Will take flake, but live and frozen foods are beneficial and should be used for conditioning for breeding.

Behavior & Care: Keep in a small school (5+) in a planted aquarium with soft, acid to neutral water, dark substrate, and subdued lighting. Males will show their best colors only if conditions are to their liking. Tankmates should be small, peaceful, and not boisterous.

Breeding: Males are larger and more colorful. Use a dimly lit tank, fine-leaved plants, and spawning mesh. The eggs are laid singly over several hours and hatch in two days. Infusoria as first food.

Metynnis argenteus Ahl, 1923
Silver Dollar

Overview: *Metynnis* are large characins that belong to the same sub-family as the infamous piranhas, but don't worry, they will only eat your plants, not other fishes or your fingers. This is the most common species in the hobby, and a school is a splendid sight.

Native Range: The Rio Tapajós drainage (Amazon system).

Maximum Length: 5.5 in (14 cm) TL.

Water: 75–82°F (24–28°C); pH: 6.5–7.5; hardness: 0–15°dGH.

Min. Tank Size: 65 gal | 48x18x18 in (240 L | 120x45x45 cm).

Feeding: Robust vegetable foods: blanched lettuce and spinach, duckweed, soft-leaved aquarium-plant prunings, herbivore pellets.

Behavior & Care: Active, peaceful schooling fishes. Keep in a group of six or more with fishes of similar size and temperament. Good tankmates for medium-sized cichlids, often equally hostile to plants, with just rocks and wood as décor.

Breeding: Males have a longer anal fin with a reddish hue. Peat filtration, and dimmed light followed by brighter, may trigger spawning. Often spawns in schools among floating plants; the eggs drop to the bottom and should be saved by spawning mesh. The fry are omnivorous: feed infusorians, then other small live foods and flake.

Metynnis fasciatus, Banded Silver Dollar.

Metynnis luna, Moon Silver Dollar, or Luna Silver Dollar.

Java Moss is perfect in a silver dollar aquarium. No matter how much the fish abuse it, it will only improve and grow as the fishes pull it apart and spread it about.

Mimagoniates microlepis (Steindachner, 1877)
Blue Tetra

Overview: An attractive tetra that requires muted light to show its colors to best effect. Note that it comes from more southerly climes than many of its kind, and is ideal for a cooler community.

Native Range: Southeastern Brazil, mainly in clear coastal rivers.

Maximum Length: 2.5 in (6 cm) TL.

Water: 66–74°F (19–23°C); pH: 6.5–7.5; hardness: 0–12°dGH.

Min. Tank Size: 38 gal | 36x16x16 in (140 L | 90x40x40 cm).

Feeding: Any small live, frozen, and manufactured foods.

Behavior & Care: This tetra tends not to school as such, but still needs to be kept in a small group as it likes the company of its own kind. A peaceful fish but a restless swimmer that needs lots of space. The back and ends of the tank should be planted, and a cover of floating greenery will provide the dim light this fish prefers. Dark substrate is also beneficial.

Breeding: Adult males are larger and more colorful, with longer fins. Condition the adults well with live foods. Plant-spawners, so use a breeding tank with Java Moss or spawning mops; soft, slightly acid water is required. Remove the adults after spawning. The fry hatch in three days and require infusoria as first food.

Moenkhausia dichroura (Kner, 1858)
Bandtail Tetra (Spot-tailed Tetra, Spot-tailed Moenkhausia)

Overview: *Moenkhausia* is a large genus of tetras, several of which are seen in the hobby. All are peaceful schooling fishes and quite easy to keep, except that some—this one included—tend not to live long in hard water. Their colors are delicate and subtle rather than gaudy, and best seen in a subdued light amid darker-colored décor. *M. intermedia* looks very similar to *M. dichroura*.

Native Range: Amazon, Paraguay, and Orinoco drainages.

Maximum Length: 1.75 in (4.5 cm) TL.

Water: 75–82°F (22–28°C); pH: 5.5–7.0; hardness: 0–8°dGH.

Min. Tank Size: 25 gal | 24x16x16 in (95 L | 60x40x40 cm).

Feeding: Like most small tetras, this species will enjoy any small live and frozen foods, and will also take flake.

Behavior & Care: Keep in a school of at least six, in a tank with a dark, hardness-free substrate and dark background, a lining of plants, and plenty of swimming space. Use surface vegetation to dim the light. Peat filtration is beneficial.

Breeding: Males are slimmer, and the swimbladder, visible through the transparent body, is pointed, not rounded. No reports of breeding available, but probably as in *M. pittieri*, the Diamond Tetra (qv).

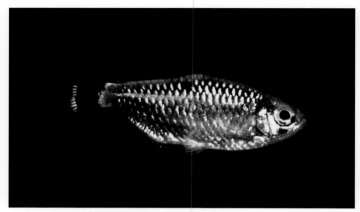

Moenkhausia oligolepis (Günther, 1864)
Glass Tetra

Overview: Although this is a peaceful fish, it grows relatively large for a tetra, so do not assume the small ones you find in the store will stay that size. It needs a good-sized tank with plenty of swimming space and tankmates its own size.

Native Range: The Guianas, Venezuela, and the Amazon drainage, in small slow-flowing streams and still pools.

Maximum Length: 5 in (13 cm) TL.

Water: 75–82°F (24–28°C); pH: 6.5–7.5; hardness: 0–15°dGH.

Min. Tank Size: 65 gal | 48x18x18 in (240 L | 120x45x45 cm).

Feeding: Like most tetras this fish is a carnivore that will enjoy live, frozen, and prepared foods, but because of its size, larger live foods such as bloodworms and mosquito larvae should be offered.

Behavior & Care: A good tetra to keep with medium-sized, peaceful, plant-friendly South American cichlids such as *Satanoperca jurupari* (qv). Keep a school of six or more in a planted tank with plenty of open space for swimming. Avoid strong filter currents.

Breeding: Males are slimmer. Use a breeding tank (24x16x16 in | 60x40x40 cm, at least) and fine-leaved plants or Java Moss, as these are plant-spawners. Remove the parents before they eat the eggs!

Moenkhausia pittieri Eigenmann, 1920
Diamond Tetra

Overview: Small, attractive fishes are often described as little gems or living jewels. And not for nothing is this sparkling fish—in its behavior as well as its appearance—called the Diamond Tetra. Probably the best-known member of its genus, this is one of the species that requires soft water to thrive.

Native Range: The Lake Valencia basin in Venezuela.

Maximum Length: 2.5 in (6 cm) TL.

Water: 75–82°F (24–28°C); pH: 6.0–7.0; hardness: 0–8°dGH.

Min. Tank Size: 25 gal | 24x16x16 in (95 L | 60x40x40 cm).

Feeding: Enjoys any small carnivore foods. As with most tetras, live food should be used to condition this species for breeding.

Behavior & Care: The ideal home for the Diamond Tetra will have dark, hardness-free substrate, soft, peaty water, dim light (or a layer of floating plants), and a backdrop of plants leaving lots of swimming space. Keep a school of six at least.

Breeding: The male has a larger, pointed, dorsal fin. Plant-spawner. Breeding tank with fine-leaved plants or Java Moss; water as for the normal tank. Put the pair into the darkened tank, then slowly increase the light to normal (dim!). Remove the parents after spawning.

Moenkhausia sanctaefilomenae (Steindachner, 1907)
Redeye Tetra (Lambari Othode-Fogo, Yellowband Moenkhausia)

Overview: The important point about this tetra is that it has a southerly, barely tropical distribution and should not be kept too warm, though nowadays most stocks are captive-bred and hardier. Unlike some *Moenkhausia* this fish does not mind hard, alkaline water, which greatly increases its versatility as a community fish.

Native Range: The Paraguay-Paraná system and other river basins in southern Brazil, Uruguay, and northern Argentina.

Maximum Length: 2.75 in (7 cm) TL.

Water: 70–77°F (21–25°C); pH: 6.5–8.0; hardness: 0–20°dGH.

Min. Tank Size: 38 gal | 36x16x16 in (140 L | 90x40x40 cm).

Feeding: Tank-bred fish will thrive on prepared foods alone, but enjoy a treat of live or frozen. The latter foods should predominate for wild fish and conditioning for breeding.

Behavior & Care: An undemanding schooling fish; keep at least five or six. A dark substrate is beneficial, and adequate swimming space, with some planting as cover, is essential.

Breeding: Ripe females are more rounded. Egg-scatterer: spawn in a breeding tank with mesh, and large floating plants like Indian Fern or Water Lettuce, as they like to spawn among the roots.

Myleus schomburgkii, Barred Silver Dollar.

Myloplus rubripinnis, Red-Hook Myleus.

Though large, silver dollars, pacus, and piranhas are best kept in large schools—this necessitates large aquaria, so let the buyer beware.

Nematobrycon lacortei Weitzman & Fink, 1971
Rainbow Tetra

Overview: Less familiar and commonplace than its cousin, the popular Emperor Tetra (*N. palmeri*), this lovely tetra is aptly named, and well worth trying if it appears in the local store, provided you are prepared to put a little effort into the water chemistry. The genus contains only these two species.

Native Range: Colombia: Rio San Juan drainage.

Maximum Length: 2 in (5 cm) TL.

Water: 73–82°F (23–28°C); pH: 5.0–7.2; hardness: 0–8°dGH.

Min. Tank Size: 25 gal | 24x16x16 in (95 L | 60x40x40 cm).

Feeding: Newly imported fish may need to be tempted with live foods, but once acclimated they will take any small carnivore and omnivore foods, including flake.

Behavior & Care: Keep in a school of at least six in a well-planted aquarium—but with ample swimming space—with a dark substrate. Floating plants are beneficial. Peaceful and a little shy, it should not be kept with boisterous tankmates. Most, if not all, stocks are wild-caught so do not assume this fish is as hardy regarding water chemistry as the Emperor Tetra.

Breeding: No reports available, but probably as for the Emperor.

Nematobrycon palmeri Eigenmann, 1911
Emperor Tetra

Overview: This lovely tetra is subtle rather than gaudy in its beauty. Although it looks just black and silver in the store, given the right conditions it will display delicate blue and other shades as well. Add in the unusual, elegant finnage and this is a fish that truly deserves its popular name.

Native Range: Colombia: Rio San Juan and Rio Atrato drainages.

Maximum Length: 2 in (5 cm) TL.

Water: 73–82°F (23–28°C); pH: 5.0–8.0; hardness: 0–15°dGH.

Min. Tank Size: 25 gal | 24x16x16 in (95 L | 60x40x40 cm).

Feeding: Any small carnivore/omnivore foods, including flake.

Behavior & Care: Although most stocks are captive bred and "water-hardy" this fish does best in soft, acid water with peat filtration (essential for breeding). Otherwise maintenance is as for *N. lacortei*, the Rainbow Tetra.

Breeding: Males larger, more colorful, with longer fins. Easy but not prolific. Use a darkened tank, spawning mesh, and Java Moss; remove the adults after spawning. Temperature in the upper part of the range given above. The eggs hatch after 1–2 days; the fry require infusoria at first, then *Artemia* nauplii after a few days.

Paracheirodon axelrodi (Schultz, 1956)
Cardinal Tetra (Red Neon Tetra)

Overview: There is no more stunning sight than a large tank with a large school of Cardinals! Almost all stocks are wild-caught as this fish requires very soft acid water to breed. Demand is such that it is an important economic resource, making a major contribution to local incomes and also to habitat conservation. A good example of why collecting wild fishes is not always a bad thing!

Native Range: Orinoco, Uaupes, and Rio Negro systems, in shaded slow-moving or still, clear and black water.

Maximum Length: 2 in (5 cm) TL.

Water: 73–82°F (23–28°C); pH: 4.6–6.2; hardness: 0–5°dGH.

Min. Tank Size: 25 gal | 24x16x16 in (95 L | 60x40x40 cm).

Feeding: Small live, frozen, and prepared foods, in variety.

Behavior & Care: Will survive for a while in hard water, but if you can't provide soft acid conditions then please keep Neons (_P. innesi_) instead. Keep in a school in a dimly lit tank with dark substrate and rooted and floating plants. Tankmates should have small mouths to avoid unwanted snacking on slim-line tetras like this one!

Breeding: Males are slimmer. (Male on right, female left in the above image.) Breeding tank and procedure as for the Neon Tetra.

Paracheirodon innesi (Myers, 1936)
Neon Tetra

Overview: Probably the most popular tetra in the hobby, available in any store. It even has a disease of tetras (*Pleistophora*) named "Neon Disease" after it. Nowadays almost all Neons are fish-farm bred, making them cheaper (and hence more popular) than the more colorful and slightly larger Cardinal Tetra (*P. axelrodi*), which is still largely wild-caught.

Native Range: Upper Amazon drainage, in clear and black water.

Maximum Length: 1.5 in (4 cm) TL.

Water: 73–82°F (23–28°C); pH: 5.0–8.0; hardness: 0–25°dGH.

Min. Tank Size: 25 gal | 24x16x16 in (95 L | 60x40x40 cm).

Feeding: Any small carnivore and omnivore aquarium foods.

Behavior & Care: Largely as for the Cardinal Tetra (qv), though vastly more tolerant with regard to water chemistry and light levels. But note, wild Neons are liable to curl up their fins and die at high hardness and pH. Avoid buying very small and cheap or full-grown (old) Neons: around 1 in (2.5 cm) is the ideal size for long life.

Breeding: Males slimmer. Very soft, acid (pH 5.0–6.0) water, dim light, spawning mesh, Java Moss. Remove adults after spawning. Hatching: 24 hours; free-swimming: five days. Infusoria as first food.

Paracheirodon simulans (Géry, 1963)
Green Neon Tetra (False Neon Tetra)

Overview: As its name suggests, this fish looks very like the ever-popular and commonplace Neon (*P. innesi*), but there the resemblance largely ends. It is rarely imported, and if anything is even trickier to keep well—if at all—than the Cardinal (*P. axelrodi*), with which it is said to be found in some parts of their ranges.

Native Range: Upper Rio Negro and Orinoco drainages.

Maximum Length: 1.5 in (4 cm) TL.

Water: 73–82°F (23–28°C); pH: 5.0–6.5; hardness: 0–6°dGH.

Min. Tank Size: 25 gal | 24x16x16 in (95 L | 60x40x40 cm).

Feeding: Best fed small live foods, but will learn to take frozen and prepared foods once acclimated.

Behavior & Care: As for the Cardinal Tetra (qv) in most respects. Soft, acid water is a must if this fish is to live long. It is also very sensitive to nitrate and other metabolic wastes, and, for reasons unknown, appears to be prone to Velvet Disease (*Piscinoodinium*)—be watchful with newly purchased fish and use a suitable proprietary remedy at the first sign of this disease.

Breeding: Largely as for the Neon (*P. innesi*, qv), but much more difficult to achieve, and not prolific. Condition with live food.

Petitella georgiae Géry & Boutière, 1964
False Rummynose Tetra (False Firehead Tetra)

Overview: Like the Firehead (*Hemigrammus bleheri*) and Rummynose (*H. rhodostomus*) Tetras, this fish, the only member of its genus, has a red nose and black and white tail. Why three small fishes from two different genera should look so alike is unknown; sometimes such "doubles" live together, so camouflage may be a benefit, but that is not the case here. Nature holds many such mysteries! Unfortunately the three are often confused in the trade.

Native Range: Upper Amazon drainage, Madeira, Purus, and Negro systems.

Maximum Length: 2 in (5 cm) TL.

Water: 73–82°F (23–28°C); pH: 5.5–7.2; hardness: 0–10°dGH.

Min. Tank Size: 25 gal | 24x16x16 in (95 L | 60x40x40 cm).

Feeding: Any small live, frozen, and prepared foods.

Behavior & Care: A peaceful schooling fish (keep six plus) for a well-planted general community with plenty of open swimming space. Floating plants, peat filtration, and dark substrate beneficial.

Breeding: Males have more contrasting tail stripes. No breeding reports available. A typical tetra breeding tank, as for the Neon Tetra (*Paracheirodon innesi*, qv) is suggested as a good starting point.

Piaractus brachypomus (Cuvier, 1818)
Red-Bellied Pacu (Pirapitinga, Giant Pacu, Black Pacu, Gamitana)

Overview: Pacus are vegetarian cousins of the notorious piranhas, but, despite a superficial resemblance, are quite harmless—unless you are a plant! There are several genera, with this and _Colossoma_ being the best known. They are gentle, schooling giants—some grow to 40 in (100 cm) long—and are valuable food fishes in their native lands. Think of them as the elephants of the fish world—you would not keep a herd of those in the back yard, and similarly, pacus have no place in the aquarium, although they are available. Public aquariums are already full of unwanted adult pacus!

Native Range: South America: Amazon and Orinoco drainages.

Maximum Length: 30 in (76 cm) TL, possibly even larger.

Water: 72-82°F (22-28°C); pH 6.5-8.0; hardness 0-20°dGH.

Min. Tank Size: 180 gal | 72x24x24 in (650 L | 180x60x60 cm). This size will suffice only for smaller specimens.

Feeding: Any robust vegetable foods, including fruit.

Behavior & Care: This fish needs to be kept in a group, making its maintenance even more impracticable. Huge tank with powerful filtration to process the vast amounts of waste generated.

Breeding: Sex differences unknown, breeding totally impracticable.

Prionobrama filigera (Cope, 1870)
Glass Bloodfin

Overview: This may not be the prettiest of the tetras that we see in the hobby, but it is not unattractive and has a lot going for it: hardy as regards water chemistry and temperature, lively but peaceful behavior, usually long-lived, and easy to breed. A very good tetra for the novice and for high-temperature tanks.

Native Range: South America: much of the Amazon drainage.

Maximum Length: 2.5 in (6 cm) TL.

Water: 72-86°F (22-30°C); pH 6.0-8.0; hardness 0-25°dGH.

Min. Tank Size: 30 gal | 36x12x16 in (105 L | 90x30x40 cm).

Feeding: Happily eats any small foods offered, including flake.

Behavior & Care: The only real demand this fish makes is the company of its own kind—it tends to be nervous and shy if kept singly, so buy at least five or six. It will also appreciate ample swimming space with a little shade from floating plants. It sometimes likes to "hang" in the current from the filter outlet.

Breeding: Males have a prolonged anal fin with a black streak. Use soft, acid water and the upper part of the temperature range cited. Surface vegetation is again beneficial. Use marbles or spawning mesh to protect the eggs, and remove the parents after spawning.

Pristella maxillaris (Ulrey, 1894)
X-ray Tetra (Pristella Riddlei, Water Goldfinch)

Overview: This little tetra has been a staple of the aquarium hobby for decades, and is one of the easiest and hardiest; ideal for the beginner's first community tank, but worthy of any aquarium with peaceful tankmates.

Native Range: Amazon and Orinoco systems, and coastal drainages in the Guianas. However, most stocks are now captive-bred. Sometimes found in brackish water in the wild.

Maximum Length: 1.75 in (4.5 cm) TL.

Water: 75-82°F (24-28°C); pH 6.0-8.0; hardness 0-25°dGH.

Min. Tank Size: 25 gal | 24x16x16 in (95 L | 60x40x40 cm).

Feeding: Any small aquarium foods; benefits from occasional vegetable flake (but doesn't harm plants.)

Behavior & Care: A peaceful schooling fish (keep six or more). Very hardy and accommodating, but to see its best colors, soft acid water, dark substrate, and dim lighting are a must.

Breeding: Easy and prolific (up to 400 eggs per spawning). Males more slender with a pointed swimbladder (female's rounded.) Best bred in a group as they like to select their own mates. Use spawning mesh to save the eggs; remove the adults after spawning.

Pygocentrus nattereri Kner, 1858
Red-bellied Piranha (Red Piranha, Serrasalmus Nattereri)

Overview: There are three species of *Pygocentrus* (the "true piranhas"), with *P. nattereri* the best-known. The other two are *P. cariba* and *P. piraya*. In nature they attack in packs only when the prey is injured or they are starving, but they cannot be trusted in the aquarium. **The true piranhas are extremely dangerous and not beginners' fishes, and are best not kept at all.** This warning, and the maintenance advice below, applies to **ALL** three species.

Native Range: Amazon, Essequibo, and Paraguay-Paraná systems.

Maximum Length: 15 in (38 cm) TL, usually smaller in captivity.

Water: 73-82°F (23-28°C); pH 6.0-7.5; hardness 0-15°dGH.

Min. Tank Size: 180 gal | 72x24x24 in (650 L | 180x60x60 cm).

Feeding: Raw meat and fish, in chunks. Must be kept well-fed.

Behavior & Care: Keep in a group of five-plus with no other fishes. Powerful filtration is required to deal with the large amounts of wastes generated. The aquarium hood **must** be child- (and unwary adult-) proof. To work on the tank, imprison the fish at one end with a stout divider. **Never risk hands with piranhas!**

Breeding: Has been achieved in very large tanks. The parents guard the eggs, which are laid in a "nest." Males have more red.

Pygocentrus cariba. This fish was named for the Caribe indians, an extinct tribe of fierce warriors. Locally it is called *Capaburro,* translation: donkey castrator.

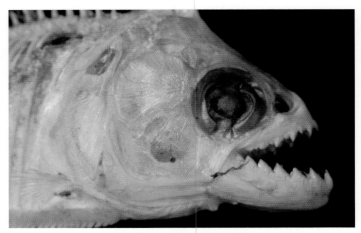

Serrasalmus hollandi. This is the business end of a piranha.

Serrasalmus are also part of the piranha group, but are less dangerous than *Pygocentrus.*

Serrasalmus rhombeus. Rhomboid, Black, or White Piranha.

Serrasalmus spilopleura. Gold Piranha.

Piranhas normally prey on other fishes, and are aroused to a feed-ing frenzy only in certain circumstances. Even so, never risk your fingers!

Thaeyeria boehlkei Weitzman, 1957
Penguinfish (Boehlke's Penguinfish, Thayeria Obliqua)

Overview: This little fish really does look rather like a penguin! For a very long time it was misidentified as its congener, *T. obliqua*, in the trade and literature. Both species have an interesting head-up, hovering mode of swimming not seen in other tetras.

Native Range: The Rio Araguaia and the upper Amazon system.

Maximum Length: 2.5 in (6 cm) TL.

Water: 72-82°F (22-28°C); pH 6.0-8.0; hardness 0-20°dGH.

Min. Tank Size: 25 gal | 24x16x16 in (95 L | 60x40x40 cm).

Feeding: Any small live, frozen, or prepared foods. Can survive very nicely on good quality flake with occasional treats.

Behavior & Care: A peaceful, hardy, community fish. Best kept in a small group. Well-planted tank, where it will often hover near plant stems or vertical leaves. Hardy as regards water chemistry but may react badly to accumulated metabolic wastes (nitrate, phosphate).

Breeding: Easy and prolific (up to 1000 eggs). Females are rounder. Use soft, acid water and spawning mesh plus Java Moss. Remove adults after spawning, and change 50% of the water as surplus milt may pollute the tank. The larvae hatch in 12–24 hours; when free-swimming the tiny fry require infusoria.

Auchenoglanis occidentalis (Valenciennes, 1840)
Giraffe Catfish (Bubu, Vacuum-Mouth Catfish)

Overview: A large but peaceful and sociable catfish. The name relates to the attractive giraffe-like markings of juveniles.
Native Range: Africa: very widespread—the Nile, Niger, Chad, Senegal, and Congo systems; Somalia; and Lake Tanganyika.
Maximum Length: 18 in (45 cm) TL., usually only half that.
Water: 75–82°F (24–28°C); pH: 6.5–8.5; hardness: 5–25°dGH.
Min. Tank Size: 180 gal | 72x24x24 in (650 L | 180x60x60 cm).
Feeding: A detritivore that sifts the bottom for food. Any sinking foods, including live food and chopped blanched greens.
Behavior & Care: The wide range means this fish occurs in different water types depending on its origins. If possible, provide water chemistry to match provenance (if known). The substrate should be fine and soft so it can be sifted without damaging mouth and barbels.
Breeding: Unlikely in captivity due to the size of the fish. In Lake Tanganyika this catfish has been observed to excavate a large nest which it fills with pebbles and shells to protect the eggs, larvae, and fry. The male guards the nest, which he fans to oxygenate the eggs. The female remains nearby.

Lophiobagrus cyclurus (Worthington & Ricardo, 1937)
Tanganyika Bullhead (Round-tailed Tanganyika Catlet,
Chrysichthys Cyclurus, Lophiobagrus Lestradei)

Overview: This little catfish is no beauty queen, and is rarely active
by day, but it is quite easily bred and practices brood care, defending its eggs and young with an enthusiasm and dedication worthy
of any cichlid!

Native Range: East Africa: endemic to Lake Tanganyika, in shallow
rocky areas, often near sand.

Maximum Length: 4 in (10 cm) TL.

Water: 75–82°F (24–28°C); pH: 7.5–9.0; hardness: 5–25°dGH.

Min. Tank Size: 25 gal | 24x16x16 in (95 L | 60x40x40 cm).

Feeding: Best fed at lights-out, on live or frozen foods.

Behavior & Care: Can be kept in a species aquarium or a Tanganyika cichlid community, bearing in mind that it will require its own
breeding territory. Requires rocky décor and well-oxygenated water.

Breeding: Females are probably deeper-bodied. A nest is dug in a cave or
between rocks and in some cases, the excavated material used to create a
protective barrier. 30–60 large eggs, defended vigorously by both parents,
hatch after 4–5 days; fry free-swimming on day 10–11 and can take
Artemia nauplii. Brood guarding continues for some time thereafter.

Amphilius atesuensis Boulenger, 1904
Golden African Kuhli (Atesu Mountain Catfish)

Overview: *Amphilius* comprises around 20 small, peaceful rheophilic catfishes found in fast-flowing upper reaches of rivers and streams over much of tropical Africa. That they are not often imported probably reflects lack of commercial profit in collecting in these often remote and relatively species-poor waters. This one is, however, available from time to time; its common name relates to a superficial resemblance; it is not related to the Kuhli loaches.

Native Range: West Africa: Liberia to Togo.

Maximum Length: 3 in (8 cm) TL.

Water: 68–77°F (20–26°C); pH: 6.5–7.5; hardness: 2–10°dGH.

Min. Tank Size: 25 gal | 24x16x16 in (95 L | 60x40x40 cm).

Feeding: Small live and frozen foods; may learn in time to take other sinking foods, including tablets.

Behavior & Care: Create a stream-bed simulation, with water-worn stones. Plants and wood can be included. Well-oxygenated water, not too warm; strong currents are unnecessary. Tankmates can be any small, peaceful fishes that don't mind the specialized conditions.

Breeding: No details available. It has been suggested that males are more colorful and females deeper-bodied.

Parailia pellucida (Boulenger, 1901)
African Glass Catfish (Nile Glass Catfish)

Overview: This catfish of the family Schilbeidae is not to be confused with the Indian Glass Catfish (*Kryptopterus bicirrhis*), though like the latter it is transparent so its skeleton and organs are visible. There are several other *Parailia*, with the smaller (4 in | 10 cm) *P. congica* also imported and similar in its requirements.

Native Range: Upper Nile, and also widespread in West Africa.

Maximum Length: 6 in (15 cm) TL.

Water: 72–82°F (22–28°C); pH: 6.5–7.5; hardness: 0–15°dGH

Min. Tank Size: 65 gal | 48x18x18 in (240 L | 120x45x45 cm).

Feeding: Live and frozen foods; can usually be acclimated to other, less natural foods. May eat very small tankmates.

Behavior & Care: *Parailia* are schooling fishes that should be kept in a group in a suitably spacious tank, with other peaceful fishes of similar size. They will appreciate a backdrop of plants and wood. They can be particularly sensitive to nitrogenous compounds (ammonia, nitrite, nitrate) so effective biological filtration and regular partial water changes are required, and monitoring is advised.

Breeding: Has been spawned accidentally, with fry appearing unexpectedly among aquarium plants. No details of spawning known.

Pareutropius buffei (Gras, 1960)
Swallow-tailed Glass Catfish

Overview: After the upside-down catfishes (*Synodontis*), *Pareutropius* are probably the African catfishes most regularly seen in the hobby. This species is probably the most common, but *P. debauwi* and *P. longifilis* are also seen and the three are often confused, with all being sold and reported in the literature as Debauwi Cats.

Native Range: West Africa: coastal rivers in Togo and Nigeria, including the lower Niger and the Cross, and freshwater lagoons.

Maximum Length: 3 in (8 cm) TL.

Water: 75–82°F (24–28°C); pH: 6.5–7.5; hardness: 0–10°dGH.

Min. Tank Size: 38 gal | 36x16x16 in (140 L | 90x40x40 cm).

Feeding: Takes all the usual aquarium fare, including dry foods.

Behavior & Care: This schilbeid catfish is an excellent fish for the softwater community tank with a backdrop of plants and wood and plenty of open swimming space. Keep in a school of at least six, with peaceful tankmates of similar size. Does best at a fairly neutral pH.

Breeding: Reports of breeding this and *P. debauwi* actually relate to *P. longifiliis*, which is an egg-scatterer that spawns at night. The eggs hatched after three days and the fry were able to manage *Artemia* nauplii. This species may well be similar in its breeding.

Schilbe intermedius Rüppell, 1832
African Butter Catfish (Silver Catfish, Schilbe Mystus)

Overview: Until recently this catfish was misidentified as *S. mystus*, under which name it will be found in older literature—and probably in aquarium stores for some time to come. It is a typical schilbeid—mainly diurnal, not particularly bottom-oriented, and with a very long anal fin. It may or may not have an adipose fin.

Native Range: Nile basin, and most of West, Central, and East Africa; in rivers and lakes, usually in calm marginal regions.

Maximum Length: 24 in (60 cm) TL. Usually half that.

Water: 72–82°F (22–28°C); pH: 6.0–9.0; hardness: 5–25°dGH.

Min. Tank Size: 65 gal | 48x18x18 in (240 L | 120x45x45 cm).

Feeding: Will take most standard aquarium carnivore foods.

Behavior & Care: Hardy as regards water conditions. Unfussy about décor, doesn't harm plants. In the wild this catfish will take fishes up to a third of its own size as prey, and any tankmates should be chosen with this in mind.

Breeding: In the wild the spawning season is February–March, and a female can contain over 60,000 eggs in her ovaries. The fry disperse during the rains, migrating with the rising waters. No records of aquarium breeding, which is probably impracticable.

Malapterurus electricus (Gmelin, 1789)
Electric Catfish (Nile Electric Catfish)

Overview: The name *M. electricus* has long been applied to a host of other species as well as the correct one. The true *electricus* is potentially a very large fish, not really suitable for the aquarium. Some of the other species, e.g. *M. beninensis, M. leonensis*, are more suitable, apparently attaining only 10–16 in (25–40 cm) or so. All *Malapterurus* have an electric organ, used to stun prey.

Native Range: Much of West and Central Africa, plus the Nile and Zambezi systems.

Maximum Length: 49 in (125 cm) TL.

Water: 72–82°F (22–28°C); pH: 6.5–8.0; hardness: 5–25°dGH.

Min. Tank Size: 180 gal | 72x24x24 in (650 L | 180x60x60 cm).

Feeding: Carnivorous and piscivorous; requires a robust diet. May need feeder fish initially, but can be acclimated to other foods.

Behavior & Care: Very undemanding in its maintenance, but needs good filtration and hiding places. Quarrelsome so best kept singly, with no other fishes. Largely nocturnal. Requires very careful and respectful treatment because of the possibility of electric shock.

Breeding: Not bred in captivity. Apparently forms pairs and breeds in holes in banks, pits, and similar. Solitary when not breeding.

Microsynodontis batesii Boulenger, 1903
Bates's Dwarf Squeaker (Bates's Bumblebee Squeaker)

Overview: As the genus name suggests, *Microsynodontis* are dwarf mochokid catfishes, with 4 in (10 cm) being the largest size for any known species. They are sometimes called bumblebee catfishes as most are dark and light barred. Almost all come from West Central Africa, and the preferred habitat is forest streams. *M. batesii* is the species most often imported.

Native Range: West Central Africa: southern Cameroon, possibly also Gabon and the northern Congo drainage.

Maximum Length: 4 in (10 cm) TL.

Water: 75–82°F (24–28°C); pH: 6.5–7.5; hardness: 0–10°dGH.

Min. Tank Size: 25 gal | 24x16x16 in (95 L | 60x40x40 cm).

Feeding: The natural diet is small aquatic organisms and algae, so feed live/frozen foods and a vegetable component.

Behavior & Care: Rather delicate and timid, and usually crepuscular in its habits. Water should be as soft and pure as possible. Provide plenty of hiding places and dense planting, and small, peaceful tank-mates to inspire confidence.

Breeding: Some *Microsynodontis* can be sexed by tail shape, and caudal variation does occur in *M. batesii*. No other details available.

Mochokiella paynei Howes, 1980
Pygmy Upside-down Catfish (Payne's Dwarf Squeaker)

Overview: This pretty little upside-down catfish is ideal for the beginner and a community tank of small peaceful fishes. It is primarily diurnal, so there are no problems with making sure it gets enough food, and it can usually be seen out and about.

Native Range: West Africa: known only from Sierra Leone, from streams in the Kasewe Forest Reserve.

Maximum Length: 4 in (10 cm) TL.

Water: 72–78°F (22–26°C); pH: 6.0–7.5; hardness: 0–12°dGH.

Min. Tank Size: 25 gal | 24x16x16 in (95 L | 60x40x40 cm).

Feeding: The natural food is aquatic invertebrates; in the aquarium this catfish enjoys live foods but will take frozen and dry foods too.

Behavior & Care: Available stocks are wild fish, so although they will tolerate hard alkaline water, soft and slightly acid to neutral is better. Nitrate is not tolerated well, so regular partial water changes are needed. Sand or water-worn gravel substrate, plants, bogwood. They do not like bright light so there should be plenty of shaded and semi-shaded areas. Floating plants are beneficial.

Breeding: There are rumors that this catfish has been bred, but unfortunately the details have not been documented.

Synodontis angelicus Schilthuis, 1891
Angel Catfish (Angelicus, Angelic Catfish, Polka-dot Catfish)

Overview: When juvenile, one of the most attractive members of its genus, and an instant hit when first imported. Unfortunately, with age the markings become paler and less distinct, and it can also grow a lot larger and more quarrelsome than most people realize. The coloration and markings are very variable.

Native Range: West Central Africa: much of the Congo basin. No details of its precise habitat preferences are available.

Maximum Length: 12 in (30 cm) TL.

Water: 72–80°F (22–27°C); pH: 6.5–7.5; hardness: 0–10°dGH.

Min. Tank Size: 65 gal | 48x18x18 in (240 L | 120x45x45 cm).

Feeding: In the wild small aquatic organisms, so may require live food initially, but readily acclimated to frozen and even dry foods.

Behavior & Care: Soft, slightly acid water is optimal, but hard and alkaline is tolerated. Soft sand or gravel substrate, plants, bogwood, plenty of hiding places. Digs. Tankmates should be fairly robust.

Breeding: Because of the desirability of this fish, attempts have been made to breed it commercially by hormone treatment—but with little success. Expensive, so most people buy only one, which is not conducive to breeding! Females can contain thousands of eggs.

Synodontis brichardi Poll, 1959
Brichard's Synodontis (Brichard's Squeaker)

Overview: An attractive, relatively small and peaceful, rheophilic catfish that shares the habitat of some popular rapids cichlids and can be kept with them in a suitably spacious biotope aquarium.

Native Range: West Central Africa: rapids of the lower Congo.

Maximum Length: 6 in (15 cm) TL.

Water: 72–80°F (22–27°C); pH: 6.5–7.5; hardness: 0–10°dGH.

Min. Tank Size: 50 gal | 48x16x16 in (190 L | 120x40x40 cm).

Feeding: Reportedly feeds on algae and any aquatic invertebrates it contains, so a suitably mixed diet is recommended. May require live foods initially as all stocks are wild fish.

Behavior & Care: The tank size cited could house a small group, or a couple plus a pair or two of small rheophilic cichlids (e.g. *Teleogramma* or *Steatocranus*). Fine, soft substrate and water-worn boulders creating plenty of hiding places. Well-oxygenated but not turbulent water. These catfishes can adhere for short periods to rocks or glass, but have no special attachment mechanism as such.

Breeding: Signs of possible breeding activity (chasing) have been seen but no spawnings reported. Sexual differences unknown. The best chance is probably a group of five or more in a biotope aquarium.

Synodontis decorus Boulenger, 1899
Clown Squeaker (Decorated Squeaker)

Overview: A very attractive species, though ultimately sizeable, with large black polka-dot body markings and striped fins. The coloration becomes less distinctive with age, but the unusual long dorsal filament gets even longer. There is also a striped form from Kisangani, sometimes known as *S. vittatus,* but thought to be the same species. In the wild this catfish is the victim of a fin-eating characiform with a taste for dorsal fins, but do not worry: if you buy one with a bitten dorsal it will grow back.

Native Range: West Central Africa: Congo drainage.

Maximum Length: 12 in (30 cm) TL.

Water: 72–80°F (22–27°C); pH: 6.5–7.5; hardness: 0–10°dGH.

Min. Tank Size: 65 gal | 48x18x18 in (240 L | 120x45x45 cm).

Feeding: Will take any regular aquarium food of suitable size.

Behavior & Care: A peaceful diurnal catfish that in nature lives in groups when adult. As all stocks are wild-caught, the water should be as soft as possible to simulate natural conditions. Otherwise easy to keep. Provide a large tank with a backdrop of plants, bogwood, and smooth rocks, and a substrate of water-worn sand or gravel.

Breeding: Nothing is known about breeding behavior.

Synodontis eupterus Boulenger, 1901
Featherfin Squeaker (Featherfin Syno)

Overview: A rather deep-bodied, fairly hardy "syno" with a "fringed" dorsal fin—hence the "featherfin" epithet. Both coloration and behavior can be highly individualistic. One of only a few species that are bred commercially, using hormone treatment

Native Range: Africa: central Nile basin, and the Niger, Chad, and Volta systems in West Africa.

Maximum Length: 8.5 in (22 cm) TL.

Water: 72–79°F (22–26°C); pH: 6.0–7.5; hardness: 2–15°dGH.

Min. Tank Size: 50 gal | 36x18x18 in (180 L | 90x45x45 cm).

Feeding: Wild fish may require live foods initially; acclimated and captive-bred specimens will take most foods.

Behavior & Care: Like many *Synodontis* this species is naturally crepuscular but will show itself readily by day if the tank is not too brightly lit. Soft substrate, plants, bogwood, with plenty of hiding places but also open space. Peat filtration is beneficial. Tankmates should be of a reasonable size, even though this is a peaceful fish.

Breeding: Unfortunately the differences between the sexes and details of the breeding process have not been documented. Photos of larval development show the young free-swimming after 7–9 days.

181

Synodontis granulosus (Boulenger, 1900)
Rough-skinned Squeaker

Overview: A large "syno" with eye-catching black and white fin markings. Arguably the most attractive member of the Lake Tanganyika *Synodontis* species flock. Rare in the wild, hence expensive.

Native Range: East Africa: endemic to Lake Tanganyika, in both rocky and sandy habitats.

Maximum Length: 17 in (43 cm) TL.

Water: 75–82°F (24–28°C); pH: 7.5–9.0; hardness: 5–25°dGH.

Min. Tank Size: 180 gal | 72x24x24 in (650 L | 180x60x60 cm).

Feeding: Carnivorous—will take most carnivore foods in captivity, though obviously the choice will need to be tailored to its size.

Behavior & Care: Very little is known about the ecology of this species. In line with its habitat, it can be offered a décor that includes both rocks and open substrate. The water should be hard and must be alkaline. Possibly a good tankmate for the large but peaceful Tanganyika cichlid *Cyphotilapia frontosa*.

Breeding: Nothing is known about breeding behavior, not even whether it is one of the species that scatters its eggs or attaches them to a substrate. No known *Synodontis* practices any form of brood care. Females are probably deeper-bodied.

Synodontis multipunctatus Boulenger, 1898
Cuckoo Catfish

Overview: The breeding habits of this fish came as a huge surprise when it first bred in captivity back in the 1970s. It parasitises some of the mouthbrooding cichlids that share its habitat, the only known "cuckoo" among the multitudinous catfishes of the world

Native Range: East Africa: endemic to Lake Tanganyika.

Maximum Length: 10 in (25 cm) TL., normally half that length.

Water: 75–82°F (24–28°C); pH: 7.5–9.0; hardness: 5–25°dGH.

Min. Tank Size: 29 gal | 30x12x18 in (100 L | 75x30x45 cm).

Feeding: In the wild this catfish pulls snails out of their shells! It also eats insect larvae in nature, but will take most foods in captivity

Behavior & Care: Best kept in a small group in a large community tank of mouthbrooding cichlids, so it can go through its unusual breeding process. Lots of rockwork and well-oxygenated water.

Breeding: Will make use of any haplochromine mouthbrooder available. Females are deeper-bodied than males. When the cichlids start to spawn, the female catfish, pursued by one or more males, swims across the site, depositing eggs, which the males fertilize. The cichlid female picks them up and broods them. The fry feed on the cichlid's own eggs and larvae, so she eventually releases only little cuckoos!

Synodontis nigriventris David, 1936
Upside-down Catfish

Overview: Until comparatively recently this was *the* Upside-down Catfish, and aquarists knew little of the many others that exist. The name is apt, as this species does spend most of its time belly-up, and its colors are reversed (dark belly, light back) from the normal camouflage pattern to reflect this. A good community fish.

Native Range: Central Africa: central Congo basin, usually in acid water with trailing bank vegetation which is used for cover.

Maximum Length: 4 in (10 cm) TL.

Water: 75–82°F (24–28°C); pH: 6.0–7.5; hardness: 2–15°dGH.

Min. Tank Size: 25 gal | 24x16x16 in (95 L | 60x40x40 cm).

Feeding: Surface feeder. Wild fish may need live foods initially; tank-breds take any floating or near-surface food, including flake.

Behavior & Care: Young fish are sociable, so keep in a group, but allow more space later as older fish are more solitary. Acid water and floating plants are advisable. Avoid boisterous tankmates.

Breeding: Bred commercially by hormone treatment, but also accidentally bred by aquarists. The eggs are attached to a substrate (many synos are egg-scatterers). No brood care. Soft acid water; spawning apparently triggered by a water and temperature change.

Synodontis njassae Keilhack, 1908
Malawi Syno (Malawi Squeaker)

Overview: Although Lake Tanganyika has a whole species flock of *Synodontis*, Lake Malawi (or Nyassa) has not been similarly blessed and has just this one, which is thus in demand by purists wanting a Malawi catfish to keep with their cichlids. However, it is worth keeping in its own right, being peaceful and attractively marked. The pattern of spots is very variable.

Native Range: East Africa: endemic to Lake Malawi, seasonally in a variety of habitats and both deep and relatively shallow water.

Maximum Length: 8 in (20 cm) TL.

Water: 72–82°F (22–28°C); pH: 7.5–8.5; hardness: 5–20°dGH.

Min. Tank Size: 38 gal | 36x16x16 in (140 L | 90x40x40 cm).

Feeding: Appears happy to eat whatever is offered to Malawi cichlid tankmates—practically anything!

Behavior & Care: Needs alkaline water and rocky hiding places. Can be kept in any sort of aquarium with tankmates of suitable size, but ideal for any Malawi cichlid community.

Breeding: Thought to spawn at the beginning of the rainy season, when it migrates from its normal rocky home to sandy or muddy areas. This suggests it is one of the egg-scattering species.

Synodontis alberti
Bigeye Squeaker
Max. Length: 8 in (20 cm).
Note the long barbels and large eyes.

Synodontis bastiani
Ivory Synodontis
Max. Length: 11 in (28 cm).
Adults will eat smaller fishes.

Synodontis congicus
Congicus Synodontis
Max. Length: 8 in (20 cm).
The number of spots is variable.

Synodontis schall
Sahel Squeaker
Max. Length: 17 in (43 cm).
Grows too large for many aquaria.

Synodontis koensis
Koe Squeaker
Max. Length: 6 in (15 cm).
An attractive smaller squeaker.

Synodontis robertsi
Roberts' Syno
Max. Length: 4 in (10 cm).
Also sold as Large-blotch Synodontis.

Synodontis petricola Matthes, 1959
Tanganyika Rock Squeaker

Overview: This catfish looks rather like the well-known Cuckoo Catfish, *S. multipunctatus*, and like it is a member of the Lake Tanganyika *Synodontis* species flock. Like the Cuckoo it is a rock-dweller, but it is smaller and has a quite different, non-parasitic method of breeding. This makes it a good catfish for keepers of Rift Valley mouthbrooders who want to produce little cichlids!

Native Range: East Africa: endemic to the northern part of Lake Tanganyika.

Maximum Length: 5 in (12 cm) TL.

Water: 75–82°F (24–28°C); pH: 7.5–9.0; hardness: 5–25°dGH.

Min. Tank Size: 29 gal | 30x12x18 in (100 L | 75x30x45 cm).

Feeding: An omnivore with a preference for insect larvae, but in captivity will eat anything offered, within reason.

Behavior & Care: Can be kept with Tanganyika cichlids or in a general community. Requires rockwork and well-oxygenated, good quality, alkaline water. Otherwise unfussy.

Breeding: Females are deeper-bodied. An egg-scatterer that produces small, sinking, transparent eggs that can be collected up (before the cichlids eat them!) and hatched/reared artificially.

Synodontis schoutedeni David, 1936
Schoutedeni (Schouteden's Squeaker)

Overview: An attractively marbled soft-water "syno," available at a reasonable price as it is now being mass-produced commercially. Also one of the very few species that have been bred by aquarists.

Native Range: West Central Africa: central Congo basin. Common in smaller rivers, but also found in the mainstream Congo at Malebo (Stanley) Pool just above the rapids at Kinshasa.

Maximum Length: 7 in (17.5 cm) TL.

Water: 72–80°F (22–27°C); pH: 6.5–7.5; hardness: 0–10°dGH.

Min. Tank Size: 38 gal | 36x16x16 in (140 L | 90x40x40 cm).

Feeding: Any standard aquarium fare is readily accepted.

Behavior & Care: Can be kept in a community aquarium of peaceful fishes of similar size. Requires soft water and plenty of hiding-places, without which it may be restless and disruptive.

Breeding: Bred commercially using hormone treatment, but captive-bred individuals have subsequently been bred naturally in a species tank with very soft water at 75°F (24°C). The fishes curved round one another in a ball at each spawning pass, laying hundreds of small sinking eggs. These hatched after about two days and were ready to take brine shrimp nauplii after six days.

Clarias batrachus (Linnaeus, 1758)
Walking Catfish

Overview: This clariid catfish is one of those fishes regularly sold for the aquarium although it is quite unsuitable for anyone but the specialist who actually wants a large fish with bad habits. The wild form is gray-brown, but it is usually the albino sport, and more recently a piebald form, that are sold to the unwary as innocuous-looking juveniles. This fish can not only breathe air, but can "walk" significant distances overland to find water if its pool dries up. It is banned in some countries as a threat to native wildlife.

Native Range: Southeast Asia: the Mekong and Chao Phraya basins, Malay Peninsula, Sumatra, Java, Borneo. Usually found in stagnant, muddy water in rivers, swamps, ditches, rice-paddies, etc.

Maximum Length: 20 in (50 cm) TL.

Water: 50–86°F (10–30°C); pH: 6.0–9.0; hardness: 0–30°dGH.

Min. Tank Size: 65 gal | 48x18x18 in (240 L | 120x45x45 cm).

Feeding: Eats anything, including tankmates—or bits of them.

Behavior & Care: Indestructible. Keep singly in a large tank with a big cave in which it can lurk and a heavy cover that it cannot lift! Handle all clariids with care—some have poisonous spines.

Breeding: Bred commercially in ponds in Asia, but not in aquaria.

Bagrichthys macracanthus (Bleeker, 1854)
Black Lancer Catfish (Humpback Catfish)

Overview: This catfish belongs to the naked catfish family Bagridae, which has members in both Africa and Asia. Bagrids are normally predatory and some reach a considerable size, so always check before buying and beware of housing with snack-sized tankmates! "Black Lancer" refers to the long dorsal spine in adults.

Native Range: Thailand to Indonesia, in upland rivers.

Maximum Length: 16 in (40 cm) TL.

Water: 68–77°F (20–25°C); pH: 6.5–8.0; hardness: 0–25°dGH.

Min. Tank Size: 180 gal | 72x24x24 in (650 L | 180x60x60 cm)

Feeding: All sorts of sinking carnivore foods. Because the mouth is small in relation to the fish, only very small fishes are at risk. Loves earthworms, which may tempt it to feed during acclimatization.

Behavior & Care: A rather shy fish that needs plenty of cover (bogwood, large clay pipes, rocky caves) to feel secure. (It is unkind to keep fish without hiding places to prevent them from hiding!) Soft sandy substrate, and plant the back and ends of the tank. Avoid bright light; and provide efficient filtration and well-oxygenated water.

Breeding: Nothing is known about breeding. Male *Bagrichthys* (and some other bagrids) have an external genital papilla.

Hemibagrus wyckioides (Fang & Chaux, 1949)
Asian Red-tail Catfish (Mystus Nemurus)

Overview: Aquarists may know this fish better as *Mystus nemurus*. The large cats formerly in *Mystus*, including the well-known *wyckii*, are now assigned to *Hemibagrus*. These are BIG catfishes that live for many years. They are voracious predators and will consume anything they can get in their mouths, including fingers!

Native Range: Mekong drainage; Chao Phraya system and peninsular rivers in Thailand. Sometimes found in brackish water.

Maximum Length: 51 in (130 cm) TL.

Water: 72–77°F (22–25°C); pH: 7.0–8.0; hardness: 5–25°dGH.

Min. Tank Size: 180 gal | 72x24x24 in (650 L | 180x60x60 cm). Will eventually require a much larger aquarium. When outspread the very long barbels should not touch the tank sides.

Feeding: Any carnivore and piscivore foods of suitable size.

Behavior & Care: Keep alone—will kill any tankmates, move substrate, and vandalize equipment. This fish can also jump and shatter thick cover glasses, so a heavy hood with protected lighting is required. Floating plants may deter leaping. Needs a large hiding place, sand substrate, powerful filtration, and good oxygenation.

Breeding: Unlikely! Males have an external genital papilla.

Mystus vittatus (Bloch, 1794)
Striped Mystus (Pyjama Catfish, Pajama Catfish)

Overview: An attractive, day-active catfish suitable for a community of medium-sized fishes, though it may hunt and eat small tank-mates. Remember that not all fish labeled "*Mystus*" are small, the name is still applied in the hobby to the much larger species now in *Hemibagrus*. Always check out any unfamiliar fish before buying.

Native Range: India, Burma, and Thailand; in still and running water.

Maximum Length: 8 in (20 cm) TL.

Water: 72–82°F (22–28°C); pH: 6.0–7.5; hardness: 0–15°dGH.

Min. Tank Size: 38 gal | 36x16x16 in (140 L | 90x40x40 cm).

Feeding: Any sinking carnivore foods of suitable size.

Behavior & Care: Keep singly, or in a small group in a large tank. Well-planted aquarium with wood, rocks, etc, creating lots of hiding places. Sandy, ideally dark-colored, substrate.

Breeding: Males are smaller and more slender than females. Court-ship is an active affair and the fish make chirruping noises while courting. The eggs number into four figures and are scattered on the bottom among plants and other décor. No brood care.

Pseudomystus siamensis (Regan, 1913)
Bumblebee Catfish (Leiocassis Siamensis)

Overview: Better known by its old genus name *Leiocassis*, this small bagrid should not be confused with the South American Bumblebee Cat, *Microglanis iheringi* (qv). Several other *Pseudomystus* are also sometimes available, and often are likewise sold as Bumblebee Cats.

Native Range: Southeast Asia: Mekong and Chao Phraya systems.

Maximum Length: 8 in (20 cm) TL.

Water: 68–79°F (20–26°C); pH: 6.0–8.0; hardness: 0–25°dGH.

Min. Tank Size: 38 gal | 36x16x16 in (140 L | 90x40x40 cm).

Feeding: Any small sinking carnivore foods, especially live and frozen. Nocturnal, so feed at lights out. Will eat small fishes.

Behavior & Care: A fairly hardy catfish suitable for a community aquarium of fishes of similar size. Territorial, so best kept singly unless the tank is very large. The aquarium should include planted areas and daytime hiding places such as bogwood, caves, and/or clay pipes. Soft sandy substrate.

Breeding: Females are deeper-bodied than males, which have an external genital papilla when adult. Egg-scatterer with no brood care. No details of rearing success. Spawns in the rainy season in the wild.

Kryptopterus bicirrhis (Valenciennes, 1840)
Glass Catfish (Ghostfish, Ghost Catfish)

Overview: A peaceful schooling catfish that, unusual for the family, is a midwater swimmer and diurnal. One of its other attractions is that it really is glassy-clear so it presents a living diagram of fish anatomy, with the skeleton and organs visible.

Native Range: Eastern India, Thailand, Malaysia, western Indonesia—Sumatra and Borneo.

Maximum Length: 6 in (15 cm) TL. Usually smaller.

Water: 70–79°F (21–26°C); pH: 6.5–7.5; hardness: 0–15°dGH.

Min. Tank Size: 38 gal | 36x16x16 in (140 L | 90x40x40 cm).

Feeding: Small live foods; will also take frozen and prepared foods in open water, but does not scavenge the bottom. May hunt fry.

Behavior & Care: An excellent fish for the general community, though it can be delicate. Requires good quality, well-oxygenated water with an element of current. Well-planted tank and floating vegetation, bogwood, and plenty of open space as this is an active swimmer. Peaceful tankmates, of similar size or smaller.

Breeding: Reputed to be farmed in the Far East but no details of spawning and rearing available, and no reports of intentional aquarium breeding, though odd fry have been seen. Males are smaller.

Chaca chaca (Hamilton, 1822)
Frogmouth Catfish (Angler Catfish)

Overview: This catfish is more of a curiosity than an ideal aquarium fish, as that large mouth can accommodate tankmates up to a third of its own size. The same applies to its similar-looking congeners, *C. bankanensis* from Indonesia and *C. burmensis* from Burma. It has been suggested that the mouth is in fact a plankton shovel, but as smaller tankmates are prone to go missing....

Native Range: Ganges drainage in India, Bangladesh, and Nepal, usually in large, sunlit but muddy rivers.

Maximum Length: 8 in (20 cm) TL.

Water: 72–77°F (22–25°C); pH: 6.0–8.0; hardness: 0–25°dGH.

Min. Tank Size: 38 gal | 36x16x16 in (140 L | 90x40x40 cm).

Feeding: May require feeder fish initially, but can usually be weaned onto worms, chopped raw fish, prawn, mussel, and tablets. Nocturnal, so feed at lights out.

Behavior & Care: Keep only with fishes too large to eat. Not fussy about water chemistry or quality. Does not harm plants. Provide daytime hiding places (wood, caves made from large flat, weathered, smooth stones) and a soft substrate.

Breeding: Nothing is known about sexing or breeding this catfish.

Agamyxis pectinifrons (Cope, 1870)
White-barred Catfish (Spotted Talking Catfish, Spotted Raphael)

Overview: The talking or thorny catfishes (Doradidae) include both fairly small species like this one, and real monsters not really suitable for aquarium maintenance. "Thorny" relates to the spines on the scutes (bony plates) on their sides, while "talking" refers to their ability to make audible sounds with their fins and/or swimbladders. All are more or less nocturnal. They are often kept with cichlids, but bear in mind that their fins are not armored.

Native Range: South America: widespread in the Amazon basin.

Maximum Length: 6 in (15 cm) TL.

Water: 72–79°F (22–26°C); pH: 6.5–7.5; hardness: 0–15°dGH.

Min. Tank Size: 38 gal | 36x16x16 in (140 L | 90x40x40 cm).

Feeding: Omnivorous. Requires sinking foods at lights out, but can be tempted out by day with food if the aquarium isn't too brightly lit. May mistake very small tankmates for food.

Behavior & Care: Best kept with its own kind in a species tank with dark hiding places (caves, bogwood) and a soft sandy substrate.

Breeding: Females wider-bodied as seen from above; males with longer dorsal and pectoral spines. Spawns among floating vegetation, the male embracing the female with his body. No records of rearing.

Amblydoras hancockii (Valenciennes, 1840)
Hancock's Catfish

Overview: Science is uncertain as to where this catfish belongs in genus terms, or even whether it is distinct at all, but aquarists have no such doubts—the species has been a staple of the catfish hobby for decades, originally as *Doras hancockii.*

Native Range: Lowland Amazon basin in Brazil, Peru, and Bolivia; also found in Guyana. Prefers smaller, quiet water courses.

Maximum Length: 6 in (15 cm) TL.

Water: 72–79°F (22–26°C); pH: 6.5–7.5; hardness: 0–15°dGH.

Min. Tank Size: 38 gal | 36x16x16 in (140 L | 90x40x40 cm).

Feeding: Said to feed on crustaceans and other invertebrates in the wild; takes most aquarium foods; nocturnal—feed at lights out.

Behavior & Care: This species does well in a well-planted aquarium with bogwood and caves where it can hide by day. Tankmates should be of similar size and peaceful temperament.

Breeding: The Hancock after whom this species is named reported as long ago as 1829 that in the wild these catfishes form pairs, then construct a nest of leaves in which the eggs are laid, then practice brood care with the nest defended by the male. Aquarium observations suggest it also spawns among aquarium plants. No records of rearing known.

Megalodoras uranoscopus (Eigenmann & Eigenmann, 1888)
Mother of Snails (Irwin's Catfish, Megalodoras Irwini)

Overview: Big doradids have their devoted fans, but it is essential to be aware how large they can grow. Provide sufficient space, and be aware that you are buying a pet that will live for many years and might not be easy to re-home. This one has been known for decades to aquarists as *M. irwini*, and will doubtless continue to be sold under that name even though its name has now been changed.

Native Range: Amazon, Tocantins, and Essequibo basins.

Maximum Length: 30 in (75 cm) TL. Usually smaller in captivity.

Water: 72–79°F (22–26°C); pH: 6.5–7.5; hardness: 0–20°dGH.

Min. Tank Size: 180 gal | 72x24x24 in (650 L | 180x60x60 cm).

Feeding: Feeds mainly on invertebrates, aquatic snails, and fruits that drop into the water. May eat very small tankmates.

Behavior & Care: Efficient filtration and adequate daytime hiding places are a must. Handle with care—in large specimens the razor-sharp spines on the lateral scutes can easily slice nets and fingers!

Breeding: For practical reasons breeding is unlikely in captivity. Females are larger than males. Like many cichlids this catfish migrates into the flooded forest when the rains come, perhaps to breed. In the dry season it lives in the main channels of permanent rivers.

Oxydoras niger (Valenciennes, 1821)
Black Doras (Ripsaw Catfish, Pseudodoras Niger)

Overview: Best known to aquarists under its old name of *Pseudodoras niger*—still in general use in the trade. Like *Megalodoras uranoscopus* this is a large doradid, and should be kept only by those with the necessary space and commitment.

Native Range: Amazon, São Francisco, and Essequibo drainages, in lowland waters. Possibly also in the Orinoco basin.

Maximum Length: 39 in (100 cm) TL., usually "only" 24 in (60 cm).

Water: 72–79°F (22–26°C); pH: 6.5–7.5; hardness: 0–20°dGH.

Min. Tank Size: 180 gal | 72x24x24 in (650 L | 180x60x60 cm) for a youngster. Be prepared to buy an even larger tank (at least 96x36x36 in | 244x90x90 cm) in due course.

Feeding: Any suitably-sized carnivore foods, plus fruit and greens. Feed at lights out. May mistake very small tankmates for food.

Behavior & Care: As for *Megalodoras uranoscopus*. While its size and diet mean efficient filtration is essential, bear in mind that this an inhabitant of the calm depths of usually slow-moving rivers and still lakes, and will not appreciate turbulence. Fast-growing, so be ready with a large tank even for the small specimens usually sold.

Breeding: The size of this fish virtually precludes captive breeding.

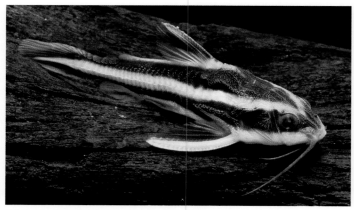

Platydoras costatus (Linnaeus, 1758)
Raphael Catfish (Chocolate Doradid, Humbug Catfish)

Overview: An attractively patterned doradid, and popular for that reason, but its night-time hunting behavior leaves a certain amount to be desired if there are any smaller fishes in the community.

Native Range: Widespread in the Amazon, Orinoco, and Essequibo drainages, plus coastal rivers in Guiana and Surinam. Prefers slow-moving or still lowland waters.

Maximum Length: 9 in (23 cm) TL.

Water: 74–79°F (23–26°C); pH: 6.5–7.5; hardness: 0–15°dGH.

Min. Tank Size: 50 gal | 48x16x16 in (190 L | 120x40x40 cm).

Feeding: A piscivore that will eat smaller tankmates at night. Feed raw fish, shrimp, prawn, and other carnivore foods at lights out.

Behavior & Care: Best kept singly, as it is highly territorial with its own kind and will also quarrel with other nocturnal catfishes. Provide daytime hiding places and a fine sand substrate. Tankmates should be too large to eat, and ideally day-active to avoid squabbles.

Breeding: No noticeable differences between the sexes, but females are probably deeper-bodied. Has been bred—the male embraces the female with his body during spawning, but no further details available, and no records of fry being reared.

Brachyplatystoma juruense (Boulenger, 1898)
Zebra Catfish (Zebra Shovelnose, Flamengo, Cunaguaro)

Overview: The pimelodid, or long-whiskered catfishes, (Pimelodidae), are characterized by long delicate barbels and unarmored skin—they are not suitable for tanks of aggressive cichlids. Some "pims"—like this one—are large and suited only to specialist aquaria.

Native Range: Lowland waters in the Amazon and Orinoco basins.

Maximum Length: 24 in (60 cm) TL.

Water: 72–80°F (22–26°C); pH: 6.0–7.5; hardness: 0–15°dGH.

Min. Tank Size: 180 gal | 72x24x24 in (650 L | 180x60x60 cm).

Feeding: A nocturnal hunter that feeds on invertebrates and small fishes in the wild. Offer prawns, mussels, earthworms, etc. May eat mouth-sized tankmates!

Behavior & Care: Keep alone or with similarly sized pims, in a dimly lit tank in a quiet spot. Provide hiding places for daytime resting; décor (including substrate) should have no sharp edges to damage the skin. Heaters must have heater guards—many catfishes hide under heaters and suffer burns. Powerful external filtration is required since copious waste is produced. Filter outlets should be sited to create flow along the length of the tank.

Breeding: For practical reasons (size!) captive breeding is unlikely.

Brachyrhamdia imitator Myers, 1927
False Corydoras (Pimelodella Imitator)

Overview: This little naked catfish, and others in its small genus, was long regarded by science as a pimelodid but has now been transferred to the family Heptapteridae. It is similar in size and color to the Mailed Catfish, *Corydoras melanistius melanistius*, and in the wild it is often found among schools of the latter. Predators soon learn that corys are not easy to eat because of their armor, and it is thought *Brachyrhamdia* spp. mimic them in order to avoid predation.

Native Range: Brazil: Unini River Basin in the upper Rio Negro River drainage.

Maximum Length: 4 in (5.5 cm) TL.

Water: 68–77°F (20–25°C); pH: 6.5–7.5; hardness: 0–15°dGH.

Min. Tank Size: 38 gal | 36x16x16 in (140 L | 90x40x40 cm).

Feeding: Omnivores that will take all standard foods.

Behavior & Care: Active swimmers that require reasonable space. Territorial towards its own kind, so keep singly or in a small group in a large tank where each can carve out its own patch. Soft sandy substrate, plants, rocky caves and bogwood as hiding places.

Breeding: Thought to be egg-scatterers but not yet bred successfully. The best chance is probably by keeping a group as above.

Microglanis iheringi Gomes, 1946
Bumblebee Catfish (Marbled Catfish)

Overview: Like *Brachyrhamdia*, the *Microglanis* species, long regarded as pimelodids, have now been reclassified in the family Pseudopimelodidae. There are several species, some rather similar in their attractive marbled patterning. This one is probably the best known in the hobby. Not to be confused with the much larger Asian Bumblebee Catfish, *Pseudomystus* (formerly *Leiocassis*) *siamensis* which is only a very distant relative (family Bagridae).

Native Range: Venezuela—Rio Turmero Basin.

Maximum Length: 4 in (10 cm) TL.

Water: 75–82°F (24–2°C); pH: 7.5–9.0; hardness: 10–25°dGH.

Min. Tank Size: 25 gal | 24x16x16 in (95 L | 60x40x40 cm).

Feeding: Live and frozen foods, but will take small prepared foods as well. May also prey on fry of other fishes.

Behavior & Care: Peaceful and an attractive fish for the general community, though unfortunately it is nocturnal. Provide plenty of cover and shade, and offer live food in a dimly lit spot to bring it out by day. Very good water quality and fine substrate required.

Breeding: Males smaller than females. Bred accidentally, but no details of procedure. Fry appeared and were removed and reared.

Phractocephalus hemioliopterus (Bloch & Schneider, 1801)
Red-tailed Catfish

Overview: This huge pim, the only member of its genus, is included here as a warning NOT to buy it. It is regularly sold to the unwary as delightful little juveniles only a few inches long, which rapidly grow to three feet or so (a meter) long—and that is only half-grown! Public aquariums and zoos have been flooded with unwanted Red-tails that have outgrown their owners' ability to house them, so unless you are prepared to provide a large heated pool for maybe 20 or 30 years, leave this fish in the store.

Native Range: Widespread in the Amazon and Orinoco systems.

Maximum Length: 72 in (185 cm) TL.

Water: 70–80°F (21–26.5°C); pH: 6.0–7.5; hardness: 0–10°dGH.

Min. Tank Size: 180 gal | 72x24x24 in (650 L | 180x60x60 cm) that will be outgrown in about a year; you will not be able to buy a tank large enough in the long-term.

Feeding: A voracious predator, even when small, that will take any carnivore food of suitable size, especially smaller fishes.

Behavior & Care: Requires a large hiding place in which to lurk; fine substrate, ideally soft acid water, gargantuan filtration system.

Breeding: Nothing known of sexing. Breeding totally impracticable.

Pimelodus maculatus Lacépède, 1803
Spotted Pim

Overview: A very attractive pimelodid that is unfortunately rather rare in the hobby. Like most members of the family it is a large-mouthed predator that cannot be trusted with smaller tankmates. Be warned, it grows a lot larger than the more familiar _P. pictus_. It also has serrated pectoral fins that can snag nets and rip fingers!

Native Range: Paraná and São Francisco basins in Argentina and southern Brazil, in lowland rivers.

Maximum Length: 15.5 in (39 cm) TL.

Water: 68–77°F (20–25°C); pH: 6.5–7.5; hardness: 0–15°dGH.

Min. Tank Size: 65 gal | 48x18x18 in (240 L | 120x45x45 cm).

Feeding: A predator that will take most carnivore foods. Nocturnal, so feed at lights out. May also feed by day if lighting is muted.

Behavior & Care: Peaceful for its size—predation isn't aggression! Needs a large tank with soft substrate and plenty of hiding places, but also lots of open space as it is an active swimmer when it does come out. Note that the southerly distribution requires fairly low temperatures, and, if possible, seasonal variation.

Breeding: Females are larger and deeper-bodied. The species has not yet bred successfully in the aquarium.

Pimelodus ornatus Kner, 1858
Ornate Pim

Overview: This attractive pim can grow rather larger than often stated in the aquarium literature. Like other *Pimelodus* (and most pims) it has very long barbels. Some species thus equipped may panic if they spread these appendages out sideways and touch the tank sides. Hiding places should also accommodate the barbels.

Native Range: Amazon, Orinoco, and Paraná basins, as well as rivers in the Guianas.

Maximum Length: 16 in (40 cm) TL. Usually smaller in captivity.

Water: 70–80°F (21–26.5°C); pH: 6.0–7.5; hardness: 0–15°dGH.

Min. Tank Size: 65 gal | 48x18x18 in (240 L | 120x45x45 cm).

Feeding: Carnivore foods of appropriate size.

Behavior & Care: Mainly diurnal and rather active. Tank décor as for *P. maculatus*. Use power filtration to create a current in the tank; choose tankmates that will thrive in this setting and accommodate the pim's active behavior, also remembering that small ones may be taken as food. Eroded barbels are a warning sign of excess nitrate.

Breeding: Females are larger and deeper-bodied, but no records of successful breeding.

Pimelodus pictus Steindachner, 1877
Angelic Pim (Polka-dot Catfish, Pictus Cat)

Overview: Probably the best-known member of its genus, and a regular in stores, but beware—it grows larger than most aquarists realize, it is a large-mouthed predator that may consume tankmates, and it is very prone to White Spot (ichthyophthiriasis or Ich) and a change of environment (such as from store to home) is often enough to trigger an outbreak. This is a nice fish as long as you know what to expect.
Native Range: Amazon and Orinoco basins in Brazil, Colombia, Peru, and Venezuela, in lowland rivers.
Maximum Length: 6 in (15 cm) TL.
Water: 73–82°F (23–28°C); pH: 6.0–7.0; hardness: 0–10°dGH.
Min. Tank Size: 38 gal | 36x16x16 in (140 L | 90x40x40 cm).
Feeding: Any carnivore foods of suitable size.
Behavior & Care: Peaceful; can be kept in a small group in a large tank. An active swimmer that requires plenty of open space. Nocturnal but will come out by day if lighting is muted. Soft, acid water. Décor as for _P. maculatus_. This species, too, has serrated pectorals.
Breeding: No records of successful breeding despite many years in the hobby. Females are larger. Said to be an egg-scatterer.

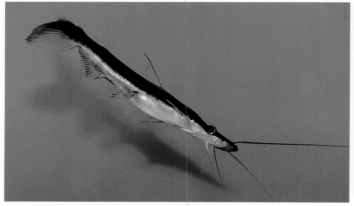

Sorubim lima (Bloch & Schneider, 1801)
Shovelnose Catfish (Lima Shovelnose, Duckbill Catfish)

Overview: A large pim that has been in the hobby for many years, albeit in small numbers. Like many cats it is nocturnal, and you might wonder what is the point of keeping a large fish that comes out only at night. The answer is, if the tank is not too brightly lit, and the catfish has a large piece of bogwood under which to sit, it will be in full view even by day. And when you have seen a Shovelnose lurking—watching you—the attraction becomes clear!

Native Range: Amazon, Orinoco, Paraná, and Parnaíba drainages.
Maximum Length: 21.5 in (55 cm) TL.
Water: 70–80°F (21–26.5°C); pH: 6.0–7.5; hardness: 0–15°dGH.
Min. Tank Size: 180 gal | 72x24x24 in (650 L | 180x60x60 cm).
Feeding: A nocturnal ambush predator that may require feeder fish but can usually be weaned onto other carnivore foods.
Behavior & Care: Given a very large tank this peaceful species can be kept in a small group if they are acquired when small. Requires suitably large hiding places, soft substrate, muted lighting, and efficient filtration. Won't harm plants as long as these are established before it is introduced; will regard smaller tankmates as food.
Breeding: Nothing known about sexing or breeding.

Pseudoplatystoma coruscans, Pintado. Ferocious and cannibalistic.

Pseudoplatystoma tigrinum, Tiger Sorubim.

These fishes are often sold young as "tiger shovelnoses," as it is difficult to distinguish the species in juveniles. Undeniably appealing, they will need a large aquarium and big, rugged tankmates.

Auchenipterichthys thoracatus (Kner, 1858)
Midnight Catfish (Zamora Catfish)

Overview: The family Auchenipteridae (woodcats and driftwood catfishes) is unusual in that, as far as is known, all its members practice internal fertilization of the eggs. They are all nocturnal, and although they rest near or on the bottom by day, they hunt near the surface when night falls. This one may not look much in the shop, but once it has settled in it is quite gorgeous.

Native Range: Peru, in small rivers and forest streams in the upper Amazon drainage. Zamora is the region where it is often collected.

Maximum Length: 5 in (13 cm) TL.

Water: 70–79°F (21–26°C); pH: 6.5–7.5; hardness: 0–10°dGH.

Min. Tank Size: 38 gal | 36x16x16 in (140 L | 90x40x40 cm).

Feeding: Small live foods, floating prepared foods, at lights out.

Behavior & Care: Peaceful, but house only with fishes too large to eat. Needs daytime hiding places (wood, caves), and plants. Does well in a small group in a large tank.

Breeding: Males are more boldly patterned and have a prolonged anal fin used for the internal fertilization. The pair curve their bodies round one another, and during this embrace insemination takes place. The female later lays her eggs on a pre-cleaned substrate.

Liosomadoras oncinus (Jardine, 1841)
Jaguar Catfish

Overview: Perhaps the most enigmatic and beautiful of all the Auchenipteridae, this fish doesn't conform fully with the genus definition but has some features of a doradid. It is also probably the most difficult woodcat to keep because of its specialized water requirements—don't keep it unless you can provide soft, acid water.

Native Range: Blackwater rivers in Brazil and Peru.

Maximum Length: 7 in (18 cm) TL.

Water: 70–77°F (21–25°C); pH: 5.0–6.5; hardness: 0–5°dGH.

Min. Tank Size: 38 gal | 36x16x16 in (140 L | 90x40x40 cm).

Feeding: Like other woodcats, this fish is a carnivore; live and frozen foods, prepared foods. Likely to eat small tankmates.

Behavior & Care: Peaceful and a good catfish for a community of similarly sized fishes. Crepuscular, so more likely to be seen by day than other woodcats, as long as lighting is low. Décor should be robust plants, fine substrate, and wood to create hiding places. Can be kept in a small group. Peat filtration advisable.

Breeding: Males are more boldly colored. As in all auchenipterids, fertilization is internal and the eggs are laid immediately afterwards. Not yet bred successfully in the aquarium.

Tatia intermedia (Steindachner, 1877)
Snowflake Woodcat

Overview: "Woodcats" and "driftwood catfishes" refer not to the appearance of these fishes but their preferred habitat among the dead wood that accumulates in South American rivers. Their main aquarium requirement should thus be obvious. *Tatia* are smaller members of the family and good community fishes—some other woodcats grow much larger and have bad habits, so research before buying.

Native Range: South America: Amazon and Guyanan rivers.

Maximum Length: 4.75 in (12 cm) TL.

Water: 70–77°F (21–25°C); pH: 6.5–7.5; hardness: 0–10°dGH.

Min. Tank Size: 25 gal | 24x16x16 in (95 L | 60x40x40 cm).

Feeding: Nocturnal—feed at lights out. Small live and frozen foods, plus prepared foods. May eat fry of other fishes.

Behavior & Care: A peaceful little catfish that will appreciate a well-planted tank with bogwood and other hiding places, soft, fine substrate, and well-oxygenated water. Ideally, keep a small group.

Breeding: As far as is known, all auchenipterids practice internal fertilization, the anal fin of the male being modified as a copulatory organ. *Tatia* are no exception. The female subsequently lays her eggs alone, usually on the underside of a piece of wood. No brood care.

Trachelyopterichthys taeniatus (Kner, 1858)
Striped Woodcat (Eel Driftwood Cat)

Overview: An attractive fish with interesting feeding and breeding behavior, suitable for a community of similar-sized tankmates. Until fairly recently it was the only member of its genus, but a second species, *T. anduzei*, was described from the upper Orinoco drainage in 1987. Note the eventual size!

Native Range: Upper Amazon drainage in Brazil and Venezuela.

Maximum Length: 12 in (30 cm) TL.

Water: 70–79°F (21–26°C); pH: 6.5–7.5; hardness: 0–10°dGH.

Min. Tank Size: 38 gal | 36x16x16 in (140 L | 90x40x40 cm).

Feeding: A nocturnal hunter that in nature takes insects that have landed on the surface, and in the aquarium may take small open-water tankmates. Live, frozen, and flake foods, at lights out.

Behavior & Care: Peaceful apart from its feeding behavior, but house only with fishes too large to eat. Needs daytime hiding places (lots of wood, caves), and plants, including floating vegetation.

Breeding: Males have a gonopodium and fertilization is internal. During spawning the male embraces the female with his body and inserts the gonopodium into her vent. Afterwards she lays the eggs on a previously cleaned surface.

Trachelyopterus galeatus (Linnaeus, 1766)
Starry Woodcat

Overview: This catfish has been sold as a general community fish for many years, but is really more suitable for the catfish specialist because of its size and rather antisocial habits.

Native Range: Very widely distributed in northern South America, usually in or among tangles of roots and dead wood.

Maximum Length: 8 in (20 cm) TL.

Water: 70–79°F (21–26°C); pH: 6.0–7.5; hardness: 0–10°dGH.

Min. Tank Size: 38 gal | 36x16x16 in (140 L | 90x40x40 cm).

Feeding: Mainly carnivorous but takes most foods. Can't be trusted with fishes small enough to eat. Nocturnal—so feed at lights out.

Behavior & Care: Not an ideal community fish as it is very active at night and may disturb resting diurnal fishes and uproot plants. Requires plenty of daytime hiding places, ideally wood, but rocky caves and clay pipes will do. Very fast-growing fish. Fairly hardy, but water quality should be good.

Breeding: Males are more colorful and have a modified anal fin for internal fertilization of the eggs. The male wraps his body around the female during mating. The eggs are not always laid immediately.

Bunocephalus coracoideus (Cope, 1874)
Banjo Catfish

Overview: Aquarists may be more familiar with members of this genus as *Dysichthys*. Banjo cats are so named because of their shape, though their rough skin—unique among South American catfishes —is not very banjo-like. Some bury themselves in the substrate, some can make sounds with their pectoral fins. Their rough skin means banjo catfishes are well-camouflaged on wood. *B. knerii* and *B. verrucosus* are similar, the latter even more rough-skinned.

Native Range: Amazon drainage.

Maximum Length: 5 in (13 cm) TL.

Water: 70–79°F (21–26°C); pH: 6.5–7.5; hardness: 0–10°dGH.

Min. Tank Size: 38 gal | 36x16x16 in (140 L | 90x40x40 cm).

Feeding: Any small sinking foods are greedily taken. Nocturnal, so feed at lights out.

Behavior & Care: A peaceful fish, and good for the general community. Provide a soft, sandy substrate, preferably dark-colored, with well-planted areas and wood as décor. If there are shady areas then this fish will be more likely to show itself by day.

Breeding: *B. coracoideus* is thought to be a group spawner, with the eggs laid on the sandy substrate.

Platystacus cotylephorus Bloch, 1794
Banded Banjo Catfish (Mottled Whiptail Banjo Catfish)

Overview: The only member of its genus. In the wild it occurs in estuaries as well as fresh water, and hence is a candidate for a brackish tank. It has unusual breeding behavior which is shared with some other members of the family Aspredinidae (Banjo Cats).

Native Range: Coastal rivers from Venezuela to northern Brazil.

Maximum Length: 12 in (30 cm) TL.

Water: 72–79°F (22–26°C); pH: 6.5–8.0; hardness: 0–20°dGH.

Min. Tank Size: 50 gal | 36x18x18 in (180 L | 90x45x45 cm).

Feeding: Small live and frozen foods; also enjoys tablet foods.

Behavior & Care: A peaceful community fish, though it may eat fry. It spends most of the day buried in the substrate, and so this should be soft sand. Plants, wood, and water-worn stones as décor. Tankmates must be salt-tolerant if brackish water is used.

Breeding: Males have a longer dorsal spine; females wider ventrals. The species practices a special form of brood care; the developing eggs are carried on "stalks" (cotylophores) attached to the underside of the female that are thought to act rather like an umbilical cord between mother and embryo. Unfortunately, this fish has not yet been successfully bred in the aquarium.

Aspidoras pauciradiatus (Weitzman & Nijssen, 1970)
Blotch-fin Aspidoras (Corydoras pauciradiatus, False Corydoras)

Overview: *Aspidoras* are members of the South American family Callichthyidae (known as the mailed catfishes), and cousins of the better-known *Corydoras*. They are generally smaller, more slender, and in some cases at least, more delicate. Like all callichthyids they are schooling fishes and should never be kept singly, and because they constantly investigate the bottom with their barbels for food, a soft substrate is important to avoid damage and infection. *A. pauciradiatus* is the species most frequently seen in the hobby.

Native Range: South America: nominally the upper Araguia drainage, Brazil, but aquarium imports originate from the Rio Negro system, and water parameters are suggested accordingly.

Maximum Length: 1.25 in (3 cm) TL.

Water: 75–82°F (24–28°C); pH: 5.5–7.0; hardness: 0–10°dGH.

Min. Tank Size: 25 gal | 24x16x16 in (95 L | 60x40x40 cm).

Feeding: Small sinking foods, including live foods.

Behavior & Care: Keep in a group of at least six in a species tank or with other very small fishes. Good quality, well-oxygenated water.

Breeding: Regularly bred. Attaches eggs to plants and hard surfaces but the adults are avid egg-eaters so remove after spawning.

Brochis britskii Nijssen & Isbrücker, 1983
Giant Brochis (Britski's Catfish)

Overview: *Brochis* look like big chunky *Corydoras*, and like them are members of the mailed catfish family Callichthyidae, but have a much longer dorsal fin with more rays, so even small specimens are unmistakable. All share an attractive metallic coloration. The popular name is apt—this species is big even by *Brochis* standards!

Native Range: South America: upper Rio Paraguay system, Brazil, also the Pantanal, where it forms huge schools during the dry season.

Maximum Length: 5.5 in (14 cm) TL, usually smaller.

Water: 70–79°F (21–26°C); pH: 6.5–7.5; hardness: 0–15°dGH.

Min. Tank Size: 38 gal | 36x16x16 in (140 L | 90x40x40 cm).

Feeding: Live and frozen foods; any other sinking foods.

Behavior & Care: Like all callichthyids these are sociable fish that should be kept in a group of five or more. Like the better-known *Corydoras* they are bottom-dwellers and search the substrate for food, so soft sand or fine gravel is essential to avoid damage to barbels. Good community fish, as long as other bottom-dwellers are of similar size. Unlikely to bother, or be bothered by, tankmates at higher levels.

Breeding: No known records; probably similar to *Brochis splendens*.

Brochis splendens (Castelnau, 1855)
Emerald Catfish (Common Brochis)

Overview: The best-known and most popular member of its genus. "Emerald" may seem an exaggeration at first glance in the store, but in full color these fish have a brilliant metallic green sheen.

Native Range: South America: Amazon drainage in Brazil, Colombia, Ecuador, and Peru. Some local color variation.

Maximum Length: 3.5 in (9 cm) TL.

Water: 72–82°F (22–28°C); pH: 6.0–7.5; hardness: 0–15°dGH.

Min. Tank Size: 38 gal | 36x16x16 in (140 L | 90x40x40 cm).

Feeding: Any sinking foods; use live foods to stimulate breeding.

Behavior & Care: As for _Brochis britskii._

Breeding: Best bred in a separate breeding aquarium to avoid egg and fry predation by tankmates. Females are larger, and rounder when full of roe. Very soft, acid water of excellent quality is required for successful hatching and larval development. Spawning is usually at night; the eggs are laid singly and attached to plant leaves and other surfaces well off the bottom. No brood care, so remove the adults after spawning. The eggs take 3–4 days to hatch depending on temperature; the fry are free-swimming after two more days. They can take _Artemia_ nauplii and microworm as first foods.

Callichthys callichthys (Linnaeus, 1758)
Cascarudo

Overview: The type species of the Callichthyidae, but rather different to most members of the family in appearance, breeding, and some other behavior. A real survivor—it can breathe air, and if its home dries up it crawls across land on its ventrals to find water.

Native Range: Most drainages in the vast area east of the Andes and north of Buenos Aires; also found on Trinidad and Tobago.

Maximum Length: 7 in (18 cm) TL.

Water: 65–82°F (18–28°C); pH: 6.0–8.0; hardness: 5–25°dGH.

Min. Tank Size: 38 gal | 36x16x16 in (140 L | 90x40x40 cm).

Feeding: Primarily a bottom-feeder; will take any sinking foods.

Behavior & Care: Keep in a small school in a well-planted tank with fine substrate, and plenty of hiding places as these cats are nocturnal and need to hide by day. The wide distribution means that nominally a wide range of water parameters is tolerated, but if the origin of specific stock is known, provide appropriate water. Peaceful, but may eat very small tankmates.

Breeding: The male has longer pectoral fins and is more colorful. He builds a bubblenest beneath floating vegetation and defends the clutch of up to 120 eggs. The young require infusoria as first food.

Corydoras aeneus (Gill, 1858)
Bronze Corydoras (Aeneus)

Overview: *Corydoras* are the best-known mailed catfishes (family Callichthyidae). These small schooling cats can breathe air and are regularly seen rising to the surface to do so; this is normal and no cause for concern. *C. aeneus* is probably the most popular of all the "corys" and is commercially bred. Albino, melanic, and long-finned forms have been created from accidental aquarium sports.

Native Range: South America: drainages east of the Andes from Colombia south to the La Plata. Also found on Trinidad.

Maximum Length: 3 in (7.5 cm) TL.

Water: 65–77°F (18–25°C); pH: 6.0–8.0; hardness: 0–25°dGH.

Min. Tank Size: 25 gal | 24x16x16 in (95 L | 60x40x40 cm).

Feeding: Bottom-feeding; takes any small sinking foods.

Behavior & Care: Keep in a small group in a well-planted tank with open, soft substrate. A hardy fish, excellent for the community.

Breeding: As with most corys, females are larger than males and have different-shaped pectoral and ventral fins. The eggs are attached to plants or other surfaces by the female. Use a bare tank with spawning mops if you want to rear fry. Remove adults after spawning. Fry are free-swimming after 6–8 days and can manage *Artemia* nauplii.

Corydoras arcuatus Elwin, 1939
Skunk Catfish (Arcuatus)

Overview: An evergreen cory. Although there are now many new species available, a school of *arcuatus* remains an attractive sight.

Native Range: Upper Amazon: Brazil, Colombia, Ecuador, Peru.

Maximum Length: 2.5 in (6 cm) TL.

Water: 68–75°F (20–25°C); pH: 6.5–8.0; hardness: 0–25°dGH.

Min. Tank Size: 25 gal | 24x12x20 in (90 L | 60x30x50 cm).

Feeding: Any small, sinking, aquarium fare. Although corys are often included in aquaria as scavengers, care must always be taken to ensure they get enough to eat, not just odd leftover scraps.

Behavior & Care: As for *C. aeneus*, and like that species an excellent hardy species for the general community.

Breeding: Easy to breed, as for *C. aeneus*. Spawning in this, and most *Corydoras*, follows a set procedure: the male grasps the female's barbels with his pectoral spines, so the pair are locked in a so-called T-position. The female expels a few eggs into a pouch formed by her folded ventral fins, then swims away to attach them to a plant leaf or solid substrate near the surface. The procedure is repeated till the clutch is complete. It is unknown how the eggs are fertilized; this apparently occurs during the "embrace." No brood care.

Corydoras elegans Steindachner, 1877
Elegant Corydoras (Elegant Catfish)

Overview: *C. elegans* is one of a small group of corys that are similar in appearance but deviate somewhat from the norm in form (more elongate) and behavior. In particular they have a tendency to swim in mid-water, and the males are quarrelsome.

Native Range: Upper Amazon basin in Brazil, Colombia, and Peru.

Maximum Length: 2.5 in (6 cm) TL.

Water: 70–82°F (21–28°C); pH: 6.5–7.5; hardness: 0–15°dGH.

Min. Tank Size: 38 gal | 36x16x16 in (140 L | 90x40x40 cm).

Feeding: Any normal aquarium foods—members of the *elegans* group are less reliant on food reaching the bottom than other corys.

Behavior & Care: As for *C. aeneus*, but allow more space because of the tendency to quarrelsomeness. Bear in mind the off-bottom swimming when selecting tankmates.

Breeding: Here too this group exhibits interesting differences. The sexes are dichromatic—males are colorful and boldly patterned. Eggs and fry are relatively small and the eggs are reported to float. It is also reported that one form of *C. elegans* does not adopt the usual T-position; the male may fertilize the eggs after the female has attached them to a pre-cleaned surface, hovering over them briefly.

Corydoras haraldschultzi, the Reticulated Cory.

Corydoras paleatus. This is a hi-fin type of cory catfish.

Catfishes are not scavengers and cannot live on garbage. When feeding your fishes, be sure there is enough of the right kinds of food to nourish these hard-working bottom-dwellers.

Corydoras hastatus Eigenmann & Eigenmann, 1888
Sickle-spot Cory (Hastatus Cory)

Overview: This tiny cory has abandoned life on the bottom to become a mid-water schooling fish. Its small size makes it vulnerable, despite its armor, so it has evolved extra defenses. The caudal spot looks like an eye, attracting predators to the "wrong" end of the fish. This trick is also practiced by a number of sympatric characin species which school with the tiny corys, so they all enjoy safety in numbers. These schools also favor so-called "floating meadows" of flooded vegetation, which provide overhead cover.

Native Range: Paraguay basin, including the Pantanal.

Maximum Length: 1.25 in (3 cm) TL.

Water: 68–79°F (20–26°C); pH: 6.5–7.5; hardness: 0–15°dGH.

Min. Tank Size: 25 gal | 24x16x16 in (95 L | 60x40x40 cm).

Feeding: Will take any small foods suited to its diminutive size. Live food is best as sinking food may be left uneaten on the bottom.

Behavior & Care: Although this is a miniature cory, it requires plenty of space and is best kept in a larger school than usual (12+) to give it confidence (safety in numbers!). Small, peaceful tankmates—ideally schools of small mid-water characins with which it can swim.

Breeding: Typical T-position spawner, but in mid-water.

Corydoras imitator Nijssen & Isbrücker, 1983
Imitator

Overview: Some corys share their habitat with "doubles"— similar-looking but not closely related species with a different head shape. As well as the normal "short-nose" types, there are (usually larger) "long-noses," and "saddle-noses" with a prolonged flattened snout. *C. imitator* is the long-nose "copycat" of *C. adolfoi*, and there is also a saddle-nose, *C. serratus*. We don't know which came first, but probably the short-noses, as they are always more numerous.

Native Range: Upper Rio Negro.

Maximum Length: 3 in (8 cm) TL.

Water: 68–77°F (20–25°C); pH: 6.5–8.0; hardness: 0–25°dGH.

Min. Tank Size: 25 gal | 24x16x16 in (95 L | 60x40x40 cm).

Feeding: The different forms feed in different ways: short-noses pick from the surface of the substrate; saddle-snouts burrow down a short way; long-noses probe deep. All require small sinking foods.

Behavior & Care: Fine, soft substrate is particularly important for the bottom-probing forms. Long-snouts are similar to short-noses in social behavior, but saddle-snouts tend to be solitary, not schooling.

Breeding: "Cory-normal" but best sexed by ventral-fin shape. Saddle-noses are trickier to breed and seem to need a strong current.

Corydoras paleatus (Jenyns, 1842)
Peppered Corydoras (Peppered Catfish)

Overview: This popular cory has a place in aquarium history—it was the third exotic fish ever to be imported for the hobby, in 1876. It was preceded by the Goldfish, *Carassius auratus*, and the Paradise Fish, *Macropodus opercularis*, and, like them, probably survived the journey because it is not strictly tropical and tolerates quite low temperatures. No insulated boxes then! Its popularity has never waned, and it is mass-produced commercially in the Far East; there are also cultivated albino, gold, and long-fin forms.

Native Range: Lower Paraná basin and coastal rivers in south Brazil and Uruguay.

Maximum Length: 3.5 in (9 cm) TL.

Water: 65–79°F (18–26°C); pH: 6.0–8.0; hardness: 0–25°dGH.

Min. Tank Size: 25 gal | 24x16x16 in (95 L | 60x40x40 cm).

Feeding: Small sinking foods of all types.

Behavior & Care: Cory-normal—an easy and hardy species for the general community. Note, however, that wild fish should be kept in the lower part of the temperature range cited, with low hardness and fairly neutral pH.

Breeding: Almost as easy to breed as to keep. Males are slimmer.

Corydoras panda Nijssen & Isbrücker, 1971
Panda Catfish (Panda Cory)

Overview: This eye-catching cory was an instant hit when first imported, and has deservedly become a staple of the aquarium hobby. Unlike many attractive fishes they are suitable for the beginner's general community tank and not restricted to experts.

Native Range: South America: upper Amazon drainage in Peru.

Maximum Length: 2.5 in (6 cm) TL.

Water: 70–79°F (21–26°C); pH: 6.5–7.5; hardness: 0–20°dGH.

Min. Tank Size: 25 gal | 24x16x16 in (95 L | 60x40x40 cm).

Feeding: Readily accepts any small sinking foods or live foods.

Behavior & Care: As for *C. aeneus*. Note that these little cats will show their best colors against a light substrate; if dark sand or gravel is used they will darken to improve their camouflage.

Breeding: Easy to breed, even by novices, and will often spawn in the community tank without any assistance from the aquarist. Not so easy to sex. Males are a little smaller, but the best method is to view them from above (e.g. in a bucket,) when the longer pectoral spines of the males are more visible, even in relatively young specimens. Not as productive as some corys, with 30 eggs being a high number (some species lay more than 100).

Corydoras pygmaeus Knaack, 1966
Pygmy Corydoras

Overview: One of the smallest corys, which, like another dwarf species *C. hastatus*, has largely abandoned bottom-foraging for a mid-water existence. Interestingly there are also dwarf corys (e.g. *C. habrosus*) that have kept their fins firmly on the bottom.

Native Range: The Madeira basin in Brazil, the Rio Nanay in Peru, and in Ecuador. This represents a disjunct distribution: the species is found in widely separated localities.

Maximum Length: 1.5 in (4 cm) TL.

Water: 70–79°F (21–26°C); pH: 6.5–7.5; hardness: 0–10°dGH.

Min. Tank Size: 25 gal | 24x16x16 in (95 L | 60x40x40 cm).

Feeding: Best fed on tiny live foods, such as *Artemia* nauplii, Cyclops, sifted *Daphnia*. Will take prepared foods but feed tiny amounts at a time and be prepared to clean up any that reaches the bottom.

Behavior & Care: Hardy despite its small size and suitable for a general community as long as tankmates aren't too large. Best kept in a fairly large school (at least 12).

Breeding: Probably the easiest cory to breed. Keep a school in an established well-planted aquarium with no other fishes, feed with live food, and change water weekly. They should then breed regularly.

Corydoras robineae Burgess, 1983
Bannertail Catfish (Flagtail Catfish)

Overview: This species is one-of-a-kind. As its common names suggests, it has a large tail, which furthermore has a striking and uncorylike pattern. The purpose of this unusual tail is unknown.

Native Range: South America: Upper Rio Negro drainage in Brazil.

Maximum Length: 3.5 in (9 cm) TL.

Water: 75–82°F (24–28°C); pH: 5.0–7.5; hardness: 0–10°dGH.

Min. Tank Size: 25 gal | 24x16x16 in (95 L | 60x40x40 cm).

Feeding: The tail is apparently not linked to diet or feeding, as this fish, like most other short-nose corys, picks over the bottom for anything edible, and will take any small sinking foods.

Behavior & Care: The main point to note is that stocks of this fish are probably entirely wild-caught, and it comes from the blackwater Rio Negro. Hence very soft, acid, peaty water is a wise choice.

Breeding: Has been bred, but few details known. One documented spawning numbered 160 eggs but hatch rate was poor. Corys are usually bred in a special tank with no other fishes, the parents removed after spawning, and methylene blue added to the water to prevent infection. The fry swim free after 7–9 days and most can take *Artemia* nauplii, microworm, or powdered food, pre-soaked so it sinks.

Corydoras trilineatus Cope, 1872
Leopard Cory (Three-line Catfish)

Overview: One of a small group of probably closely-related corys known as leopard catfishes because of their markings, and similar in their requirements. They include *C. julii*, though the real *julii* is rare in the hobby and other species (including *trilineatus*) are incorrectly sold under its name. There is also a *C. leopardus*, but it is a long-snout (see under *C. imitator*) and not a close relative.

Native Range: Central and Peruvian Amazon drainage.

Maximum Length: 2.5 in (6.5 cm) TL.

Water: 75-82°F (24-28°C); pH 6.5-7.5; hardness 0-15°dGH.

Min. Tank Size: 25 gal | 24x16x16 in (95 L | 60x40x40 cm).

Feeding: Bottom-feeder—small sinking foods.

Behavior & Care: An easy, hardy species, but one of those that needs to be kept fairly warm in line with its natural range.

Breeding: Although Leopard Corys are easy to keep, they are less cooperative as regards breeding. A water change, with colder water to cause a large temperature drop, will sometimes trigger breeding. Live food can be helpful, as is very soft, slightly acid water. Corys from shady, poorly lit biotopes may respond to leaving the light off and covering the tank so only a glimmer of light enters.

231

Dianema urostriatum (Miranda Ribeiro, 1912)
Flagtail Catfish

Overview: This fish could easily have borrowed its tail from *Corydoras robinae*, as well as sharing a common name, but there the resemblance ends. Although this species is also a callichthyid, it is more closely related to *Callichthys* than to *Corydoras*.

Native Range: Amazon drainage in Brazil, lower Rio Negro.

Maximum Length: 4.5 in (11.5 cm) TL.

Water: 75–82°F (24–28°C); pH: 6.5–7.5; hardness: 0–15°dGH.

Min. Tank Size: 38 gal | 36x16x16 in (140 L | 90x40x40 cm).

Feeding: Mainly nocturnal, so should be fed at lights out. Prefers sinking carnivore foods; enjoys food tablets.

Behavior & Care: Peaceful and sociable, so keep in a school of six or more. Because they are nocturnal, the tank should offer plenty of daytime hiding places. Although this fish is found in the Rio Negro, it inhabits only the lower reaches, where the upstream blackwater chemistry has been modified by the massive influx of whitewater from the Rio Branco. Hence they are not too fussy about water.

Breeding: Females are deeper-bodied when ripe. Bubble-nest spawner like *Callichthys*, with brood care by the male. Provide floating vegetation to which the nest can be attached.

Megalechis thoracata (Valenciennes, 1840)
Tamboata (Tamboatá, Hoplosternum Thoracatum)

Overview: This callichthyid catfish is that rare creature—a fish that has benefited from pollution by humans. Its natural habitat is muddy areas with dense vegetation, and waste-water discharge provides just the right conditions, so it is sometimes found in schools of up to a thousand near areas of human habitation.

Native Range: South America: Amazon and Orinoco drainages as well as coastal rivers in the Guianas and north-east Brazil.

Maximum Length: 7 in (18 cm) TL.

Water: 75–82°F (24–28°C); pH: 6.0–8.0; hardness: 0–25°dGH.

Min. Tank Size: 38 gal | 36x16x16 in (140 L | 90x40x40 cm).

Feeding: Eats any sinking food of suitable size. Nocturnal, so feed at lights out. Tablet food is ideal for this.

Behavior & Care: Close to indestructible, but since the margin for error is smaller in the limited amount of water in a glass box, aim for good quality. Requires hiding places for retreat by day.

Breeding: A bubble-nester like *Callichthys*, so floating vegetation is required. Males are very aggressive when breeding, so use a breeding tank and remove the female after spawning. The male guards the spawn, but may turn cannibal in captivity—if so, remove him!

Scleromystax barbatus (Quoy & Gaimard, 1824)
Bearded Cory (Bearded Catfish, Barbatus, Checkerboard Cory)

Overview: Better known as *Corydoras barbatus*, this species is now assigned to a separate genus. Some of the generic characteristicss are visible to the amateur: the pectoral spine and dorsal fin are much longer in adult males than in females; in some species sexually active males develop a "beard" of bristles (odontodes) on the cheeks, hence the common and scientific names of this species. There is an albino form, though why anyone should want an albino of such an attractively marked species is a mystery.

Native Range: South America: upland rivers in southeast Brazil.

Maximum Length: 5 in (12 cm) TL.

Water: 60–72°F (15–22°C); pH: 4.5–7.2; hardness: 0–10°dGH.

Min. Tank Size: 38 gal | 36x16x16 in (140 L | 90x40x40 cm).

Feeding: Will take any small sinking foods.

Behavior & Care: Small school, soft substrate, not too warm.

Breeding: As well as the sex differences mentioned above, males are larger than females and more boldly patterned. Apparently very soft, acid water is needed for egg viability. Spawning has been triggered by a water change and temperature drop. The eggs are laid a few at a time, unusually all in a single clump, off the bottom.

Acanthicus adonis Isbrücker & Nijssen, 1988
Adonis Catfish (Adonis)

Overview: Within the family Loricariidae (mailed suckermouth cat-fishes), *Acanthicus* forms part of the subfamily Ancistrinae, which also includes the much smaller *Ancistrus*. *Acanthicus adonis* is a very attractive fish, but its eventual huge size must be considered. The same applies to *A. hystrix*, which lacks the attractive spots. There are plenty of smaller loricariids with similar coloration.

Native Range: South America: lower Tocantins drainage.

Maximum Length: 39 in (100 cm) TL.

Water: 72–80°F (22–27°C); pH: 6.0–7.5; hardness: 0–15°dGH.

Min. Tank Size: 180 gal | 72x24x24 in (650 L | 180x60x60 cm). A full-grown specimen will need a much larger tank.

Feeding: Omnivorous with strong vegetarian tendencies so feed plenty of green foods.

Behavior & Care: Produces huge amounts of waste so a powerful filter system is needed. Keep singly or with other large fishes, but note, this species can be aggressive towards other large loricariids.

Breeding: Males are larger with longer bristles behind the gills. A similar, undescribed species has been bred in a 16,000 gal (55,000 L) public aquarium. The fry were 1.25 in (3 cm) at free-swimming!

Ancistrus claro Knaack, 1999
Claro Bristlenose (Reticulated Bristlenose, LDA8)

Overview: Many aquarists, familiar only with the Common Bristlenose, (*Ancistrus* sp.) think of *Ancistrus* as hardy, gray-brown little loricariids. But nothing could be further from the truth, as this one shows. There are more than 50 described species (and a lot as yet undescribed), from almost every type of habitat and representing various degrees of difficulty of maintenance and breeding.

Native Range: Southern Brazil: fast-flowing waters in the Rio Cuiabá basin in the upper Paraguay drainage.

Maximum Length: 4.5 in (11 cm) TL.

Water: 72–77°F (22–27°C); pH: 6.5–7.5; hardness: 0–15°dGH.

Min. Tank Size: 25 gal | 24x16x16 in (95 L | 60x40x40 cm).

Feeding: Any sinking foods, but requires plenty of vegetable fare.

Behavior & Care: A peaceful community fish that can be kept singly as a scavenger but is more rewarding in a group. Well-planted tank with caves, soft substrate, well-oxygenated water, not too warm.

Breeding: Fairly easy. In all *Ancistrus* species breeding males have longer "tentacles" on the head. In this species males are usually more colorful, though color varies. Cave-brooder with parental care by the male. Up to 40 eggs; fry growth (feed tablets and greens) is slow.

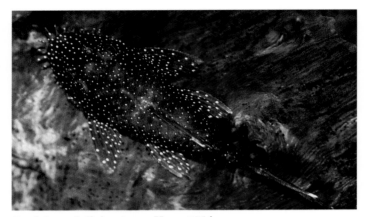

Ancistrus dolichopterus Kner, 1854
White-edged Bristlenose (Ancistrus Hoplogenys, L183)

Overview: Because the first *Ancistrus* to be regularly imported was misidentified as *A. dolichopterus*, this catfish was not initially recognized as that species. Like many unidentified loricariids it was given an L number (L183), a system devised in Germany to create a universal identification method for the large number of "mystery" armored cats imported in recent years. LDA numbers are a similar system. Not all *Ancistrus* are dwarf catfishes—this one is often sold at 2.5–3 in (6–7 cm) but can grow to more than four times that size.

Native Range: Brazil: Rio Negro drainage.

Maximum Length: 12 in (30 cm) TL.

Water: 72–79°F (22–26°C); pH: 5.5–7.5; hardness: 0–15°dGH.

Min. Tank Size: 50 gal | 48x16x16 in (190L | 120x40x40 cm).

Feeding: Bottom-feeder—sinking foods, including vegetable matter.

Behavior & Care: From the Rio Negro, so although the species is water-tolerant, very soft, acid water and peat filtration are suggested, especially for breeding. Décor as for *A. claro*. Good community fish.

Breeding: Males have longer tentacles and tend the brood. Mature at about 3 in (8 cm). Tricky to breed and said to be choosy about breeding caves, so offer a good variety. Up to 100 eggs; rear fry on tablets.

Ancistrus ranunculus Muller, Rapp Py-Daniel & Zuanon, 1994
Frog Bristlenose (L34)

Overview: This catfish wins no prizes for color, but is one of the most bizarre bristlenoses in form. Viewed from above it looks like a tadpole. ("Frog" is a mistranslation of its German name of Tadpole Catfish.) From the side it is extremely flattened, apparently an adaptation to allow it to fit into narrow crannies where deeper-bodied fishes cannot enter.

Native Range: Brazil: Rio Xingu and Rio Tocantins basins.

Maximum Length: 8 in (20 cm) TL.

Water: 75–82°F (24–28°C); pH: 6.0–7.0; hardness: 0–10°dGH.

Min. Tank Size: 50 gal | 48x16x16 in (190L | 120x40x40 cm).

Feeding: Apparently not as herbivorous as most *Ancistrus*. Feed an omnivore diet of sinking foods.

Behavior & Care: Difficult and not a general community fish. Very sociable, so keep a group in a species tank (though small characins can be housed in the upper levels) with sandy substrate and rocks (slate is ideal) arranged to create very low-ceilinged caves. Well-oxygenated, very soft, acid water. White patches denote ill health.

Breeding: Bred only once, by accident. Males have longer bristles, and again this is apparently a cave-brooder with male brood care.

Ancistrus temminckii (Valenciennes, 1840)
Temminck's Bristlenose

Overview: Probably the best-known species after the Common Bristlenose Catfish, and like it one of the easier, accommodating species that will live and breed in hard, alkaline water even though that of the natural habitat is soft and acid.

Native Range: The rivers Saramacca, Surinam, and Maroni, in Surinam; also found on the Guianan side of the Maroni.

Maximum Length: 5.5 in (14 cm) TL.

Water: 75–82°F (24–28°C); pH: 6.0–8.0; hardness: 0–15°dGH.

Min. Tank Size: 25 gal | 24x16x16 in (95 L | 60x40x40 cm).

Feeding: Like most *Ancistrus*, a bottom-feeding omnivore which requires plenty of vegetable matter in its diet.

Behavior & Care: An easy, peaceful community fish that can be kept singly but is more rewarding in a group as then it is quite likely to breed. Obviously a group requires a larger tank than that cited above, which is intended for a small general community with one *Ancistrus*. Plants, caves, soft substrate, moderate light.

Breeding: Sexing and brood care as for *A. claro*. It has been reported that brood growth is sometimes uneven, so the fry need to be size-sorted into groups else the smaller ones will waste away and die.

***Ancistrus* sp. "Aquarium Dolichopterus"**
Common Bristlenose (Bushymouth Catfish, Blue Bristlenose)

Overview: When first imported, this popular, easy-to-keep little loricariid was wrongly identified as *A. dolichopterus*, and has been sold as such ever since. It has not been possible to match it to any wild species, described or undescribed. The stocks we have now may have hybrid blood from in-crosses of other species, or may have shifted genetically away from the original form. After all, it is available in various color strains and even a long-finned form.

Native Range: South America: precise origin unknown.

Maximum Length: 5 in (13 cm) TL.

Water: 72–82°F (23–28°C); pH: 6.0–8.0; hardness: 0–20°dGH.

Min. Tank Size: 25 gal | 24x16x16 in (95 L | 60x40x40 cm).

Feeding: Any regular sinking aquarium foods.

Behavior & Care: The best *Ancistrus* for the beginner who wants a small hardy catfish to scavenge and eat algae in a general community, and far better for that purpose than the larger "plecs" which are really too large in relation to tankmates to keep in such a tank. Peaceful, though males may squabble harmlessly among themselves.

Breeding: If you have a male, a female, and a cave, fry are almost inevitable, but in a community they may be eaten by other fishes.

Baryancistrus sp. "Gold Nugget"
Golden Nugget Pleco (L18, L85, LDA60)

Overview: There are a couple of dozen species in this genus, most of them dark with light spots, but only two of them described and neither regular in the hobby. The Golden Nugget is by far the best known of the undescribed forms. Varies with locality and age, hence the three identification numbers. L177 from the Rio Iriri is similar in looks, much easier, and a better choice for the non-specialist.

Native Range: Lower Rio Xingu, Brazil. Found in shallow water that is sunlit by day and hence abundant in algae.

Maximum Length: 12 in (30 cm) TL.

Water: 79–86°F (26–30°C); pH: 6.0–7.5; hardness: 0–10°dGH.

Min. Tank Size: 50 gal | 48x16x16 in (190 L | 120x40x40 cm).

Feeding: Strongly herbivorous and needs an almost constant supply of green food. Can be given small amounts of live and frozen foods.

Behavior & Care: Difficult and tends not to thrive unless given the correct diet and conditions, which it rarely enjoys in captivity. Very clean, warm, soft, acid, oxygen-rich water. Nocturnal, so provide daytime hiding places. Wild adults are territorial, but youngsters kept together will tolerate one another better when grown.

Breeding: Adult males have more heavily built heads. Not bred.

***Baryancistrus* sp. 'Snowball'**
Snowball Plec (L142, LDA33)

Overview: This gorgeous loricariid has the largest spots—white on black—of any known member of the genus, and was an instant hit when introduced; it is regularly imported though not as common as the Golden Nugget. Sadly it too is difficult. Maybe in time aquarists will unlock the secrets of keeping this genus.

Native Range: Brazil: rapids in the lower Rio Tapajos.

Maximum Length: 12 in (30 cm) TL.

Water: 79–86°F (26–30°C); pH: 6.0–7.5; hardness: 0–10°dGH.

Min. Tank Size: 50 gal | 48x16x16 in (190 L | 120x40x40 cm).

Feeding: Like the Golden Nugget, this species feeds on algae on stones and any invertebrate life it contains, and so needs lots of green food and small amounts of live and frozen foods.

Behavior & Care: As for the Golden Nugget. Remember that a large amount of food going in means copious wastes, so efficient mechanical and biological filtration is essential, plus regular water changes to keep nitrate at bay.

Breeding: Males more heavily built in the head region. Not bred. Probably the best chance of breeding any *Baryancistrus* is to grow on a few youngsters in a very large tank with optimal conditions.

Chaetostoma tachiraense Schultz, 1944
Bulldog Catfish (Chaetostoma Thomsoni, Chaetostoma Thomasi)

Overview: *Chaetostoma* is a large genus, but only a couple of species are common in the hobby. They live in fast-flowing mountain streams, and have special adaptations to this habitat. One of these is a huge suckermouth that allows them to stay attached to rocks in the current, giving them a very broad-nosed appearance.

Native Range: Rio Catatumbo basin in the Maracaibo drainage.

Maximum Length: 4 in (10 cm) TL.

Water: 70–80°F (21–27°C); pH: 6.0–7.5; hardness: 0–15°dGH.

Min. Tank Size: 25 gal | 24x16x16 in (95 L | 60x40x40 cm).

Feeding: Feeds on algae and any invertebrates it contains, so should be given a diet of green food with some live and frozen fare.

Behavior & Care: Sandy substrate, water-worn stones, very well-oxygenated water are the main prerequisites. An excellent tankmate for rheophilic cichlids (e.g. *Steatocranus*, *Teleogramma*) of similar size, as long as sufficient territory and caves for all are allowed.

Breeding: Quite easy. Males are larger, with a more angular head, more attractive pattern, and enlarged ventral fins. At breeding time the male excavates a cave beneath a rock and the eggs are laid on the ceiling. Eggs and fry are large; fry can safely be left with the parents.

Farlowella vittata Myers, 1942
Whiptail Catfish (Twig Catfish)

Overview: *Farlowella* are long, slender catfishes that look rather like twigs, and are well camouflaged when they rest on wood. The species are difficult to separate and the name *F. acus* is applied indiscriminately though that species is probably rarely if ever imported. *F. vittata* is probably the most common species in the hobby.

Native Range: Orinoco system in Colombia and Venezuela.

Maximum Length: 6 in (15 cm) TL.

Water: 75–82°F (24–28°C); pH: 6.0–7.5; hardness: 0–15°dGH.

Min. Tank Size: 38 gal | 36x16x16 in (140 L | 90x40x40 cm).

Feeding: Green foods, small live and frozen foods, scattered on off-bottom décor (e.g. plants and wood).

Behavior & Care: Well-planted tank with wood among the plants. If possible, establish the origin of the fish and adjust water parameters accordingly; in all cases well-oxygenated water is required. Does best in tanks established for some months. Do not keep with more robust catfishes that may outcompete it for food. House with dwarf cichlids, *Corydoras*, *Sturisoma*, and small characins.

Breeding: Males have odontodes (spines) on the snout. Best bred as a pair in a separate tank. The fry are tiny and difficult to rear.

Glyptoperichthys gibbiceps (Kner, 1854)
Sailfin Plec (Gibbiceps, Pterygoplichthys Gibbiceps)

Overview: An excellent scavenger and algae eater but it grows larger than novices realize, and is territorial when adult. As it is commercially bred, juveniles are often available to attract the unwary. Other members of the genus are also on the large side.

Native Range: Upper and middle Amazon and Orinoco drainages.

Maximum Length: 24 in (60 cm) TL. Usually half that.

Water: 75–82°F (24–28°C); pH: 5.5–7.5; hardness: 0–15°dGH.

Min. Tank Size: 50 gal | 48x16x16 in (190 L | 120x40x40 cm).

Feeding: Will eat almost anything, but not aquarium plants!

Behavior & Care: Hardy as regards water chemistry, but does best in soft acid conditions. Décor should include plenty of wood, its preferred cover in nature. The only problem area is eventual size, as a large specimen in full flight can uproot plants as it swims, and scare smaller tankmates. Best kept in large, unplanted tanks with other large fishes. Large specimens require robust filtration.

Breeding: Males have larger fins, especially the dorsal. Has been bred in the aquarium. Spawning was triggered by a large water change and took place on a piece of wood. The male guarded and fanned the 120 or so eggs. The fry were reared separately on tablets.

Hemiloricara lanceolata (Günther, 1868)
Chocolate Whiptail Catfish (Lanceolate Whiptail Cat)

Overview: The genus *Rineloricaria*, long known to aquarists, has been split into four genera, with many species—including the Chocolate Whiptail—now belonging in *Hemiloricaria*. The other two genera are *Fonchiiichthys* and *Leliella*. All are peaceful and mainly easy-to-keep catfishes, similar in their requirements with the proviso that there is geographical variation in water chemistry and temperature, so "homework" on individual species is required.

Native Range: South America: upper Amazon drainage.

Maximum Length: 4.75 in (12 cm) TL.

Water: 75–82°F (24–28°C); pH: 6.0–7.5; hardness: 0–10°dGH.

Min. Tank Size: 38 gal | 36x16x16 in (140 L | 90x40x40 cm).

Feeding: Sinking green foods, small amounts of live and frozen fare.

Behavior & Care: Excellent community fish. Well-planted tank, soft sandy substrate, wood and water-worn rocks, shaded areas.

Breeding: *Hemiloricaria* usually spawn in hollow logs—clay pipes are a good substitute. The eggs are guarded by the male, who is more boldly patterned and slimmer (from above), and has "whiskers" on his cheeks at breeding time. Feed him well or he may eat the eggs, or tip him out of the pipe and remove him if he makes a habit of it!

Hypancistrus zebra Isbrücker & Nijssen, 1991
Zebra Plec

Overview: This fish was a sensation when first imported, and the price astronomical. It is now bred routinely in captivity and has become affordable; just as well, as overfishing was endangering the species and there is now a ban on wild exports. Other *Hypancistrus* require similar conditions and are often equally attractive.

Native Range: Rio Xingu in Brazil, in deep water near rapids, which may be why this striking fish was not discovered earlier.

Maximum Length: 4 in (10 cm) TL.

Water: 77–86°F (25–30°C); pH: 6.0–7.5; hardness: 0–15°dGH.

Min. Tank Size: 25 gal | 24x16x16 in (95 L | 60x40x40 cm).

Feeding: Omnivore—feed a mix of green plus live and frozen foods.

Behavior & Care: Quite accommodating as regards water chemistry, but requires warm, well-oxygenated water and current. Peaceful—can be kept in groups and with other non-aggressive fishes in a suitable large tank. Requires hiding places, ideally rocky caves.

Breeding: Relatively easy. Male larger, with a wider head. Spawns in caves, with brood care by the male for two weeks or more. The young require plenty of vegetable food, but will also readily take small live foods. Water quality must be impeccable during rearing.

Leporacanthicus galaxias Isbrücker & Nijssen, 1989
Galaxy Vampire Catfish (Galaxias, Milky-Way Pleco)

Overview: *Leporacanthicus* all have fangs on their suckermouths, hence Vampire Catfishes, which is not entirely a misnomer since there are reports of fangs being sunk into fingers, other fishes—and even silicone sealant! The galactic connection in this species is the mass of white "stars" scattered on a black background. It appears that in the trade the name may conceal a number of very similar species from the lower Amazon drainage, but they are all largish, rheophilic plecs that are best for a specialist aquarium.

Native Range: Rio Tocantins, Brazil.

Maximum Length: 12 in (30 cm) TL.

Water: 77–84°F (25–29°C); pH: 6.0–7.5; hardness: 0–15°dGH.

Min. Tank Size: 65 gal | 48x18x18 in (240 L | 120x45x45 cm).

Feeding: Omnivorous, requiring carnivore as well as green foods.

Behavior & Care: Not difficult, but best kept in a species aquarium or with other similarly-sized armored cats that like a décor of boulders and wood and a strong current. Monitor silicone seals!

Breeding: Breeding recorded several times. Males are more elongate but with wider heads and a "stubble" of bristles on the snout. Cave-brooder; brood care by male, who may eat the spawn if disturbed.

Liposarcus pardalis (Castelnau, 1855)
Common Plec (Hypostomus Plecostomus, Common Pleco)

Overview: It may come as a surprise to learn that the true *H. plecostomus* has probably never been imported for the aquarium hobby. The name is used indiscriminately for many large unidentified suckermouths, in particular this one, *Liposarcus pardalis*. Now that so many properly identified, often more attractive loricariids are available—many far more suitable for the aquarium community in terms of size—it is best to buy an alternative whose requirements have been researched and can be satisfied.

Native Range: Almost the entire Amazon drainage.

Maximum Length: 24 in (60 cm) TL. Usually somewhat smaller.

Water: 70–82°F (21–28°C); pH: 6.0–8.0; hardness: 0–25°dGH.

Min. Tank Size: 65 gal | 48x18x18 in (240 L | 120x45x45 cm).

Feeding: Primarily herbivorous. Often hangs from the aquarium glass to scrape algae, and may also attach to large flat-sided fishes such as Discus (*Symphysodon* spp.). Some find the mucus of their victim to their taste and come back for more, causing major damage.

Behavior & Care: Virtually indestructible—rare to hear of a Common Plec dying even though they are kept in almost any conditions.

Breeding: Pond farmed in the Far East, but not bred in aquaria.

Loricaria simillima Regan, 1904
Marbled Whiptail

Overview: *Loricaria* is the genus for which the family Loricariidae is named. It once contained numerous species but is now restricted to about 10, this one being probably the most common in the hobby. Like its congeners, it has a long whip-like posterior body and tail. Coloration is variable, apparently determined by habitat.

Native Range: Amazon, Orinoco, and La Plata basins.

Maximum Length: 10 in (25 cm) TL. Mature at half that length.

Water: 70–82°F (21–28°C); pH: 6.0–7.5; hardness: 0–15°dGH.

Min. Tank Size: 50 gal | 48x16x16 in (190 L | 120x40x40 cm).

Feeding: Omnivorous with a strong herbivorous tendency.

Behavior & Care: Wild fish require careful acclimatization (they come from a wide range of habitats and water types and are often transport-stressed) and are best left in the shop for a while to see if they live. Thereafter unfussy, though water quality must be excellent and current is required. Wood and plants as décor; sand substrate.

Breeding: Regularly bred and very interesting in its behavior. The eggs are laid in an elongate mass which the male carries beneath his body, attached to his suckermouth—a sort of mouthbrooder! The larvae hatch after about 12 days of brooding; the fry are easy to rear.

Otocinclus vestitus Cope, 1872
Striped Otocinclus

Overview: *Otocinclus* (and their cousins, *Parotocinclus*) are dwarf loricariids that are frequently kept as algae eaters in communities of small fishes. Unfortunately, like the Sucking Loach (*Gyrinocheilus aymonieri*) and some other suckermouths they may "graze" the mucus of flat-sided fishes (e.g. Discus [*Symphysodon* spp.]), so small *Ancistrus* are a better choice for tanks containing such fishes.

Native Range: Amazon and lower Paraná drainages, usually in shallow vegetated bank zones.

Maximum Length: 1.5 in (4 cm) TL.

Water: 75–82°F (24–28°C); pH: 6.0–7.5; hardness: 0–10°dGH.

Min. Tank Size: 25 gal | 24x16x16 in (95 L | 60x40x40 cm).

Feeding: Extra greens unless there is plenty of algae. Small live and frozen foods in small quantities.

Behavior & Care: Densely planted tank with surface vegetation to give shade, dark substrate, well-oxygenated water and an element of current. Small peaceful tankmates.

Breeding: The sexes differ in size. Use a breeding tank with more males than females. Adhesive eggs are laid on surfaces all over the tank, a few at a time, and fertilized by the male. No brood care.

Panaqolus albomaculatus (Kanazawa, 1958)
White-spotted Panaque (LDA31)

Overview: The genus *Panaqolus* was erected for a group of species formerly included in *Panaque* because their dentition was similar, even though their form is quite different. Both consume large amounts of wood, which explains the similar teeth. They are relatively small and thus better suited than *Panaque* to many aquaria. Most are attractively striped; a few, like this one, spotted.

Native Range: Upper Amazon drainage in Peru and Ecuador.

Maximum Length: 5.5 in (14 cm) TL.

Water: 77–84°F (25–29°C); pH: 6.0–7.5; hardness: 0–15°dGH.

Min. Tank Size: 38 gal | 36x16x16 in (140 L | 90x40x40 cm).

Feeding: MUST have plenty of bogwood available. In addition, provide plenty of greens and avoid too much protein-rich food.

Behavior & Care: Peaceful and hardy, but tankmates need to be herbivores to prevent a protein overdose which can cause ill-health. Digested wood reappears as large amounts of fine brown powdery waste so filtration must be mechanically efficient. Will eat plants!

Breeding: Males have more odontodes (spines) on the caudal peduncle. Not bred, but a number of other species have proved to be cave-brooders with small clutches of eggs, tended by the male.

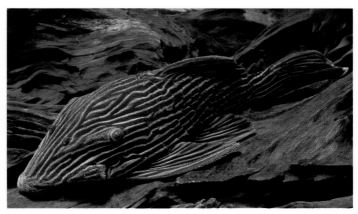

Panaque nigrolineatus (Peters, 1877)
Royal Pleco

Overview: Members of the genus *Panaque* (the native name for these eye-catching plecs) live mainly on rotting wood. But there the similarity ends. They are much larger, and have remarkably big heads with, in most cases, brilliant red eyes. Their popularity is immense, but they are best left to more experienced aquarists.

Native Range: Widespread in the Orinoco system.

Maximum Length: 24 in (60 cm) TL.

Water: 77–84°F (25–29°C); pH: 6.0–7.5; hardness: 0–15°dGH.

Min. Tank Size: 180 gal | 72x24x24 in (650 L | 180x60x60 cm).

Feeding: MUST have plenty of bogwood available. Supplement with a low-protein diet consisting mainly of green foods.

Behavior & Care: Similar to *Panaqolus albomaculatus*, but with even more efficient mechanical filtration and regular water changes

Breeding: Adult males have longer, broader heads and longer odontodes behind the gill-cover. Not bred, but *P. cochliodon* has bred at just 7 in (18 cm). The male nibbled a depression 3 in (8 cm) across in a piece of wood, and guarded it for weeks till the female was ripe. Spawning was at night. The eggs hatched after 8 days, the larvae fell to the gravel, and the male then guarded them in a hole under a slate.

Peckoltia brevis (La Monte, 1935)
Spotted Peckoltia

Overview: *Peckoltia* are fairly small plecos, suitable for keeping with other fishes of similar size and needs, which are not stringent. The main problem is that some species in the hobby are misidentified, with two different species being wrongly sold as *P. vittata*, one of them a *Panaqolus*, which has very specialized needs! So obtain fish (and advice) from a catfish specialist store.

Native Range: South America: Rio Purus drainage in Brazil.

Maximum Length: 5 in (13 cm) TL.

Water: 77–86°F (25–30°C); pH: 6.0–7.5; hardness: 0–10°dGH.

Min. Tank Size: 38 gal | 36x16x16 in (140 L | 90x40x40 cm).

Feeding: Requires plenty of green foods with some live or frozen.

Behavior & Care: Very peaceful and does well in a group. Usually found in slow-moving, rather shallow—and hence warm—water where it grazes algae from stones. Water-worn rocks, wood, plants. Requires well-oxygenated water because of the high temperature.

Breeding: No reports of breeding. Other *Peckoltia* have proved to be cave brooders that prefer a cave with only one opening. Sexually active males have more bristles on the caudal area. The clutch is small, and guarded by the male. Rear fry on tablets and small live foods.

Pseudacanthicus sp. aff. 'leopardus'
L114 (Leopard Cactus Catfish, Demini Cactus Catfish, LDA7)

Overview: Not all suckermouths are herbivores! Cactus catfishes are out-and-out carnivores that are thought to rasp flesh from dead animals and fishes. They are large, often very attractive fishes, covered all over in spines as their name suggests. Handle with care! This undescribed species is very popular, and usually sold as *Ps. leopardus*, a similar fish but with a different distribution.

Native Range: The Rio Demini, a tributary of the Rio Negro, Brazil.

Maximum Length: 16 in (40 cm) TL.

Water: 77–86°F (25–30°C); pH: 6.0–7.5; hardness: 0–10°dGH.

Min. Tank Size: 180 gal | 72x24x24 in (650 L | 180x60x60 cm).

Feeding: Frozen foods, chopped fish, shrimp, mussel.

Behavior & Care: Not as territorial as some cactus cats, but create line-of-sight barriers if more than one is kept. Soft substrate, roomy hiding places, warm, well-oxygenated water, and efficient filtration.

Breeding: Mature at 6 in (15 cm). Males have longer, broader heads and a larger dorsal fin. Cave brooder; thought to breed in tunnels in the bank in the wild. The male "mounts" the female, biting her, as a prelude to mating, which takes place in the cave. He then protects the 100 or so eggs by blocking the entrance with his body.

Scobinancistrus aureatus Burgess, 1994
Sunshine Suckermouth (Golden Peacock Catfish, L14)

Overview: Like *Pseudancanthicus* (cactus catfishes), the members of this small genus are also carnivorous but in this case the food is thought to be live and include aquatic snails. *Scobinancistrus* are a recent discovery; they are found only in the rios Xingu (this one), Tapajós, and Tocantins. They are very attractive but rather large.
Native Range: Brazil: lower and middle Rio Xingu drainage, in warm, shallow marginal water with a stony substrate.
Maximum Length: 16 in (40 cm) TL.
Water: 77–86°F (25–30°C); pH: 6.0–7.5; hardness: 0–10°dGH.
Min. Tank Size: 180 gal | 72x24x24 in (650 L | 180x60x60 cm).
Feeding: Frozen foods, chopped shrimp and mussel. Aquatic snails.
Behavior & Care: Quite territorial—try to break up the line of sight along the tank if more than one is kept. Water-worn rocks, sand, roomy caves, warm, well-oxygenated water, and efficient filtration.
Breeding: Males are more heavily built in the head region and there may also be color differences at breeding time. Unlike in many suckermouths, the length of odontodes is not a secondary sexual characteristic. Cave-brooder, with brood care by the male, who guards not just the eggs but the young for a week after hatching. Easy to rear.

Sturisoma festivum Myers, 1942
Giant Whiptail (Long-Finned Whiptail, Sturisoma Aureum)

Overview: *Sturisoma* species are not all that easy to tell apart, and for many years this one was sold as *S. aureum*, the error being discovered when the real thing was collected from its type locality. The genus is widespread in South America.

Native Range: Venezuela and Colombia: Maracaibo basin and Rio Catatumbo respectively. Regularly imported from Colombia.

Maximum Length: 7 in (18 cm) TL.

Water: 75–82°F (24–28°C); pH: 6.5–7.5; hardness: 0–10°dGH.

Min. Tank Size: 38 gal | 36x16x16 in (140 L | 90x40x40 cm).

Feeding: Tablets; small sinking green, live, and frozen foods.

Behavior & Care: *Sturisoma* fall into two groups—wood-dwellers and sand-dwellers. This one lives on wood. In all cases a well-planted tank with wood, sandy substrate, and well-oxygenated, top quality water are advised, in case the fish kept is wrongly named.

Breeding: The eggs are laid on plants, wood, or the aquarium glass. Brood care by the male till the eggs hatch. Rearing the fry is a challenge much debated among fans. A good growth of algae may help.

Eigenmannia virescens (Valenciennes, 1836)
Glass Knifefish (Green Knifefish, Eigenmannia Humboldtii)

Overview: This is a curious, gentle, mostly nocturnal fish that is well liked for its transparent coloration, unique body shape, and an effortless backward/forward swimming style. It has an electrical organ, and the discharge enables it to "see" in the dark, locating food and mates.

Native Range: South America: Orinoco and La Plata river basins.

Maximum Length: 18 in (45 cm) TL.

Water: 73–82°F (23–28°C); pH: 6.0–7.0; hardness: 2–15°dGH.

Min. Tank Size: 90 gal | 48x18x24 in (320 L | 120x45x60 cm).

Feeding: Omnivore. Feeds on plant detritus as well as small live, frozen, and prepared foods.

Behavior & Care: Though nocturnal, the Glass Knifefish will become more active during the daylight hours if it is given enough cover in the form of plants, driftwood, etc, and provided it is fed while the tank is lit. Though large, it does best in a group of six or more.

Breeding: Glass Knifefish are egglayers that spawn in the early morning following a large water change and reduction in the pH of the water. A dominant male fertilizes the eggs of one or more females who have laid 100–200 eggs each among the plants.

Apteronotus albifrons (Linnaeus, 1766)
Black Ghost

Overview: A fish of moving water in rivers and streams, the Black Ghost is believed by some natives in its range to contain the souls of fallen warriors. It generates a weak electrical field around its body, and can sense prey in all directions.

Native Range: South America: Ecuador, Colombia, Guyana, Surinam, French Guiana, Venezuela, Paraguay, Peru, Bolivia, and Brazil.

Maximum Length: 20 in (50 cm) TL.

Water: 73–82°F (23–28°C); pH: 6.0–8.0; hardness: 5–20°dGH.

Min. Tank Size: 75 gal | 48x18x20 in (270 L | 120x45x50 cm).

Feeding: Live and frozen meaty foods, especially fond of Tubifex. Feed in the evening.

Behavior & Care: Use plenty of cover in the form of plants and driftwood. Prefers a sandy substrate and subdued lighting. Water quality is critical, and while turbulence is not required, well-oxygenated water is. It is quite timid, and peaceful among fishes too small to be considered food, though it is not happily kept with conspecifics. Otherwise, tankmates should be large and gentle. Be sure it gets enough food, and that other fishes are not taking advantage.

Breeding: Not reported in the aquarium.

The Black Ghost, *Apteronotus albifrons,* a nocturnal fish, has poor eyesight and tiny eyes. They can always be found looking for food at night. Though shy, they can be trained to feed from your hand.

Apteronotus leptorhynchus, Brown Ghost. Ghost fishes can detect prey and conspecifics from as close as 4 in (10 cm) through their sensors. The presence of other ghost fishes evokes chirping sounds. There are six distinct chirps.

Dermogenys pusilla Kuhl & van Hasselt, 1823
Malayan Halfbeak (Wrestling Halfbeak)

Overview: With such an unusual appearance, frisky nature, and modest size, the halfbeaks are interesting fishes even for beginners. They are a bit delicate and skittish until they settle into a new environment, so it behooves the aquarist to keep a close eye on recent arrivals. Once acclimated, however, they are among the easiest of aquarium fishes to keep. Transport carefully to protect the "beak." Males are inclined to "wrestle" by locking beaks.

Native Range: Southeast Asia.

Maximum Length: 2.5 in (7 cm) TL.

Water: 75–82°F (24–28°C); pH: 7.0–8.0; hardness: 10–20°dGH. Found in both fresh and brackish waters.

Min. Tank Size: 20 gal | 30x12x12 in (65 L | 75x30x30 cm).

Feeding: Surface feeder which will take small live, frozen, and prepared aquarium foods. Requires additional vitamins A and D in diet.

Behavior & Care: Protect the fragile lower jaw of halfbeaks by planting around the sides of the tank and use floating plants as well. This will help to buffer the "beak." Injuries are fatal if they become infected.

Breeding: Livebearers eat the young if given the chance. Start fry on *Artemia* nauplii, graduating to larger foods as they grow.

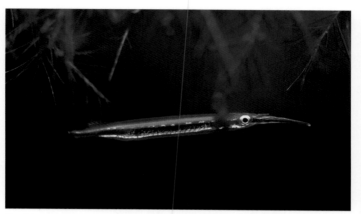

Hemirhamphodon tengah, Dwarf Halfbeak, Max. Length: 1.5 in (3.5 cm).

Nomorhamphus liemi, Black-finned Halfbeak, Max. Length: 2.5 in (6 cm).

The halfbeaks are a bit skittish and can easily damage their fragile beaks. A growth of algae on the sides and back of the tank glass helps to show them where the glass is so they can avoid it.

Oryzias latipes (Temminck & Schlegel, 1850)
Japanese Rice Fish (Medaka)

Overview: This fish has been in the hobby since at least 1895. Like other members of its genus it has colonized the rice paddies of Southeast Asia, hence the popular name. Long regarded as killifishes, *Oryzias* are now thought to be closer to the halfbeaks. This is an easy, peaceful fish for the cooler general community. Several color morphs are known.

Native Range: Asia: Japan, China, South Korea, perhaps elsewhere.

Maximum Length: 1.5 in (4 cm) TL.

Water: 64–75°F (18–24°C); pH: 6.5–7.5; hardness: 5–12°dGH.

Min. Tank Size: 25 gal | 24x16x16 in (95 L | 60x40x40 cm).

Feeding: Almost any small carnivore and omnivore foods.

Behavior & Care: Keep in a small school (five plus) in a well-planted tank with peaceful tankmates of roughly its own size. Appreciates reasonably well oxygenated water with a slight current.

Breeding: Not easy to sex; males slimmer with a larger anal fin. Use a planted breeding tank with a small group. The eggs are laid in a clump that remains attached to the female until it brushes off against a plant. The parents can be removed, or the clumps of eggs collected and hatched separately. This takes 10–12 days.

Aphyosemion australe (Rachow, 1921)
Cape Lopez Lyretail (Australe, Chocolate Killie, Lyretail Panchax)

Overview: One of the loveliest African killies, available in both a chocolate and a golden form. "Aphys" are generally seen as specialist fishes, but some, including this one, are excellent for a community or as dither fishes for dwarf cichlids—if the right water is used. Not an annual fish (see *A. gardneri*).

Native Range: Africa—Angola, Gabon, Cameroon, and Congo.

Maximum Length: 2.25 in (6 cm) TL.

Water: 70–77°F (21–25°C); pH: 6.0–6.8; hardness: 0–5°dGH.

Min. Tank Size: 15 gal | 24x12x12 in (50 L | 60x30x30 cm).

Feeding: Prefers live foods, will take frozen, sometimes flake. Like most killies, needs live food to condition females for breeding.

Behavior & Care: A proficient escape artist—tight-fitting cover vital. Well-planted tank, surface vegetation, peaceful tankmates.

Breeding: Males are colorful. Spawns for 1–2 weeks. Use floating spawning mops. Remove eggs from mops daily (gently run fingernails along strands) and place in containers with shallow water from the breeding tank; hatching takes two weeks. Feed the fry on infusoria. Don't discard any healthy (clear) unhatched eggs—some may hatch later as Nature's precaution against loss of the first hatching.

Aphyosemion bivittatum (Lönnberg, 1895)
Twostriped Lyretail (Bivittatum, Red Panchax)

Overview: A beautiful killie, but difficult and not for the community. A lively fish that can live 2–3 years given optimal conditions.

Native Range: Africa—southeastern Nigeria and southwestern Cameroon, in rainforest streams.

Maximum Length: 2 in (5 cm) TL.

Water: 70–77°F (21–25°C); pH: 6.0–6.8; hardness: 0–5°dGH.

Min. Tank Size: 15 gal | 24x12x12 in (50 L | 60x30x30 cm.

Feeding: Very reluctant to take anything but live foods, so do not keep this fish unless you have a permanent supply. *Tubifex* should not be on the menu as this killie is susceptible to bacteria.

Behavior & Care: Species tank with soft dark substrate (fine sand or peat). Lighting subdued, with a layer of floating plants. Water should be of exceptionally good quality. Like most killies this is an accomplished jumper that will find the tiniest exit from the tank.

Breeding: Males are colorful with a lyrate tail. Use non-floating spawning mops; remove and hatch eggs as for *A. australe.* "Aphys" attach eggs to plants (surface or lower down) or (in annual species, see *A. gardneri*) bury them in the substrate. If unsure whether mops should be floating or not, use both, or guess and swap if wrong!

Aphyosemion calliurum, Banner Lyretail.

Aphyosemion poliaki, Orange-Fringed Killie.

Aphyosemion species sometimes spawn on plants, sometimes in the substrate, so if in doubt provide peat on the bottom and both floating and non-floating spawning mops.

Aphyosemion gardneri (Boulenger, 1911)
Blue Lyretail (Gardneri, Steel-blue Killie)

Overview: *Aphyosemion* includes around 50 species, and some, like this one, have subspecies. *A. gardneri gardneri* is the commonest in the hobby. It is one of the "annual killies" from waters that dry up seasonally; before this happens it spawns in the soft substrate. The adults die, then when the rains come the eggs hatch and the cycle starts again. However, it may live rather longer in captivity.

Native Range: Southern Nigeria to southwestern Cameroon.

Maximum Length: 2.5 in (6.5 cm) TL.

Water: 70–77°F (21–25°C); pH: 6.0–6.8; hardness: 0–5°dGH.

Min. Tank Size: 15 gal | 24x12x12 in (50 L | 60x30x30 cm).

Feeding: Live foods; some specimens may take frozen and flake.

Behavior & Care: Males can be quite aggressive. Annual killies are best kept in species tanks with a substrate of peat, pre-boiled so it stays in place. Some unrooted greenery can be included, such as stems of *Cabomba* or *Hygrophila*. As with all killies, use a tight cover!

Breeding: Feed heavily during the spawning period. Afterwards remove the peat, squeeze out the water, and store in a plastic box in a warm place. After a month add water. If no fry appear, repeat the whole process. Hatching periods vary a lot, even within a species!

Aphyosemion sjoestedti (Lönnberg, 1895)
Blue Gularis (Golden Pheasant, Fundulopanchax Sjoestedti)

Overview: One of the larger "Aphys" and an easy, hardy killie. Though not necessarily an "annual," it is a substrate spawner and not long-lived, so its habitat probably dries up now and then.
Native Range: Ghana to southern Nigeria (including the Niger Delta) and southwestern Cameroon; swamps, pools, sluggish streams.
Maximum Length: 5.5 in (14 cm) TL.
Water: 73–79°F (23–26°C); pH: 6.0–7.5; hardness: 0–10°dGH.
Min. Tank Size: 20 gal | 30x12x12 in (65 L | 75x30x30 cm).
Feeding: Reputed to eat only live foods, but will learn to take frozen and flake by example, as it is a greedy fish. May eat small fishes!
Behavior & Care: Likes cover, so best kept in a decorated tank (e.g. a community), and bred in a separate breeding tank. Jumps!
Breeding: Males are colorful. Procedure as for *A. gardneri*. Use water of suitable chemistry and temperature for wetting. Fry can manage *Artemia* nauplii. Once you have hatched annual killie eggs, don't discard the peat but repeat the storing and wetting process. In the wild there is often a period of rain then further drying, with loss of any fry that have hatched, so some eggs "wait" for a second or even a third wetting to ensure survival of the species.

Aplocheilus lineatus (Valenciennes, 1846)
Striped Panchax (Sparkling Panchax, Panchax Lineatus)

Overview: *Aplocheilus* is an Asian killifish genus, and *A. lineatus* probably its best-known species. Killifishes is the name used for all egg-laying members of the order Cyprinodontiformes (toothcarps) (there are also livebearing toothcarps, or livebearers.) All are small(ish) fishes, with an upward-pointing mouth for surface-feeding, and are found throughout the tropics.

Native Range: Southern India and Sri Lanka.

Maximum Length: 4 in (10 cm) TL.

Water: 72–77°F (22–25°C); pH: 6.0–7.5; hardness: 0–10°dGH.

Min. Tank Size: 15 gal | 24x12x12 in (50 L | 60x30x30 cm).

Feeding: Small live and frozen foods, carnivore/omnivore flake.

Behavior & Care: Another jumper, so a tight-fitting cover is vital. Well-planted tank with surface vegetation and peaceful tankmates. May eat very small fishes. Rather hardy compared to some killies.

Breeding: Females are larger. Spawns on floating spawning mops or plants (e.g. *Riccia*), over a period of 2–3 weeks. To avoid cannibalism, transfer plants/mops daily to separate darkened containers and replace, or carefully remove eggs from the mops. Hatch in shallow water; this takes 12–14 days. Feed the fry with infusorians.

Epiplatys dageti Poll, 1953
Daget's Panchax (Dageti, Epiplatys Chaperi)

Overview: *Epiplatys* are similar to *Aplocheilus* in some respects, but restricted to Africa. Because some killies are difficult and require special breeding techniques, and some are short-lived, the group has the reputation for being reserved for experts, but *Epiplatys*, for example, are hardy and make good community fishes, or much more interesting "dither fish" for soft-water dwarf cichlids than the usual tetras!

Native Range: West Africa—Sierra Leone and Liberia; southern Ivory Coast and Ghana. Still or slow-flowing waters.

Maximum Length: 3 in (7.5 cm) TL.

Water: 70–77°F (21–25°C); pH: 6.0–7.5; hardness: 0–10°dGH.

Min. Tank Size: 15 gal | 24x12x12 in (50 L | 60x30x30 cm).

Feeding: Small live foods. Usually learns to accept frozen and flake foods when hungry enough, especially if other fishes eating same.

Behavior & Care: Plant with rooted and floating vegetation. Dark substrate. Like most killies this is an accomplished leaper, so the cover must offer no chance of escape. Does not like "raw" water— age tap water for at least a week and do only small changes.

Breeding: Males larger and more colorful. Breed as for *Aplocheilus lineatus*, but hatches sooner, in 8–10 days.

Lamprichthys tanganicanus (Boulenger, 1898)
Tanganyika Killifish

Overview: This, the largest African killie, is an interesting as well as a beautiful fish, and can be mixed with some of the smaller cichlids that share its habitat in Lake Tanganyika (e.g. *Julidochromis, Altolamprologus*, small *Lamprologus*). The Cuckoo Catfish, *Synodontis multipunctatus*, is another suitable tankmate.

Native Range: East Africa—endemic to areas of rocky shoreline in Lake Tanganyika.

Maximum Length: 6 in (15 cm) TL.

Water: 73–82°F (23–28°C); pH: 7.5–9.0; hardness: 10–25°dGH.

Min. Tank Size: 38 gal | 36x16x16 in (140 L | 90x40x40 cm).

Feeding: Small live or frozen foods are the preferred diet, but will usually learn to take anything cichlid tankmates are eating.

Behavior & Care: Requires hard, alkaline, well-oxygenated, very pure water and rocky décor with narrow vertical cracks. Keep in a group, which one male will dominate. Not an annual species.

Breeding: Males larger with blue spots, females with silver spots. A bottom spawner that lays its eggs in vertical cracks in or among rocks, where they are relatively safe from predation. In a cichlid community the fry are likely to be eaten when they emerge.

271

Nothobranchius rachovii Ahl, 1926
Rachov's Notho (Bluefin Notho, Rachovii, Rachow's Notho)

Overview: "Nothos" really are killies for the expert, as they are very short-lived annuals with often stringent water requirements. While *Aphyosemion* are slender and found in West Africa, nothos are "chunk-ier" and from the mid- and south-east of the continent. Rarely seen in shops, and more often passed from fan to fan. The dormant eggs of annual killies (and some non-annuals) can be mailed in damp peat! Joining a killifish club is the best way to obtain stock.

Native Range: Africa: Mozambique and South Africa, in temporary pools, streams, and swamps in coastal savannahs.

Maximum Length: 2.25 in (6 cm) TL.

Water: 68-75°F (20-24°C); pH 5.5-6.5; hardness 0-5°dGH.

Min. Tank Size: 15 gal | 24x12x12 in (50 L | 60x30x30 cm).

Feeding: Small live foods; will sometimes accept frozen and flake.

Behavior & Care: Peaceful, though males can be quarrelsome and territorial. Species tank with plants and wood. Very soft, acid water essential. Jumps, though not as prone to this as some killies.

Breeding: Males colorful, females drab. Bottom spawner—proceed as for *Aphyosemion gardneri* and *A. sjoestedti*. Dormant period 3–4 months or more. Young are sexually mature in 12 weeks.

Pachypanchax playfairii (Günther, 1866)
Playfair's Panchax (Panchax Playfairii)

Overview: An easy, hardy beginner's killie, excellent for the general community, though its large mouth is adept at snapping up fry of other fishes. Not the most colorful, but quite long-lived and hence more likely to be found in shops that hesitate to stock killies in case they die of "old age" before they are sold.

Native Range: Madagascar, Zanzibar, Seychelles.

Maximum Length: 4 in (10 cm) TL.

Water: 72–79°F (22–26°C); pH: 6.5–7.8; hardness: 5–15°dGH.

Min. Tank Size: 15 gal | 24x12x12 in (50 L | 60x30x30 cm).

Feeding: May require live foods when first imported, but in a community setting this fish soon learns to eat almost anything. Loves small or chopped earthworms.

Behavior & Care: Prefers a well-planted tank with subdued light. In older males the scales protrude slightly; this is normal and not dropsy or any other disease.

Breeding: Males are larger and more colorful. Breeding tank with fairly neutral water and mops or Java Moss. Spawns for 6–8 days. Collect and hatch eggs as for *Aplocheilus lineatus*. Fry hatch in 12 days; their mouths are already large enough to take *Artemia* nauplii!

Pseudepiplatys annulatus (Boulenger, 1915)
Clown Killie (Epiplatys Annulatus, Chocolate Killie, Rocket Panchax)

Overview: Some killies are easy, some not—this is one of the latter. It's a tiny predator, feeding on tiny aquatic invertebrates, but more in danger of becoming prey unless you are very careful about tank-mates! But what a little stunner! Well worth a lot of effort.

Native Range: West Africa—Guinea to Nigeria. Said to be rare.

Maximum Length: 1.5 in (4 cm) TL.

Water: 72–79°F (22–26°C); pH: 5.5–6.8; hardness: 0–5°dGH.

Min. Tank Size: 10 gal | 20x10x12 (35 L | 50x25x30 cm).

Feeding: Tiny live foods such as _Cyclops_ and sifted _Daphnia_. Often reluctant to take flake, though may learn in time.

Behavior & Care: If you want this fish to live, use very soft, slightly acid water, with the very lowest nitrate reading (<10 ppm essential)—and a tight-fitting cover, as it jumps. Totally peaceful, and best kept in a small group in a species tank as it is difficult to find tankmates safe enough, though _Corydoras_ are a possibility.

Breeding: Difficult. Males larger, with more colorful finnage. Raise the temperature, drop the pH, slightly. Eggs are attached to plants or mops as in _Aplocheilus lineatus_ (qv), but can be safely left with the parents. Hatching 8–10 days, infusorians required as first food.

Aphyolebias peruensis (Myers, 1954)
Peruvian Longfin (Pterolebias Peruensis)

Overview: *Aphyolebias* are short-lived, so-called "annual fishes" that live in small pools which dry up seasonally. Before this happens they spawn in the soft substrate. The adults die, then when the rains come the eggs hatch and the cycle starts again.

Native Range: South America—Amazon drainage in Peru.

Maximum Length: 4 in (10 cm) TL.

Water: 73–79°F (23–26°C); pH: 6.0–6.8; hardness: 0–5°dGH.

Min. Tank Size: 15 gal | 24x12x12 in (50 L | 60x30x30 cm).

Feeding: Small live foods; may accept frozen and flake.

Behavior & Care: Annual killies are best kept in species tanks, either in pairs or in a group. Because they may spawn in their normal quarters, the substrate should be loose peat, pre-boiled so it stays on the bottom (keep the water—homemade peat extract). A few stems of plants can be included. As with all killies, use a tight cover!

Breeding: Spawning may continue for several weeks during which heavy feeding is needed. Then remove the adults, collect up the peat, squeeze out the water, and store in a plastic box in a warm place. After a month add water. If no fry appear, repeat the whole process. Hatching periods vary a lot, even within a species!

Austrolebias bellottii (Steindachner, 1881)
Argentine Pearlfish (Cynolebias Bellottii)

Overview: For many years most South American "annual" killies were assigned to *Cynolebias*, which has now been split into several genera. *Austrolebias* are the southerly species, distributed from southern Brazil south to Argentina. They can be kept in unheated tanks with seasonal variation. This one is an old favorite.

Native Range: Lower Paraná and Uruguay drainages in Argentina and Uruguay.

Maximum Length: 2.75 in (7 cm) TL.

Water: 64–77°F (18–25°C); pH: 6.0–6.8; hardness: 0–5°dGH.

Min. Tank Size: 15 gal | 24x12x12 in (50 L | 60x30x30 cm).

Feeding: Almost any small live foods; also takes frozen and flake.

Behavior & Care: Species tank with boiled peat substrate and a few small-leaved plant stems, such as *Cabomba*. Floating plants are beneficial. Males can be quite aggressive when they want to spawn, so keep one male and 2–3 females. Close-fitting cover!

Breeding: As usual with killies, the male is more colorful. A temperature rise may trigger breeding. Separate the adults after spawning so the female can recover in peace. Egg care as for *Aphyolebias peruensis*, but with an incubation period of 3–4 months.

Jordanella floridae Goode & Bean, 1879
American Flagfish (Florida Flagfish, Cyprinodon Floridae)

Overview: This native American fish is both comely and intelligent. When alarmed, the group scoots, leaving the dominant male to position himself between the threat and the family. He hovers motionless, coloration blending into the background, until "all clear." They are shy and elusive and quite territorial. Very alert to room activity.

Native Range: North America—from southeastern USA to the Yucatan in Mexico, in slow-moving or still waters of variable chemistry.

Maximum Length: 2.5 in (6 cm) TL.

Water: 64–77°F (18–25°C); pH: 6.5–8.0; hardness: 5–25°dGH.

Min. Tank Size: 20 gal | 30x12x12 in (65 L | 75x30x30 cm).

Feeding: Will take almost any small foods, and nibbles algae.

Behavior & Care: Heavy planting (especially mosses), a dark substrate and background, and indirect morning light. Prefers the lower part of the tank. Best in a species tank as they can be quite nippy.

Breeding: Females and juvenile males have a dark spot on the dorsal. Marimo Balls and Java Moss are favorite spawning sites. The male lures the female to his nest, where she lays a few eggs a day over several days. The male is devoted, fanning and protecting the eggs until hatching in about a week. Fry are tiny and need microscopic foods.

Lucania goodei Jordan, 1880
Bluefin Killifish

Overview: The genus *Lucania* contains just three species, with this one and the very variable *L. parva* sometimes seen in the hobby. They are not seasonal, and usually swim lower in the water than most killies. Note that they are not strictly tropical and should not be kept too warm, and tankmates should be chosen to match.

Native Range: North America—southeastern USA, in still or slow-moving waters such as lakes, swamps, and backwaters.

Maximum Length: 2.5 in (6.5 cm) TL.

Water: 54–72°F (12–22°C); pH: 6.5–6.8; hardness: 0–5°dGH.

Min. Tank Size: 25 gal | 24x16x16 in (95 L | 60x40x40 cm).

Feeding: Ideally small live foods, but will take frozen and prepared.

Behavior & Care: Peaceful, and easy to maintain. Requires a well-planted aquarium. Should not be buffeted by strong filtration. An air-driven sponge filter should be adequate, or no filter at all. Keep several females per male if possible, to prevent excessive chasing.

Breeding: Males are larger and more colorful than females. Spawns on plant leaves in the wild. Use a separate breeding tank with spawning mops so the eggs can be collected and hatched separately. Hatching normally takes place after about two weeks. Not very prolific.

Nematolebias whitei (Myers, 1942)
Rio Pearlfish (Cynolebias Whitei)

Overview: Like *Austrolebias*, this genus was once part of *Cynolebias*. Once again these are "annual" fishes that usually live for less than a year. Try to buy the youngest specimens possible, ideally from a breeder, as "old" fish may not live long enough to settle in and breed. *N. whitei* is an old favorite with killie fans.

Native Range: Southeastern Brazil, in the Rio de Janeiro region.

Maximum Length: 3 in (8 cm) TL.

Water: 68–73°F (20–23°C); pH: 6.0–6.8; hardness: 0–5°dGH.

Min. Tank Size: 15 gal | 24x12x12 in (50 L | 60x30x30 cm).

Feeding: Small live foods, may take frozen, not keen on flake.

Behavior & Care: As for *Austrolebias bellottii* and *Aphyolebias peruensis*. *N. whitei* is a bit of a "bruiser" but damage is usually limited to torn fins and not serious.

Breeding: Again as for *Austrolebias*. Always use water of suitable temperature for wetting. Once you have hatched annual killie eggs, don't discard the peat but repeat the store and wet process. In the wild there is often a period of rain then further drying out, wiping out fry that hatched, so some eggs "wait" for a second or even a third wetting to ensure survival of the species. One of Nature's miracles!

Rivulus hartii (Boulenger, 1890)
Hart's Rivulus (Giant Rivulus)

Overview: The genus *Rivulus* has representatives from the USA south to the Amazon region, and in the Caribbean. Almost all are found in flowing streams with vegetation, though other water parameters may vary so always check. These are not annual fishes and they spawn on plants.

Native Range: Trinidad, Venezuela, eastern Colombia.

Maximum Length: 4 in (10 cm) TL.

Water: 72–79°F (22–26°C); pH 6.5–7.5; hardness 5–10°dGH.

Min. Tank Size: 30 gal | 36x12x16 in (105 L | 90x30x40 cm).

Feeding: Prefers live foods but quite accommodating about frozen and flake.

Behavior & Care: Dark substrate, rooted and floating plants, slight current. Not a good community fish as it may eat smaller tankmates but is shy with fishes its own size. Very individualistic—some become tame, others remain timid. Accomplished jumper.

Breeding: *Rivulus* are plant spawners like the African *Aplocheilus*, and require similar treatment of the eggs. Males are more colorful. Spawns are larger following a diet of live foods. Breed with two females and one male.

Ameca splendens Miller & Fitzsimons, 1971
Butterfly Goodeid (Butterfly Splitfin)

Overview: This lovely goodeid is extinct in the wild, but appears to be safe in captivity—nevertheless buy only if you intend to breed it and help its survival. Like the better-known poeciliids, such as the Guppy (*Poecilia reticulata*), goodeids are livebearers that practice internal fertilization and give birth to live young.

Native Range: North America—Jalisco, western Mexico.

Maximum Length: 3.25 in (8 cm) TL.

Water: 79–90°F (26–32°C); pH: 6.0–8.0; hardness: 5–20°dGH.

Min. Tank Size: 30 gal | 36x12x16 in (105 L | 90x30x40 cm).

Feeding: A well-varied diet of green, live, and frozen foods. This fish benefits from availability of algae as a natural food supply.

Behavior & Care: Keep warm. Use dark substrate and rocks alternating with thick clumps of plants; encourage algae by bright lighting. Males are territorial; all goodeids should be packed singly for transportation to avoid mayhem or murder in the bags.

Breeding: The male *A. splendens* has a modified anal fin (andropodium) for insemination, and a striped tail. The young are born about 55 days after mating and are easy to rear. They can take *Artemia* nauplii as first food; algae should be available to nibble.

Anableps anableps (Linnaeus, 1758)
Four-eyes (Largescale Foureyes)

Overview: Anableps are unusual fishes—their eyes are divided into an upper part for seeing above the water's surface (primarily for spotting predators, e.g., herons), and a lower for normal "sub-aqua" activities. Hence their popular name. These peaceful, schooling live-bearers can also survive out of water on the wet mud at low tide.

Native Range: Trinidad, and coastal drainages from Venezuela to the Amazon delta in Brazil, in fresh and brackish water.

Maximum Length: 12 in (30 cm) TL.

Water: 75–82 °F (24–28 °C); pH: 6.5–8.0; hardness: 5–20 °dGH.

Min. Tank Size: 55 gal | 48x20x13 in (195 L | 120x50x33 cm).

Feeding: Live/frozen foods; also takes flake. May eat small fishes!

Behavior & Care: Usually kept in brackish water—plants and tank-mates should then be salt-tolerant. Fine gravel, plenty of swimming space. Use a shallow tank with an air space above the water. Tight-fitting cover, to keep the air warm and humid and the fish from jumping out! Sociable, so keep a small school.

Breeding: The male's anal fin is modified as a gonopodium, to inseminate the female. Mature when half-grown. Fry measure about 1 in (2.5 cm) at birth, so feeding them is easy on any small foods.

Belonesox belizanus Kner, 1860
Pike Topminnow (Pike Livebearer)

Overview: You have only to look at the mouth of this fish to recognize it as a predator. This is not a species for the general community, it needs tankmates too large to eat and able to look after themselves, eg medium-sized Central American cichlids.

Native Range: Central Mexico, south along the Atlantic side to Costa Rica, in sluggish vegetated waters, sometimes brackish.

Maximum Length: 8 in (20 cm) TL.

Water: 77–85°F (25–29°C); pH: 7.5–8.5; hardness: 10–25°dGH.

Min. Tank Size: 65 gal | 48x18x18 in (240 L | 120x45x45 cm).

Feeding: Feeder fish, chopped raw fish or shrimp, other robust live foods. Will regard small tankmates as extra meals.

Behavior & Care: Large tank with plants and wood as décor, rocks optional. Benefits from the addition of salt as long as plants and tankmates are salt-tolerant. Avoid filter turbulence. Adults can be rather aggressive as well as predatory.

Breeding: Females are much larger (almost double the size of males) and have yellow or orange at the anal-fin base. Livebearer: the female produces up to 100 young almost an inch (2.5 cm) long, and, remarkably for a piscivore, doesn't molest them.

Heterandria formosa Girard, 1859
Mosquito Fish (Dwarf Livebearer, Dwarf Topminnow)

Overview: Males of this species are among the smallest fishes in the world, but females are much larger. They are very attractive, and ideal if you want a small livebearer that hasn't been man-modified. Short-lived (1-2 years) but readily breeds replacements!

Native Range: USA: Cape Fear River drainage in North Carolina to southern Louisiana; vegetated, sluggish, fresh and brackish water.

Maximum Length: 1.75 in (4.5 cm) TL.

Water: 68–79°F (20–26°C); pH: 7.0–8.0; hardness: 10–20°dGH.

Min. Tank Size: 25 gal | 24x16x16 in (95 L | 60x40x40 cm).

Feeding: Small live and frozen foods; readily accepts flake.

Behavior & Care: A very easy, hardy, peaceful little fish for a small community tank with dense vegetation. Tankmates should be of similar size or smaller. Can be kept in slightly brackish water if plants and tankmates are salt-tolerant.

Breeding: Males are only half the size of females and have the anal fin modified as a gonopodium for internal fertilization. Young are born every two weeks or so, sometimes at longer intervals. Not cannibalistic, but if bred in a community fry should have dense plants among which to hide from other fishes!

Poecilia latipinna (Lesueur, 1821)
Sailfin Molly

Overview: This poeciliid livebearer is found in fresh, brackish and even salt water. Often confused with and sold as the similar *P. velifera* (Mexican Sailfin Molly) and some aquarium stocks are hybrids. Very variable in color, with black and albino forms known.

Native Range: Cape Fear, North Carolina to Veracruz, Mexico.

Maximum Length: 6 in (15 cm) TL.

Water: 72–82°F (22–28°C); pH: 7.0–8.5; hardness: 5–25°dGH.

Min. Tank Size: 40 gal | 48x13x16 in (155 L | 120x32.55x40 cm).

Feeding: Live, frozen, prepared foods; high vegetable component.

Behavior & Care: Sailfins benefit from the addition of salt, so tankmates should be salt-tolerant, ditto plants (and able to withstand nibbling—Java Fern, Java Moss). Plenty of swimming space or the male's sailfin will not develop fully. Well-lit tank.

Breeding: Males have a larger dorsal. All poeciliid livebearers have the male anal fin modified to a gonopodium for internal insemination and can be sexed by this feature. Fry measure 0.5 in (1.25 cm) at birth; likely to be eaten by adults so move the female to a breeding trap in a separate tank. Handle her with care, as in this species there is a tendency to give birth prematurely in the event of stress.

Poecilia reticulata Peters, 1859
Guppy (Millions Fish)

Overview: The Guppy is easy to keep, beautiful, and inexpensive, and will breed as long as you have both sexes. Ideal for the beginner with one small tank, to see if he enjoys the hobby. Decades of selective breeding have produced "fancy" Guppies in a staggering array of colors and finnage, and the wild form is now rarely seen.

Native Range: Venezuela and several Caribbean islands. Introduced elsewhere, sometimes to control mosquitoes (feeds on their larvae).

Maximum Length: 2.5 in (6 cm) TL.

Water: 72–82°F (22–28°C); pH: 7.0–8.5; hardness: 5–25°dGH.

Min. Tank Size: 15 gal | 24x12x12 in (50 L | 60x30x30 cm).

Feeding: Guppies will accept just about anything offered.

Behavior & Care: Unfussy, but prefers a well-lit tank, densely planted along sides and back. Avoid fin-nipping tankmates!

Breeding: Males are smaller and more colorful, and have a gonopodium. Use a breeding trap as for _P. latipinna_. One mating allows a female to produce multiple broods over a period of months, and the father may not be the male you think, so if parentage is important, separate off young "virgin" females at as early an age as possible and then add the desired male.

Poecilia reticulata, Fancy Red Veiltail Guppy, Max. Length: 2.5 in (6 cm).

Poecilia reticulata, Fancy Veiltail Guppy, Max. Length: 2.5 in (6 cm).

Guppy breeding can be done by youngsters but some become life-long enthusiasts. Serious amateur breeders annually produce new and sometimes startlingly unusual colors and strains.

Poecilia sphenops Valenciennes, 1846
Black Molly (Short-finned Molly)

Overview: The wild form of this fish is blue, and found in fresh, brackish, and even salt water; it is rarely seen in the hobby. The popular "Black Molly" is a cultivated form that may even have hybrid blood—it was "created" so long ago that nobody knows.

Native Range: Central to South America: Mexico to Colombia.

Maximum Length: 2.5 in (6 cm) TL.

Water: 64–86°F (18–30°C); pH: 7.0–8.5; hardness: 5–25°dGH.

Min. Tank Size: 15 gal | 24x12x12 in (50 L | 60x30x30 cm).

Feeding: Varied diet with a high vegetable component.

Behavior & Care: Black Mollies require temperatures in the upper part of the range given above, wild fish are hardier. The black form also tends to be disease-prone and short-lived, probably due to its origins, but will produce plenty of young so there is no need to restock. Should have a little salt added, so tankmates and plants should be salt-tolerant (many catfishes, some other fishes, and most plants are not, and will die). May nibble soft foliage. Plastic plants are a possible solution to both problems.

Breeding: As for *P. latipinna.* Easy and very prolific. Black parents may produce "throwbacks"—spotted fish closer to the wild type.

Poecilia wingei Poeser, Kempkes & Isbrücker, 2005
Endler's Guppy (Endler's Livebearer)

Overview: This is a cousin to the fancy Guppy, more like the wild *P. reticulata* and much less ornate than its flamboyantly finned domestic relatives. Only recently recognized by science as a distinct species. Easy to keep, and of particular interest to the livebearer enthusiast who wants something a bit different.

Native Range: South America: northeastern Venezuela.

Maximum Length: 2 in (5 cm) TL.

Water: 72–82°F (22–28°C); pH: 7.0–8.2; hardness: 8–20°dGH.

Min. Tank Size: 15 gal | 24x12x12 in (50 L | 60x30x30 cm).

Feeding: Unfussy omnivore. Like other poeciliids and many other small fishes, this species benefits from several small feeds per day.

Behavior & Care: A peaceful fish, as suited to community life as the Guppy. Likes a well-lit tank with planting on sides and back. More active than its tail-heavy cousins, needs lots of open space.

Breeding: As for the common Guppy; note that the two species will hybridize and should be kept separate. Surplus livebearer fry are often used as live food for other fishes, but this species is sufficiently scarce in the hobby that the young are worth rearing and selling to stores or giving to other hobbyists.

Xiphophorus helleri Heckel, 1848
Swordtail

Overview: The Swordtail takes its name from the long, sword-like extension of the lower lobe of the male's tail, which is rounded in females. The wild form of this fish is green, but as with many popular poeciliid livebearers there are cultivated color variants. The sword itself comes in a variety of shades. The species has been selectively bred to produce finnage variations as well, including an upper, or "top," sword.

Native Range: Central America, from Veracruz in Mexico to northwestern Honduras.

Maximum Length: 5 in (12.5 cm) TL. A lot of this is the sword!

Water: 64–82°F (18–28°C); pH: 7.0–8.5; hardness: 5–25°dGH.

Min. Tank Size: 15 gal | 24x12x12 in (50 L | 60x30x30 cm).

Feeding: Any small aquarium foods; requires some green food.

Behavior & Care: A hardy fish for any hard-water community. Males are quite quarrelsome among themselves and one will become dominant, but injuries are unlikely.

Breeding: Will hybridize with the closely related Platy, *X. maculatus*, so do not mix the two. Breed as for other poeciliid livebearers. Color forms may or may not breed true.

Xiphophorus maculatus (Günther, 1866)
Platy (Moonfish)

Overview: Platies are hardy fishes and this, along with their vibrant coloration, makes them ideal for beginners. They lack the "sword" of their otherwise very similar close relative, the Swordtail, *X. helleri*. Many "fancy" variations have been developed, including the red, sunset, wagtail, and tuxedo Platies. Some of these have been produced by hybridizing this species with others.

Native Range: Veracruz in Mexico to northern Belize.

Maximum Length: 3 in (7.5 cm) TL.

Water: 68–79°F (20–26°C); pH: 7.0–8.5; hardness: 10–25°dGH.

Min. Tank Size: 15 gal | 24x12x12 in (50 L | 60x30x30 cm).

Feeding: Omnivore with a high vegetable requirement.

Behavior & Care: Keep Platies in a tank with live plants, as they may pick at them—and algae—to supplement their diet. Provide good lighting and lots of open space in the center for swimming.

Breeding: Males have a gonopodium. Extremely easy to breed. If the parents are well fed they are less likely to cannibalize the young. Platies, Guppies, & Co. are so easy to breed and prolific that some aquarists keep a few with dwarf pike cichlids or killies, for example, to provide a steady source of youngsters as live food.

Xiphophorus variatus (Meek, 1904)
Variatus Platy (Platy Variatus, Variegated Platy)

Overview: Unfortunately not often seen nowadays, the Variatus Platy is an interesting alternative to its commoner cousin, *X. maculatus*. The two should not be mixed—or with *X. helleri*—as they may hybridize.

Native Range: Central America: eastern central Mexico.

Maximum Length: 2.5 in (6.5 cm) TL.

Water: 68–79°F (20–26°C); pH: 7.0–8.5; hardness: 10–25°dGH.

Min. Tank Size: 15 gal | 24x12x12 in (50 L | 60x30x30 cm).

Feeding: Omnivore, with a high vegetable requirement. Eats most aquarium foods.

Behavior & Care: This fish is often recommended for an unheated aquarium, but this does not accord with its natural range and the temperatures given above are more appropriate. Requires a planted aquarium with open swimming space, and will appreciate algae being allowed to grow as a food supplement. An excellent, peaceful, and hardy community fish.

Breeding: Females larger, males have a gonopodium. Breeding as for other poeciliid livebearers above. Like Endler's Guppy (*Poecilia wingei*) this species is worth rearing for other hobbyists to enjoy.

Alfaro cultratus, Knife-edge Livebearer.

Gambusia holbrooki, Holbrook's Mosquitofish.

Sometimes regarded as a subspecies of *G. affinis*, this little live-bearer is sold under both names.

Limia melanogaster, Blackbelly or Blue Limia. Max. Length: 1.5 in (4 cm).

Xenotoca eiseni, Redtail Goodeid or Redtail Splitfin. Max. Length: 2.5 in (6 cm).

Limia species are an interesting alternative to the more common-place livebearers. *L. melanogaster* is endemic to Jamaica, while the chunky Redtail Goodeid is found in Central America.

Bedotia geayi Regan, 1903
Madagascar Rainbowfish (Red-tailed Silverside)

Overview: This is a lively, peaceful community fish that is easy to keep and house; best in groups of six or more. Like many Madagascan fishes it is endangered in its natural habitat.

Native Range: Africa: eastern Madagascar.

Maximum Length: 6 in (15 cm) TL.

Water: 68–75°F (20–24°C); pH: 7.0–7.5; hardness: 8–15°dGH.

Min. Tank Size: 38 gal | 48x12x16 in (140 L | 120x30x40 cm).

Feeding: Omnivore. Small live, frozen, and prepared foods are taken midwater. Will not follow food to bottom. Include vegetable foods.

Behavior & Care: Can be timid so keep only with peaceful, non-boisterous tankmates. Requires plenty of swimming space. Comes from running water so gentle water movement is desirable to improve the oxygen level. Dark substrate; rooted and floating plants.

Breeding: The male is more colorful with red tips on the lobes of the caudal fin and a pointed dorsal fin. Condition with live foods. The pair will lay a few eggs each day, attaching them to surface and near-surface vegetation by fine threads. The parents will not eat eggs or fry, which are of sufficient size to take newly hatched brine shrimp.

Marosatherina ladigesi (Ahl, 1936)
Celebes Rainbowfish (Telmatherina Ladigesi)

Overview: This charming beauty is a bit demanding, but when properly kept it is a stunning addition to a peaceful community tank.

Native Range: Sulawesi, Indonesia, in fresh and brackish waters.

Maximum Length: 3 in (8.0 cm) TL.

Water: 72–78°F (22–26°C); pH: 7.0–8.0; hardness: 12–20°dGH.

Min. Tank Size: 20 gal | 30x12x12 in (65 L | 75x30x30 cm).

Feeding: Omnivores. Small live, frozen, and prepared foods that can be taken from the surface or midwater.

Behavior & Care: Requires floating and rooted plants and open swimming space. Keep the water pristine with regular partial water changes, never too much at one time, as the fish are as sensitive to sudden change as they are to poor water quality. Use gentle water flow, but efficient filtration. Benefits from the addition of salt, but tankmates and plants must be salt-tolerant.

Breeding: Males are larger with longer, pointed fins. Breeds continuously for several months. Use a breeding tank with very clean water and floating plants, to which the eggs are attached by threads. The parents will eat eggs and fry, so swap the vegetation (or use spawning mops) and hatch the eggs separately. Infusorians as first food.

Chilatherina bleheri Allen, 1985
Bleher's Rainbowfish

Overview: Rainbowfishes are peaceful, active schoolers with many admirable qualities. They are best kept in groups of two females for every male—or larger schools in bigger tanks—and are excellent community fishes. This lovely species is relatively rare, and slow to color up, requiring maturity and a mate to develop full coloration.

Native Range: Indonesia: western Papua New Guinea.

Maximum Length: 5 in (13 cm) TL.

Water: 72–81°F (22–27°C); pH: 6.5–8.5; hardness: 5–25°dGH.

Min. Tank Size: 30 gal | 36x12x16 in (105 L | 90x30x40 cm).

Feeding: Omnivore. Takes prepared, frozen and live foods with equal enthusiasm. It is an active hunter that will capture live prey the instant it hits the water.

Behavior & Care: Decorate sparingly with rocks, driftwood, a dark substrate, and a planted backdrop, leaving plenty of open swimming room in the center. A layer of floating plants is advised. These fishes enjoy an element of water movement.

Breeding: Easy to breed. Females are smaller, paler, and deeper-bodied than males. A continuous spawner that scatters a few eggs per day among plants, to which they adhere by fine threads.

Glossolepis incisus Weber, 1907
Red Rainbowfish (Lake Sentani Rainbowfish)

Overview: This species becomes truly flamboyant when in spawning condition. The high back and full color come only with maturity. Can be rather timid for a fish its size.

Native Range: Indonesia: Lake Sentani in Papua New Guinea.

Maximum Length: 6 in (15 cm) TL.

Water: 72–79°F (22–26°C); pH: 7.0–8.0; hardness: 10–25°dGH.

Min. Tank Size: 50 gal | 48x16x16 in (190 L | 120x40x40 cm).

Feeding: Live, frozen, and prepared foods. Use foods containing carotenoids to enhance the red color of males to optimum.

Behavior & Care: Like all rainbowfishes this is a peaceful schooling fish and should be kept in a group of five or more. Tankmates should be peaceful community fishes with differing swimming habits and occupying different zones in the aquarium. Rocks, wood, plants, but above all plenty of swimming space. Jumps!

Breeding: Sexes colored differently. Easy to breed. Spawns in the morning. The eggs are scattered and adhere to fine-leaved vegetation and the roots of floating plants such as Indian Fern. Java Moss is also an excellent spawning medium for this species. The fry are free-swimming in 7–8 days and require infusoria as first food.

Iriatherina werneri Meinken, 1974
Threadfin Rainbowfish

Overview: A unique and unmistakable little Australasian rainbowfish with a high wow factor!

Native Range: Southern New Guinea (Fly River area) and the extreme northern tip of Australia (Cape York).

Maximum Length: 2 in (5 cm) TL.

Water: 75–82°F (24–28°C); pH: 7.0–7.5; hardness: 10–15°dGH.

Min. Tank Size: 25 gal | 24x16x16 in (95 L | 60x40x40 cm).

Feeding: Small live and frozen foods, plus occasional flake.

Behavior & Care: Species tank or peaceful community of small fishes. Do not keep with fin-nippers! Mixes well with other small rainbows. School of at least six, fine substrate, background décor, and plenty of open swimming space.

Breeding: Males are larger with much longer finnage. Continuous spawner. Use a breeding tank with a bottom covering of Java Moss in which the eggs will be laid. Condition the pair or group with live food and keep up this conditioning throughout the breeding period. Periodically transfer (and replace) the moss to a small, bare tank with water from the breeding tank. Hatching takes 8–12 days; the tiny fry swim near the surface and are best started on rotifers.

Melanotaenia boesemani Allen & Cross, 1980
Boeseman's Rainbowfish

Overview: This is a beautiful species from the former Irian Jaya, now captive-bred for the hobby. Young rainbows do not show much color and are often overlooked in the store by aquarists ignorant of their adult splendor. Don't make that mistake!

Native Range: Indonesia: Ajamaru lakes in western New Guinea.

Maximum Length: 4 in (10 cm) TL.

Water: 77–86°F (25–30°C); pH: 7.5–8.5; hardness: 10–25°dGH.

Min. Tank Size: 30 gal | 36x12x16 in (105 L | 90x30x40 cm).

Feeding: Rainbows generally take any aquarium foods of suitable size, but prefer carnivore foods. The orange color of males will benefit from the inclusion of chopped shrimp and adult *Artemia*.

Behavior & Care: A peaceful community fish that should be kept in a school of at least six. Plenty of swimming space, bordered sparingly with rocks, wood, and plants. Dark substrate. Warm water important. Close-fitting cover as this fish is an accomplished jumper.

Breeding: Males are larger and more colorful. Like other *Melanotaenia*, this species scatters small batches of eggs among plants, where they attach to the foliage by short threads. Spawning takes place daily for weeks or months, usually in the morning.

Melanotaenia goldiei (Macleay, 1883)
Goldie River Rainbowfish

Overview: This is one of the larger rainbowfishes and deserves along aquarium where it can use its swimming muscles. A long black band that gives the genus its name (*melano* = black, *taenia* = band) is particularly prominent in this lovely species.

Native Range: Indonesia: Papua New Guinea and the Aru Islands. One of the more widespread New Guinea rainbows.

Maximum Length: 5 in (13 cm) TL.

Water: 75–82°F (24–28°C); pH: 7.0–7.8; hardness: 8–15°dGH.

Min. Tank Size: 50 gal | 48x16x16 in (190 L | 120x40x40 cm).

Feeding: Wild fish require live foods but will learn to take frozen and prepared foods once quarantined and acclimated to their new home. Peaceful tankmates, feeding eagerly, will show the way.

Behavior & Care: Largely as for *M. boesemani*. A layer of floating plants will help deter nervousness and jumping.

Breeding: Males are larger and more colorful. Spawns like *M. boesemani*. Rainbows generally spawn in the morning and they can be encouraged to breed by siting the tank where it catches the early rays of the sun. Because spawning continues for a long period, feed mainly live food to breeders to maintain their condition.

Melanotaenia herbertaxelrodi Allen, 1981
Lake Tebera Rainbowfish

Overview: This fish gradually grows into a show-stopper, with large males having deep golden hues at certain times of day and when courting. Named in honor of Dr. Herbert R. Axelrod, founder of _Tropical Fish Hobbyist_ magazine.

Native Range: Indonesia: endemic to the Lake Tebera basin in the southern highlands of Papua New Guinea.

Maximum Length: 4 in (10 cm) TL.

Water: 72–79°F (22–26°C); pH: 7.2–8.0; hardness: 8–15°dGH.

Min. Tank Size: 30 gal | 36x12x16 in (105 L | 90x30x40 cm).

Feeding: Readily takes live, frozen, and prepared foods.

Behavior & Care: This species requires somewhat cooler conditions than _M. boesemani_ but maintenance is otherwise similar.

Breeding: Males are more colorful. Like other rainbows this fish scatters eggs among plants daily over an extended period. Many species are cannibalistic, but can be outwitted in the same way as plant-spawning killifishes—by using spawning mops and removing the eggs daily after the early morning spawning session. An alternative is to swap the plants for new ones. Hatch the eggs separately in a small tank filled with water from the breeding tank.

Melanotaenia lacustris, Lake Kutubu Rainbowfish.

Melanotaenia praecox, Dwarf Rainbowfish. Measures only 2 in (5 cm).

Like many New Guinea rainbows the Lake Kutubu Rainbowfish has a limited distribution, but most stocks are now tank-bred. The Dwarf Rainfbowfish is gem for smaller, peaceful communities.

303

Melanotaenia maccullochi Ogilby, 1915
McCulloch's Rainbowfish (Black-lined Rainbow)

Overview: The genus *Melanotaenia* is Australasian in its distribution, being found in both Indonesia and Australia. This species has a foot in both camps, and exhibits some geographical color variation. It is characterized by a host of narrow black longitudinal bands. Like most rainbows it is an "ugly duckling" that develops its fine colors only when mature.

Native Range: Southern Papua New Guinea and NE Australia.

Maximum Length: 2.75 in (7 cm) TL.

Water: 70–84°F (21–29°C); pH: 5.5–8.0; hardness: 0–25°dGH.

Min. Tank Size: 30 gal | 36x12x16 in (105 L | 90x30x40 cm).

Feeding: Smaller than many rainbows—small mouth means small foods. Takes live, frozen, and prepared foods readily.

Behavior & Care: Water chemistry varies with geography, with the pH down to 5.5 in Australia (with correspondingly low hardness), 6.5–7.5 in New Guinea. In practice the entire range is tolerated, but best to provide the right conditions for newly acquired wild stock. Otherwise maintenance similar to that for *M. boesemani*.

Breeding: Males brighter with slightly longer fins. Spawning can be triggered by a partial water change. Breed as for other rainbows.

Melanotaenia parkinsoni, Parkinson's Rainbowfish.

Melanotaenia splendida rubrostriata, Red-striped Rainbowfish.

Parkinson's Rainbowfish is a lovely species with a limited distribution in Papua New Guinea. The Red-striped Rainbowfish is one of several subspecies of *M. splendida* with varying color patterns.

Melanotaenia trifasciata (Rendahl, 1922)
Banded Rainbowfish

Overview: This Australian rainbow, like its cousin *M. splendida*, occurs in several color variants depending on the river of origin. The commonest in the hobby is the Goyder River form, resplendent with red fins, purplish body, and black midlateral band. Some of these variants also differ in shape so they may be distinct species.

Native Range: Australia: Northern Territory and Queensland.

Maximum Length: 5 in (13 cm) TL.

Water: 74–84°F (24–29°C); pH: 7.0–8.0; hardness: 10–20°dGH.

Min. Tank Size: 50 gal | 48x16x16 in (190 L | 120x40x40 cm).

Feeding: Like other rainbows, an unfussy fish that will take live, frozen, and flake foods.

Behavior & Care: The water parameters given are for the Goyder River variant; some others prefer cooler, softer water. Like other rainbows it should be maintained in a school, ideally with two females per male. General maintenance as for *M. boesemani*.

Breeding: Males are more colorful, and in some variants deeper-bodied. Avoid keeping different variants together in case they cross-breed. Even if they are the same species it is better to keep the wild forms pure. Breeding as for other *Melanotaenia*.

Pseudomugil furcatus Nichols, 1955
Forktail Rainbowfish

Overview: The blue-eyes are, if possible, even more gorgeous than other rainbows, but rather rare in the hobby, which is a pity as they are easy to keep and breed and need only a small tank.

Native Range: Indonesia: known only from the lowlands of eastern Papua New Guinea from Dyke Ackland Bay to Collingwood Bay.

Maximum Length: 2.25 in (5.5 cm) TL.

Water: 75–79°F (24–26°C); pH: 7.5–8.0; hardness: 10–25°dGH.

Min. Tank Size: 25 gal | 24x16x16 in (95 L | 60x40x40 cm).

Feeding: Blue-eyes are little carnivores that should be fed mainly live (and/or frozen) foods but will also take some flake.

Behavior & Care: Small, active, peaceful fish that are best kept in a school of six or more in a species tank. Decor largely as for *Melanotaenia* except that blue-eyes relish dense planting.

Breeding: Males are larger, more colorful, and have a longer first dorsal fin. Breed in a group (best) or as a pair, with Java Moss and floating plants. Males can be aggressive; if this is a problem add extra females. The eggs are large and hang from plants by adhesive threads. Free-swimming in 15–20 days; infusoria as first food. The parents are cannibalistic so remove them or the eggs.

Parambassis ranga (Hamilton-Buchanan, 1822)
Indian Glassfish (Chanda Ranga)

Overview: One of a number of aquarium fishes whose main attraction is their "see-through" bodies. A territorial but peaceful, shoaling fish with a tendency to timidity. Its cousin, *C. wolfii*, is also sometimes available but grows to more than twice the size.

Native Range: India to Malaysia, in fresh and brackish water.

Maximum Length: 3 in (8 cm) TL.

Water: 68–86°F (20–30°C); pH: 7.5–8.5; hardness: 10–25°dGH.

Min. Tank Size: 29 gal | 30x12x18 in (100 L | 75x30x45 cm).

Foods & Feeding: Any small live foods or the frozen equivalent. Will take flake but doesn't thrive on a diet of prepared foods alone.

Behavior & Care: Benefits from the addition of salt, so plants and tankmates must be salt-tolerant. Keep in a school of six-plus, with quiet tankmates, in a mature, well-planted tank with rocks and wood as hiding places. Site the tank to catch the morning sun.

Breeding: Males are darker yellow with blue edges to dorsal and anal fins. Breeding can be triggered by a water change followed by an increase in temperature and morning sunlight. Lays adhesive eggs among plants. Hatching in 24 hours, free-swimming in 48. The fry are tiny (infusoria required) and difficult to rear.

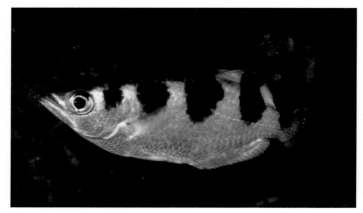

Toxotes jaculatrix (Pallas, 1766)
Archerfish (Toxotes Jaculator, Banded Archerfish)

Overview: *Toxotes* (the Latin means "archer") have a remarkable way of feeding—they fire a jet of water at insects on twigs above the water, shooting them down to the surface to be snapped up.

Native Range: Coastally from India via SE Asia to Indonesia and northern Australia, in tidal waters, in particular mangrove swamps.

Maximum Length: 12 in (30 cm) TL.

Water: 75–86°F (24–30°C); pH: 7.5–8.5; hardness: 10–25°dGH.

Min. Tank Size: 65 gal | 48x18x18 in (240 L | 120x45x45 cm).

Foods & Feeding: Live foods such as flies, crickets, beetles. Will take food from the surface without shooting it down first!

Behavior & Care: Tolerates fresh and sea water, but best kept in brackish conditions, which precludes most live plants. Tankmates must be salt-tolerant. Large tank, decorated with rocks and old, weathered wood that has long since leached out any tannins it once contained. If you want to see this fish "at work" then allow a large air space above the water with branches where prey can "sit" until shot. Lighting and other electricals must be protected from fall-out! Best kept in a group of similar-sized individuals.

Breeding: Sex differences unknown; probably not bred in captivity.

Badis badis (Hamilton, 1822)
Badis

Overview: This distant relative of the cichlids is often mistaken for one, but belongs to a different family. It was long thought there was just one species with a number of subspecies or color forms, but recently a host of separate species have been recognized.

Native Range: India, Pakistan, and Bhutan, in standing water.

Maximum Length: 3 in (8 cm) TL.

Water: 73–86°F (23–30°C); pH: 7.5–9.0; hardness: 10–25°dGH.

Min. Tank Size: 20 gal | 30x12x12 in (65 L | 75x30x30 cm).

Foods & Feeding: Live, frozen, and other carnivore fare.

Behavior & Care: Well-planted tank with sandy substrate and caves. Can be territorial but unlikely to harm other fishes in a roomy community. The tank size cited is a species tank for a pair. A hardy little fish that can survive poor water quality, but such treatment may be responsible for its supposed susceptibility to fish tuberculosis, an incurable disease known to be encouraged by poor conditions.

Breeding: Females have a rounder lower body profile. Usually spawns in a cave, laying up to 100 eggs. Eggs and larvae are tended by the male until free-swimming. The fry are best removed (with a pipette) to a rearing tank. Feed with *Artemia* nauplii initially.

Aequidens pulcher (Gill, 1858)
Blue Acara

Overview: A hardy, medium-sized beginner's cichlid, long popular because of its character, color, and ease of maintenance. In cichlid terms it is rather peaceful for its size, though it will defend its young vigorously, digs a lot, and may consume smaller tankmates. The only real downside is that it is hard to sex.

Native Range: Northern Venezuela and Colombia; and the Caribbean island of Trinidad.

Maximum Length: 8 in (20 cm) TL.

Water: 75–82°F (24–28°C); pH: 6.5–8.0; hardness: 5–20°dGH.

Min. Tank Size: 30 gal | 36x12x16 in (105 L | 90x30x40 cm).

Feeding: Will readily accept any manufactured foods of suitable size, but also enjoys fresh foods—particularly earthworms.

Behavior & Care: Best kept as a pair in a species tank. Although this fish uses vegetation as cover in the wild, plants are unlikely to survive its digging in captivity, so caves (e.g. flowerpots) or bogwood should be provided as shelter.

Breeding: Blue Acaras form pairs to breed, laying several hundred eggs on a rock in the open. Males are larger and have longer un-paired fins, but these differences are relative and far from clear-cut.

Aequidens rivulatus (Günther, 1860)
Green Terror (Goldsaum, Silversaum)

Overview: A medium-large cichlid, whose common name is rather unfair, although it is more aggressive than its cousin, the Blue Acara. Several geographical variants are known, with orange (Goldsaum) or white (Silversaum) fin edgings. It is at present unclear whether these are just forms or separate species.

Native Range: South America: Pacific-coast drainages in Ecuador and northern Peru, possibly also Colombia.

Maximum Length: 10 in (25 cm) TL.

Water: 75–82°F (24–28°C); pH: 6.8–7.5; hardness: 5–15°dGH.

Min. Tank Size: 50 gal | 48x16x16 in (190 L |120x40x40 cm).

Feeding: An omnivore that will take any manufactured, fresh, or live foods of suitable size.

Behavior & Care: Easy to keep, ideally as a pair in a species tank as males are likely to harm or fight with tankmates, especially when breeding. Provide shelter in the form of caves (e.g. flowerpots) or bogwood. Digs a lot, and may uproot plants.

Breeding: A pair-forming substrate-spawner that lays several hundred eggs on a rock in the open. Males are appreciably larger than females and have longer fins, and may develop a nuchal hump.

Altolamprologus calvus (Poll, 1978)
Calvus (Pearly Compressiceps)

Overview: A rather difficult cichlid, with a highly compressed body that enables it to lurk in cracks waiting for prey—mainly the tiny fry of other fishes. The pearly spots and strange shape are very attractive. There are several geographical forms, the Black Calvus being particularly sought-after. *A. compressiceps* is similar.

Native Range: East Africa: endemic to Lake Tanganyika where it is found only in rocky habitat in the southwest of the lake.

Maximum Length: 6 in (15 cm) TL.

Water: 77–82°F (25–28°C); pH: 7.5–9.0; hardness: 10–25°dGH.

Min. Tank Size: 29 gal | 30x12x18 (100 L | 75x30x45 cm).

Feeding: Often reluctant to take flake, and best fed live and frozen foods such as *Daphnia*, bloodworms, and adult brine shrimp.

Behavior & Care: Can be kept with other small Tanganyikans in a large, sparsely populated community with lots of rockwork and well-oxygenated (but not turbulent), very good quality water.

Breeding: Females are much smaller than males. The eggs are laid in a crevice which the female blocks, head-first, with her body till the fry are free-swimming; the male guards her rear. She then leaves them to fend for themselves—but they often fall prey to the male!

Amphilophus citrinellus (Günther, 1864)
Midas Cichlid (Yellow Devil, Citrinellum)

Overview: This is a large species, with the devilish habits suggested by its common name but popular with big-cichlid fans because of its color and character. Youngsters are striped, but later change color to white or yellow or orange, sometimes with a few black markings. The change does not take place at any fixed age or size.

Native Range: Central America: the Nicaraguan lakes as well as Atlantic-slope drainages in Costa Rica.

Maximum Length: 12 in (30 cm) TL.

Water: 75–82°F (24–28°C); pH: 7.0–8.5; hardness: 5–25°dGH.

Min. Tank Size: 65 gal | 48x18x18 in (240 L |120x45x45 cm).

Feeding: An omnivore that will take virtually any food of suitable size, including smaller tankmates.

Behavior & Care: Very hardy, but territorial and aggressive, as well as digging enthusiastically. No special demands regarding décor.

Breeding: Midas Cichlids are open-brooding substrate spawners. Males are larger and develop a nuchal hump. Unfortunately, male aggression is often directed at the female, and a divider may be necessary much of the time, but otherwise they are easy to breed. Both parents produce a skin secretion on which the 1,000-plus fry feed.

Anomalochromis thomasi (Boulenger, 1915)
African Butterfly Dwarf Cichlid (Thomasi)

Overview: A popular dwarf cichlid that can be kept in a general community aquarium provided there is plenty of space for the other fishes to retreat to when the Thomasi breed. Rarely shows any color in aquarium-store tanks, but blossoms into an attractive little fish once settled in a decorated aquarium.

Native Range: West Africa: lowland savannah regions in Guinea, Liberia, and Sierra Leone.

Maximum Length: 3.5 in (8.5 cm) TL.

Water: 75–82°F (24–28°C); pH: 6.0–7.5; hardness: 5–10°dGH.

Min. Tank Size: 15 gal | 24x12x12 in (50 L | 60x30x30 cm).

Feeding: Thomasi will take any foods of suitable size. Live or frozen foods (e.g. *Daphnia*, mosquito larvae) will encourage breeding.

Behavior & Care: These little cichlids are normally peaceful and often rather shy, but can become little terrors when defending a brood. Requires a well-planted tank with plenty of caves.

Breeding: A biparental substrate spawner that lays up to 400 eggs (usually less) on a stone, piece of wood, or plant leaf. Soft, slightly acid to neutral water is required for egg development. The fry are too small to take *Artemia* nauplii and need infusorians as first food.

Apistogramma agassizii (Steindachner, 1875)
Agassiz's Dwarf Cichlid (Agassizii, Aggie)

Overview: An old favorite dwarf cichlid, but quite demanding in its maintenance and breeding. The tail-form in males is unique, within the genus and among cichlids in general. Coloration is very variable and several forms have been line-bred, notably the red-tailed. These are not geographical forms as often stated.

Native Range: Small clear and blackwater forest streams along almost the entire Ucayali and main Amazon drainages.

Maximum Length: 4 in (10 cm) TL.

Water: 77–82°F (24–28°C); pH: 6.0–6.8; hardness: 0–5°dGH.

Min. Tank Size: 15 gal | 24x12x12 in (50 L | 60x30x30 cm).

Feeding: Tank-breds will take flake but wild fish require live foods, such as _Daphnia_ and bloodworms. Frozen foods may also be accepted.

Behavior & Care: Requires a well-planted tank with fine substrate. Susceptible to incorrect water chemistry and less-than-perfect water quality. Prefers muted lighting so ensure the décor provides shade. Can be kept with other small peaceful fishes.

Breeding: The sexes differ in size, color, and finnage. Can be bred in pairs or harems, with brood care by the females. Provide caves with small entrances and low ceilings, on which the eggs are laid.

Apistogramma borellii (Regan, 1906)
Borelli's Dwarf Cichlid (Reitzigi, Umbrella Dwarf Cichlid)

Overview: A fairly hardy and easy-to-breed *Apistogramma*, in which females are tiny compared to males. The latter occur in a number of different geographical color variants. Male finnage is relatively "cichlid normal" compared to many Apistos. Still sometimes sold as *A. reitzigi*, which is a synonym.

Native Range: Brazil, Paraguay, Bolivia: upper/central Rio Paraguay system, Pantanal, and the Mato Grosso area.

Maximum Length: 3.5 in (8.5 cm) TL.

Water: 75–82°F (24–28°C); pH: 6.0–7.2; hardness: 0–5°dGH.

Min. Tank Size: 15 gal | 24x12x12 in (50 L | 60x30x30 cm).

Feeding: Most stocks are tank-bred and will take flake but wild fish may require live or frozen foods, e.g. *Daphnia* and bloodworms.

Behavior & Care: Tolerates hard, alkaline water but shows better color in optimal conditions. Sensitive to poor water quality. Provide a well-planted tank with fine substrate and caves with low ceilings and small entrances. Can be kept with small, peaceful tankmates.

Breeding: Easy to breed. The sexes differ in size, color, and finnage. A cave-spawner that usually breeds in pairs. The male may help with brood care, sometimes "kidnapping" all or part of the brood.

Apistogramma cacatuoides Hoedeman, 1951
Cockatoo Dwarf Cichlid (Big-mouth Apisto)

Overview: A fairly hardy dwarf cichlid, in which males have extended anterior dorsal fin spines like the crest of a cockatoo—hence the scientific and hobby names. Unfortunately the species is rather short-lived. The extent of the caudal- and dorsal-fin spotting is variable; there is an aquarium strain bred for enhanced spotting.

Native Range: Rio Ucayali basin in northeastern Peru; Amazon basin in southeastern Colombia and western Brazil.

Maximum Length: 3.5 in (8.5 cm) TL.

Water: 75–82°F (24–28°C); pH: 6.0–7.5; hardness: 0–10°dGH.

Min. Tank Size: 15 gal | 24x12x12 in (50 L | 60x30x30 cm).

Feeding: Tank-bred stocks will take flake but wild fish may refuse all but live or frozen foods (e.g. *Daphnia*), initially at least.

Behavior & Care: Tolerates, and will breed in, hard, alkaline water. Sensitive to poor water quality. Requires a well-planted tank with fine substrate and caves with low ceilings and small entrances. Can be kept with small, peaceful tankmates.

Breeding: An easy-to-breed cave-spawner, ideally kept in harems of 3–4 females per male. The sexes differ in size and finnage. Tends to produce more males than females in hard, alkaline water.

Apistogramma nijsseni Kullander, 1979
Panda Dwarf Cichlid (Nijsseni, Nijssen's Dwarf Cichlid)

Overview: This little fish created a sensation when it was first introduced to the hobby, and remains very popular, along with its very similar cousin, _A. panduro_. Males are quite colorful, but it is the black panda markings of the breeding female that are the main attraction. Will survive, but not thrive and breed, in hard water.

Native Range: South America: a rather limited area of small forest waters in the Rio Ucayali drainage in eastern Peru.

Maximum Length: 3.5 in (9 cm) TL.

Water: 75–82°F (24–28°C); pH: 5.5–7.0; hardness: 0–10°dGH.

Min. Tank Size: 20 gal | 30x12x12 in (65 L | 75x30x30 cm).

Feeding: Most stocks are tank-bred and will take flake, but live or frozen foods will encourage breeding.

Behavior & Care: Quite robust for the genus, including in its behavior towards tankmates if the tank is too small. Requires a well-planted tank with fine substrate and plenty of caves.

Breeding: A cave-brooder that forms pairs or harems depending on space and female availability. The sex ratio of the brood is affected by temperature and pH: low pH and high temperature (within the range given) produces more males, and the reverse more females.

Astatotilapia latifasciata (Regan, 1929)
Zebra Obliquidens (Haplochromis Obliquidens)

Overview: A colorful "hap" (haplochromine cichlid), for a long time misidentified as the Lake Victoria species, *Haplochromis obliquidens.* A good mouthbrooder for beginners, as it is relatively peaceful and can be kept in a species tank or as part of a community of "haps" of similar temperament.

Native Range: East Africa: Lake Nawampasa and other lakes in the Kyoga basin in Uganda. Endangered in the wild.

Maximum Length: 5 in (12.5 cm) TL.

Water: 75–82°F (24–28°C); pH: 7.0–7.5; hardness: 5–15°dGH.

Min. Tank Size: 38 gal | 36x16x16 in (140 L | 90x40x40 cm).

Feeding: The natural diet is algae and aquatic invertebrates; does well on small feeds of *Spirulina* flake and live/frozen foods.

Behavior & Care: Best kept in a group of one male and 2–4 females in a well-planted tank with open gravel where the male may dig a spawning pit.

Breeding: Like all "haps," this fish is a maternal mouthbrooder, and pairs only for the duration of spawning. The female then seeks a quiet spot to brood eggs and fry for 20–22 days. Both sexes are colorful, but males are larger and more vividly colored.

Astronotus ocellatus (Agassiz, 1831)
Oscar (Peacock Cichlid, Marbled Cichlid, Velvet Cichlid)

Overview: A large cichlid, often purchased as a juvenile in ignorance of its eventual size. Can be destructive of equipment and décor, and will eat smaller tankmates. Nevertheless, a fish of great character that makes an excellent pet. Available in several man-made color varieties.

Native Range: South America: mainstream Ucayali-Amazon as well as the lower parts of some major Amazon tributaries.

Maximum Length: 12 in (30 cm) TL.

Water: 75–82°F (24–28°C); pH: 6.0–8.0; hardness: 5–20°dGH.

Min. Tank Size: 65 gal | 48x18x18 in (240 L | 20x45x45 cm).

Feeding: Live or raw fish, shrimps, mussels, earthworms, pellets. A varied diet is required to avoid digestive problems.

Behavior & Care: Effective filtration is essential for this greedy, messy feeder. Although it is aquarium-hardy, optimal conditions are soft, acid water and muted lighting. Providing "toys" (ping-pong balls, plastic plants) helps reduce destructive behavior.

Breeding: Oscars are pair-forming substrate spawners that may produce more than a thousand fry per brood. Almost impossible to sex, and two females may "pair" if no male is present.

Astronotus ocellatus. This is a juvenile common Oscar.

Astronotus ocellatus. Albino Oscar, juvenile.

These appealing babies beg like puppies to be taken home from the pet shop. Like puppies, they grow up—while you don't need a fenced yard to keep an Oscar, you do need quite a large tank.

Aulonocara sp., possibly one of the many forms of *A. stuartgranti."*

Aulonocara maylandia, Sulfurhead Aulonocara.

Aulonocara spp. are Malawi cichlids, but they are not mbuna. They are less aggressive than mbuna and do not generally fare well when kept with them.

Aulonocara jacobfreibergi (Johnson, 1974)
Malawi Butterfly (Jacobfreibergi, Trevori, Reginae, and others)

Overview: A rather peaceful cichlid that occurs in a number of geographical color variants, many of which have been given individual trade names. As with all *Aulonocara*, only the males are colorful, but their brilliance and their elegant form more than make up for the drab females.

Native Range: East Africa: endemic to Lake Malawi, where it is found in areas where rocks meet sand.

Maximum Length: 5.5 in (14 cm) TL.

Water: 77–85°F (25–28°C); pH: 7.5–8.5; hardness: 5–20°dGH.

Min. Tank Size: 38 gal | 36x16x16 in (140 L | 90x40x40 cm).

Feeding: The natural food is aquatic invertebrates taken from the sand; best fed on live or frozen foods such as *Daphnia*, *Artemia*.

Behavior & Care: Can be kept in a group in a species tank, or in a larger tank with other Malawis of similar temperament and size. Never mix with aggressive rock-dwelling mbuna. Décor should be rockwork and open sand. Well-oxygenated water is essential.

Breeding: A maternal mouthbrooder in which male and female associate only to spawn. The female then retires to a quiet spot to brood for about 21 days, then releases the fry.

Aulonocara stuartgranti Meyer & Riehl, 1985
Malawi Peacock (Aulonocara Nyassae, Blue Neon, etc.)

Overview: This rather peaceful cichlid is still erroneously sold as *A. nyassae*, a species probably never imported. There are various geographical color forms, most with their own hobby names. Like all *Aulonocara* it uses a sonar-like system to locate invertebrates in the sand, then dives headfirst into the substrate to catch them.

Native Range: East Africa: endemic to Lake Malawi, where it is found in the "intermediate zone"—areas where rocks meet sand.

Maximum Length: 5.5 in (14 cm) TL.

Water: 77–82°F (35–38°C); pH: 7.5–8.5; hardness: 5–20°dGH.

Min. Tank Size: 38 gal | 36x16x16 in (140 L | 90x40x40 cm).

Feeding: Avoid too much dry food; best fed on live or frozen foods such as *Daphnia*, bloodworms, *Artemia*, etc, plus chopped shrimp.

Behavior & Care: Can be kept in a species tank (2–3 females per male), or in a larger tank with other peaceful Malawis. Never mix with the aggressive rock-dwelling mbuna. Well-oxygenated water is essential. The décor should be rockwork and sand or fine gravel.

Breeding: As for *A. jacobfreibergi*. Females are similar to those of some other *Aulonocara*, and males (as well as aquarists) cannot tell them apart, so avoid mixing species—otherwise hybrids may occur.

Chalinochromis brichardi Poll, 1974
Bridled Cichlid

Overview: Although this cichlid isn't brilliantly colored, its attractive facial markings have won it popularity. In nature it lives solitary except when breeding, and hence wild fishes can be rather aggressive in the confines of the aquarium. This can be avoided by growing on several young tank-breds so they are used to company.

Native Range: East Africa: endemic to Lake Tanganyika, in rocky habitat at the northern and southern extremes of the lake.

Maximum Length: 6.5 in (16 cm).

Water: 77–82°F (25–28°C); pH 7.5–9.0; hardness 10–25°dGH.

Min. Tank Size: 38 gal | 36x16x16 in (140 L | 90x40x40 cm).

Feeding: In nature this species picks aquatic invertebrates from rocks. Feed live or frozen foods as staple, with occasional flake.

Behavior & Care: Can be kept as a pair in the tank size cited, or as part of a low-population Tanganyikan community in larger quarters. Tankmates should be of similar temperament. Provide plenty of rockwork, plus well-oxygenated (not turbulent), top quality water.

Breeding: These cichlids are pair-forming cave-brooders, and both parents defend their young vigorously. Males are larger but there are no color differences between the sexes.

Copadichromis borleyi (Iles, 1960)
Borleyi (Borley's Cichlid, Kadango Redfin, Red Empress)

Overview: One of most colorful of the utaka, the plankton-feeding open-water cichlids of Lake Malawi, which are typically found in huge mixed species shoals following the inshore plankton. Males are only territorial for short periods (else they would starve!), and so these are relatively peaceful cichlids.

Native Range: East Africa: endemic to Lake Malawi. Found lake-wide, usually near rocks, in various geographical color variants.

Maximum Length: 7 in (16 cm) TL.

Water: 75–82°F (24–28°C); pH: 7.5–8.5; hardness: 5–20°dGH.

Min. Tank Size: 65 gal | 48x18x18 in (240 L | 120x45x45 cm).

Feeding: Ideally planktonic live (and frozen) foods such as *Daphnia*, *Cyclops*, *Artemia*, mosquito larvae. Avoid too much dry food.

Behavior & Care: Keep a male and two-plus females with other utaka or peaceful sand-dwellers, e.g. *Aulonocara*. Mix only species found together in nature or with clearly different females, else hybrids may occur. Provide a rocky backdrop and well-oxygenated water.

Breeding: Maternal mouthbrooder. Spawning typically takes place against a vertical rock face. Dominant males are larger and more colorful than females, but subdominant males may be deceptive.

Crenicichla compressiceps Ploeg, 1986
Compressiceps Dwarf Pike Cichlid

Overview: The pike cichlids of the genus *Crenicichla* include not only large piscivorous species, but also dwarfs like this one, whose menu consists largely of aquatic invertebrates. They are often very attractive, but despite their small size, they can be rather thuggish during courtship, and require plenty of space.

Native Range: South America: the Rio Tocantins drainage.

Maximum Length: 3.5 in (9 cm) TL.

Water: 77–82°F (25–28°C); pH: 6.0–6.8; hardness: 0–5°dGH.

Min. Tank Size: 50 gal | 48x16x16 in (190 L | 120x40x40 cm).

Feeding: Best fed on live or frozen foods to simulate the natural diet, though will take flake once acclimated to aquarium life.

Behavior & Care: Best kept in a large tank in a group so there is partner choice. Provide plenty of hiding places (bogwood and rockwork) and top quality water. The tank can be shared with small non-cichlid tankmates requiring similar water and décor.

Breeding: This cichlid is virtually unsexable—a further reason for keeping a group. Pairs, once formed, are usually permanent and compatible. 40–80 eggs are laid on the ceiling of a cave. Care of eggs and larvae is mainly by the female, but both parents guard the fry.

Cryptoheros nigrofasciatus (Günther, 1867)
Convict Cichlid (Cichlasoma Nigrofasciatum)

Overview: A well-known ichthyologist once remarked that you can keep and breed Convicts in a Coke bottle on your desk. That may be an exaggeration, but this is one of the hardiest and easiest cichlids, ideal for beginners. However, it is quite feisty and not for the general community, though sometimes sold as such. There is an albino aquarium variety as well as the natural striped form.

Native Range: Central America: Atlantic-slope drainages from Honduras to Panama, Pacific-slope from Guatemala to Costa Rica.

Maximum Length: 5.5 in (14 cm) TL.

Water: 75–82°F (24–28°C); pH: 7.0–9.0; hardness: 5–30°dGH.

Min. Tank Size: 20 gal | 24x12x16 in (70 L | 60x30x40 cm).

Feeding: Will eat anything with gusto, and thrive on it.

Behavior & Care: Best kept as a pair in a species tank, as likely to harass tankmates, even larger ones. Provide a cave or two (clay flowerpots or pipes are liked), but no plants, as Convicts dig a lot.

Breeding: There has to be something very wrong for Convicts not to breed. Males are larger with longer fins; females have a metallic area in the dorsal fin. 60–200 eggs are laid in a cave and tended by the female. Excellent parents that guard their fry assiduously.

Cryptoheros sajica (Bussing, 1974)
T-Bar Cichlid (Sajica)

Overview: A cousin of the Convict Cichlid, rather more demanding though still quite hardy. Very similar in appearance to some other *Cryptoheros*, especially the Blue- or Jade-Eyed Cichlid, *C. spilurus*, but always recognizable by the on-its-side T-marking on the flank. The smallest member of its genus.

Native Range: Central America: small watercourses in Pacific-slope drainages in Costa Rica, in rather soft, slightly acid water.

Maximum Length: 4.5 in (11.25 cm) TL.

Water: 75–82°F (24–28°C); pH: 6.5–7.5; hardness: 5–10°dGH.

Min. Tank Size: 20 gal | 24x12x16 in (70 L | 60x30x40 cm).

Feeding: Omnivorous with a herbivore bias in nature. Will take most foods, but ensure there is a reasonable vegetable element.

Behavior & Care: Like most Central American cichlids, best kept as a pair in a species tank. Unlike most "Centrals", can be touchy about water conditions—chemistry and quality. Unfussy about décor as long as caves are available. Likely to dig pits when breeding.

Breeding: In common with other *Cryptoheros*, this is a pair-forming cave-brooder, in which males are larger and females have a metallic area in the dorsal. Excellent parents that produce up to 200 fry.

Cyphotilapia frontosa (Boulenger, 1906)
Frontosa (Tanganyika Humphead)

Overview: A popular cichlid that grows a lot larger than many aquarists realize! In nature adults are active only at dawn and dusk, and in captivity they like to spend the day lazing in a cave—often several huddled together in one large cave. Ridiculously peaceful for its size, and can be kept in groups with more than one male.

Native Range: East Africa: endemic to Lake Tanganyika, where it is found lake-wide in rocky habitat, often at some depth.

Maximum Length: 16 in (40 cm) TL. Mostly 12 in (30 cm) in aquaria.

Water: 75–80°F (24–27°C); pH: 7.5–9.0; hardness: 10–25°dGH.

Min. Tank Size: 65 gal | 48x18x18 in (240 L | 120x45x45 cm).

Feeding: In the wild (and sometimes in the aquarium!) the diet is small cichlids, taken when drowsy at dawn and dusk. The menu should include raw fish, but shrimps, earthworms, and pellets are taken too.

Behavior & Care: Its slothful existence means this cichlid doesn't need a lot of space in relative terms, and 5–6 can be kept in the tank size cited. Provide large caves and well-oxygenated water.

Breeding: Maternal mouthbrooder. If more than one male is kept, one will become dominant after an unnoticeable power struggle, and father any young. The brooding period is an unusually long 5 weeks.

Cyprichromis leptosoma (Boulenger, 1898)
Leptosoma (Blue Flash Cypricichlid)

Overview: *Cyprichromis* and the similar *Paracyprichromis* are rather delicate cichlids that look more like cyprinids, hence their collective name cypricichlid. Males hold territories in open water near rocks by day, then at dusk descend to the bottom, where they are the main element in the diet of *Cyphotilapia frontosa*!

Native Range: East Africa: endemic to Lake Tanganyika. Several geographical variants in male coloration are known.

Maximum Length: 3.5 in (9 cm) TL.

Water: 75–82°F (24–28°C); pH: 7.5–9.0; hardness: 10–25°dGH.

Min. Tank Size: 65 gal | 48x18x18 in (240 L | 120x45x45 cm).

Feeding: A zooplankton feeder, so wild specimens may take only swimming live foods such as *Daphnia*, at least initially. Even tank-breds often won't follow food down but take it only as it passes.

Behavior & Care: Best kept in a shoal of 10 or more in a deep tank, with small Tanganyikan rock- and shell-dwellers below to fill the space and eat any food that reaches lower levels. Requires a rocky backdrop and well-oxygenated, very good quality water.

Breeding: A maternal mouthbrooder in which male and female get together only to spawn. Females are smaller and not colorful.

Cyrtocara moorii Boulenger, 1902
Blue Dolphin Cichlid (Malawi Humphead)

Overview: Behaviorally one of the most interesting Malawi species. In the wild it follows large sand-sifting cichlids, feeding on anything edible they stir up. Dominant males treat their "host" sifter as a mobile territory, which they defend against rivals, but allowing females and subdominant males to share.

Native Range: East Africa: endemic to Lake Malawi where it is found lake-wide over sandy bottoms in fairly shallow water.

Maximum Length: 8 in (20 cm) TL.

Water: 77–82°F (25–28°C); pH: 7.5–8.5; hardness: 5–20°dGH.

Min. Tank Size: 65 gal | 48x18x18 in (240 L | 120x45x45 cm).

Feeding: Live and frozen foods, chopped shrimp and mussel, and dried foods—but feed the last of these only in small amounts.

Behavior & Care: It is impossible to simulate the natural, mobile, environment, but this fish does well in captivity provided it has plenty of open space and other peaceful Malawi "haps" as tankmates—never the aggressive mbuna. Well-oxygenated water essential.

Breeding: Males are larger, with a larger hump. Because the sexes live together in nature there is no problem with male aggression. A maternal mouthbrooder with an incubation period of 20–22 days.

Dicrossus filamentosus (Ladiges, 1959)
Lyre-tailed Checkerboard Cichlid

Overview: A very attractive dwarf cichlid in its coloration and form, but rather tricky to keep and even trickier to breed, and best tried after practicing on some of the hardier *Apistogramma* species. Water chemistry and quality are particularly important.

Native Range: South America: Rio Negro and Rio Orinoco.

Maximum Length: 3.5 in (8.5 cm) TL.

Water: 77–82°F (25–28°C); pH: 4.5–6.5; hardness: 0–3°dGH.

Min. Tank Size: 38 gal | 36x16x16 in (140 L | 90x40x40 cm).

Feeding: Although these cichlids will usually take flake, they benefit tremendously from a diet of live and frozen foods.

Behavior & Care: Best kept in a small group in a roomy tank with plenty of cover (plants, bogwood, caves). The water must be very soft and acid and of exceptional quality. *Corydoras* catfishes and small characins are useful to give these little cichlids confidence.

Breeding: Easily sexed by the long tail filaments in males. Breeds in pairs or harems. The eggs are usually attached to a plant leaf and guarded by the female alone. A pH of 4.5–5.5 is required for viability. Brood care is of short duration and the fry are best removed and reared separately to avoid predation by tankmates.

Dimidichromis compressiceps (Boulenger, 1908)
Malawi Eye-biter

Overview: Do not be put off by the common name of this fish! Its main food in nature is the fry of other cichlids, which it stalks by lurking among reeds. Its bizarre, highly compressed body and angular, pointed head are ideally suited to this way of life. It is actually rather timid and more likely to be victim than bully.

Native Range: East Africa: only in lakes Malawi and Malombe.

Maximum Length: 9 in (23 cm) TL.

Water: 77–82°F (25–28°C); pH: 7.5–8.5; hardness: 5–20°dGH.

Min. Tank Size: 65 gal | 48x18x18 in (240 L | 120x45x45 cm).

Feeding: Chopped raw fish and shrimp; live and frozen foods. Will eat flake and small pellets but feed these sparingly.

Behavior & Care: Keep a male and two or more females in a community of Malawi "haps" of similar size. Do not keep with the aggressive rock-dwelling mbuna. Ideally provide thickets of long-leaved plants such as *Vallisneria*. Well-oxygenated water.

Breeding: Males are larger and more colorful. A maternal mouthbrooder with no permanent pairing. Males dig shallow pits in which to spawn. The female broods in a secluded spot for 20–22 days, in nature releasing her fry into shoals of the young of other cichlids.

Eretmodus cyanostictus Boulenger, 1898
Horseface Goby Cichlid

Overview: The goby cichlids are a small group of species that live in the surf zone in Lake Tanganyika, and are characterized by a rather comical appearance and by having a reduced swimbladder so that they move in hops. Quite difficult to keep, aggressive for their size, and unusual in being biparental mouthbrooders.

Native Range: East Africa: endemic to Lake Tanganyika, and found in the upper levels of rocky habitats in the south of the lake.

Maximum Length: 3.5 in (9 cm) TL.

Water: 77–82°F (25–28°C); pH: 7.5–9.0; hardness: 10–25°dGH.

Min. Tank Size: 38 gal | 36x16x16 in (140 L | 90x40x40 cm).

Feeding: The natural diet is algae and aquatic invertebrates, so feed *Spirulina* flake and live/frozen foods such as bloodworm.

Behavior & Care: Best kept in pairs or a group of six or more. Provide a large amount of rockwork extending close to the surface in places, and very well oxygenated, good quality water. Can form part of a community of small Tanganyikan rock-dwellers.

Breeding: The sexes look identical. The female broods for the first 10–12 days, then transfers them to the male who broods them for a further period of similar length. Broods are small.

Etroplus maculatus (Bloch, 1795)
Orange Chromide (Red Chromide, Yellow Chromide)

Overview: The chromides are three closely-related cichlids found in Asia, their closest relatives being found in Madagascar. The Orange and the much larger Green (or Silver) Chromide (*E. suratensis*) are found in brackish water and occur together, sharing a fascinating symbiotic relationship.

Native Range: Asia: Sri Lanka and the southern part of India, in coastal lagoons and estuaries, sometimes some distance upriver.

Maximum Length: 4 in (10 cm) TL.

Water: 75–82°F (24–28°C); pH: 7.5–9.0; hardness: 10–25°dGH.

Min. Tank Size: 25 gal | 24x16x16 in (95 L | 60x40x40 cm).

Feeding: Will take any carnivore or omnivore food of suitable size.

Behavior & Care: Brackish water not essential, but the addition of salt is beneficial. Unfussy about décor but requires hiding places. Do not use real wood or live plants in brackish water. May eat very small tankmates. Several pairs can be obtained and kept together in a large tank by growing on 6–8 (unsexable) youngsters.

Breeding: In the wild, breeds in colonies of pairs, laying eggs on a stone, usually sheltered by plants or wood. Males are larger; mature females have white on the upper and lower edges of the tail.

Geophagus steindachneri Eigenmann & Hildebrand, 1910
Redhump Geophagus (Redhump Eartheater)

Overview: "Eartheaters" is the name given to a group of South American cichlids, the geophagines, that sift the bottom for food and whose main range lies east of the Andes. The Redhump is one of a group of three that have settled among the cordilleras of the north west. All are highly evolved maternal mouthbrooders, like those found in Africa—an example of parallel evolution.

Native Range: South America: northern Colombia and Venezuela.

Maximum Length: 8 in (20 cm) TL.

Water: 75–82°F (24–28°C); pH: 6.5–7.5; hardness: 5–15°dGH.

Min. Tank Size: 38 gal | 36x16x16 in (140L | 90x40x40 cm).

Feeding: Despite their size, eartheaters are designed to feed on small particles (animal and vegetable); any small foods will suit. Feed the fry on *Artemia* nauplii and microworm.

Behavior & Care: Can be kept as a pair, but males develop their magnificent mob-cap-like humps only if multiple males are kept, in a suitably spacious tank. Sandy, siftable, substrate required.

Breeding: Males are larger and more colorful, and always have a reddish crown, even before the hump develops. The eggs are laid on a flat stone and picked up by the female, who broods for 19–22 days.

Gymnogeophagus balzanii (Perugia, 1891)
Balzani's Cichlid

Overview: *Gymnogeophagus* are also eartheaters, with a southerly, partly sub-tropical distribution in eastern South America. Most require a "winter rest" at reduced temperature to stay healthy, but this one is the exception. Possibly aquarium stocks originate from the warmer part of its range. A larvophilous mouthbrooder.

Native Range: South America: the Paraguay-Paraná and Uruguay systems, and the upper Rio Guaporé in Brazil and Bolivia.

Maximum Length: 8 in (20 cm) TL.

Water: 70–82°F (21–28°C); pH: 6.0–7.0; hardness: 2–10°dGH.

Min. Tank Size: 38 gal | 36x16x16 in (140L | 90x40x40 cm).

Feeding: Any small foods will suit, but a varied diet is optimal: live and frozen foods, chopped shrimp and earthworms, flake.

Behavior & Care: Can be kept as a pair but a group is better, in a suitably large tank. Tends to be shy, so any tankmates must be non-boisterous. Requires an open area of fine, siftable substrate, and plenty of cover round the tank margins. Avoid bright lighting.

Breeding: Males are larger and more colorful, and have a humped head. The eggs are laid on a stone and covered with sand; when they hatch the female picks up and mouthbroods the larvae for 7–8 days.

***Haplochromis* sp. 'Flameback'**
Flameback

Overview: One of the few Lake Victoria "haps" that has achieved wide popularity, no doubt because of its brilliant colors and ease of maintenance. The colors often do not show in aquarium-store tanks, but this fish will blossom in the home aquarium once it has settled in. Only the males are colorful.

Native Range: East Africa: Lake Victoria.

Maximum Length: 3.5 in (9 cm) TL.

Water: 77–82°F (25–28°C); pH: 7.0–8.0; hardness: 5–15°dGH.

Min. Tank Size: 38 gal | 36x16x16 in (140L | 90x40x40 cm).

Feeding: Will take almost any aquarium foods of suitable size.

Behavior & Care: Males are not very territorial so more than one can be kept (allow at least 16 in (40 cm) of tank length per male). The ideal sex ratio is two or more females per male. Plenty of cover is needed as the species is shy, and the back and ends of the tank should be "blocked out" for security. Can be mixed with other peaceful "haps" but make sure the females are different enough to avoid hybrids.

Breeding: Maternal mouthbrooder with no pair bond. The female broods the 50–80 eggs and larvae for 20–22 days.

__Hemichromis lifalili__ Loiselle, 1979
Dwarf Red Jewel Cichlid (Lifalili)

Overview: The Jewel Cichlid (*H. guttatus*) was a popular cichlid before the introduction of colorful Rift Lake cichlids, because of its stunning coloration and despite its atrocious (aggressive) behavior. This slightly smaller but equally colorful species is far better behaved and has gained quite a following.

Native Range: Central Africa: Congo and Democratic Republic of Congo, Central African Republic; mainly in forest waters.

Maximum Length: 4 in (10 cm) TL.

Water: 75–82°F (24–28°C); pH: 6.0–7.5; hardness: 5–10°dGH.

Min. Tank Size: 38 gal | 36x16x16 in (140L | 90x40x40 cm).

Feeding: In nature, aquatic invertebrates and fish fry. Feed live and frozen foods, chopped worms and shrimp, and good quality flake.

Behavior & Care: No more than one pair per tank, when adult, as this species is still quite territorial. Can be kept with other fishes as long as there is plenty of escape space. Planted tank with caves.

Breeding: Unsexable, so best to grow on half a dozen young until a pair forms naturally. Spawns on a stone in the open but near shelter. Excellent parents that defend the brood against all comers. The fry can take newly hatched brine shrimp and microworm as first foods.

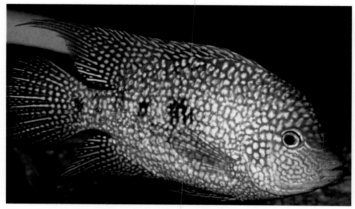

Herichthys carpintis (Jordan & Snyder, 1899)
Texas Cichlid (Carpinte)

Overview: The true Texas Cichlid, found in that state, is in fact *H. cyanoguttatus*, but this one (once thought a subspecies) has carried the name in the hobby for decades. It is also a far more stunningly colored cichlid, deservedly an evergreen.

Native Range: Central America: Atlantic slope drainages in northern Mexico. Has extended its range via irrigation channels.

Maximum Length: 10 in (25 cm) TL.

Water: 75–82°F (24–28°C); pH: 7.5–8.5; hardness: 10–30°dGH.

Min. Tank Size: 65 gal | 48x18x18 in (240 L | 120x45x45 cm).

Feeding: Omnivorous with herbivore tendencies. Feed a mixed diet including vegetable foods (e.g. veggie pellets). Loves earthworms.

Behavior & Care: Relatively peaceful for its size but not a community fish; keep as a pair in a species tank, with an armored (loricariid) catfish or two if desired. Hardy and not fussy about décor but should have hiding places. Likely to uproot plants.

Breeding: Male and female coloration is similar, but males are larger with longer finnage, and develop a humped head with age. Both sexes change color dramatically when breeding, showing lots of black. Up to 600 eggs are laid on a stone in the open.

Heros efasciatus Heckel, 1840
Severum (Deacon, Poor Man's Discus)

Overview: Long thought to be *H. severus* (formerly *Cichlasoma severum*, hence the common name). The latter is now known to be a mouthbrooder, restricted to the upper Rio Negro, while this is a substrate spawner. Most "unusual" (and expensive) *Heros* that crop up in the trade are just geographical variants of this species. There is a "man-made" gold form derived from an aquarium sport.

Native Range: South America: Rios Ucayali and Amazon in Peru and Brazil, and lower parts of tributaries, including the Rio Negro.

Maximum Length: 12 in (30 cm) TL.

Water: 75–82°F (24–28°C); pH: 6.5–8.0; hardness: 3–20°dGH.

Min. Tank Size: 65 gal | 48x18x18 in (240 L | 120x45x45 cm).

Feeding: Any of the usual aquarium fare; include vegetable foods.

Behavior & Care: One of a few large neotropical cichlids that can be kept in groups or with others of similar temperament, though a full-grown male may decide otherwise! Aquarium strains are hardy, but soft acid water is needed for breeding and for wild fish.

Breeding: Males usually have spotted scales, females unspotted, when adult. Up to 1000 eggs are laid on a solid substrate, by preference well off the bottom (e.g. on top of bogwood).

Herotilapia multispinosa (Günther, 1867)
Rainbow Cichlid

Overview: The nearest Central America has to offer to a peaceful cichlid, as it lives in small groups in nature. The common name relates to the variability of its color pattern, apparently depending on whether it wishes to be camouflaged or conspicuous.

Native Range: Central America: Honduras, Costa Rica, and Nicaragua (including the Nicaraguan lakes). Prefers vegetated zones in shallow, still or slow-moving water.

Maximum Length: 6 in (15 cm) TL.

Water: 75–82°F (24–28°C); pH: 7.5–9.0; hardness: 5–25°dGH.

Min. Tank Size: 30 gal | 36x12x16 in (105 L | 90x30x40 cm).

Feeding: Primarily herbivorous in the wild, but enjoys small carnivore foods and in practice will eat almost anything.

Behavior & Care: More than one pair can be kept, or can be mixed with pairs of *Cryptoheros* or *Thorichthys* (allow 18 in [45 cm] of tank length per cichlid pair) or resilient non-cichlid tankmates. Very temperature tolerant, and generally extremely hardy.

Breeding: Difficult to sex, so it is beneficial to grow on 5–6 youngsters and maintain a group. Spawns on a semi-sheltered hard substrate (e.g. a stone among plants), and will breed almost continuously.

Hypsophrys nicaraguensis (Günther, 1864)
Nicaraguan Cichlid (Nica)

Overview: A very attractive and interesting cichlid. Although nominally a substrate-brooder, it appears to be in the early stages of evolving mouthbrooding as the eggs are non-adhesive and are laid in a pit, and sometimes taken into the mouth temporarily.

Native Range: Central America: Costa Rica and Nicaragua, including the Nicaraguan lakes. Prefers moving water.

Maximum Length: 10 in (25 cm) TL, in exceptional circumstances.

Water: 75–82°F (24–28°C); pH: 7.5–9.0; hardness: 10–25°dGH.

Min. Tank Size: 30 gal | 36x12x16 in (105 L | 90x30x40 cm).

Feeding: An algae-browser in nature, so requires some vegetable food, but will take all the usual aquarium fare.

Behavior & Care: Ideally keep a single pair of Nicas in a species tank, even though they are peaceful for their size. Appreciates plenty of rockwork providing large caves both fish can enter together, and requires diggable substrate for spawning pits. Easy and hardy.

Breeding: Males larger, with a reticulated pattern when adult, losing the bright green and orange of the female. Pairs are usually very harmonious. The spawning pit is by preference dug in a large cave. Avoid strong water current as it will wash the fry away.

Julidochromis marlieri Poll, 1956
Checkered Julie (Marlier's Juli, Marlieri)

Overview: The "Julies" are among the most popular—but tricky —Tanganyikans. This species, *J. regani*, and *J.* sp. 'Gombi' are very similar in size, form, and facial markings, but differ in body pattern. They may be just forms of one species, with Gombi a geographical variant and *regani* a habitat-determined colour variant, occurring where rocks meet sand rather than over pure rocks.

Native Range: East Africa: endemic to Lake Tanganyika.

Maximum Length: 5 in (13 cm).

Water: 75-82°F (24-28°C); pH: 7.5-9.0; hardness: 10-30°dGH.

Min. Tank Size: 30 gal | 30x16x16 in (120 L | 75x40x40 cm).

Feeding: Will take flake and granules, but live/frozen food better.

Behavior & Care: The water must be well oxygenated and very good quality. Masses of rockwork providing small caves. One pair of one Julie species per tank is the rule, and the larger Julies are best kept in species tanks rather than a Tanganyikan community.

Breeding: May produce largish broods at long intervals or "trickle spawn" a few regularly. Mated Julies, especially once they have young, often react to any disturbance by "divorcing" with one killing the other. Even water changes require care and delicacy of touch.

Julidochromis ornatus Boulenger, 1898
Ornate Julie (Ornatus)

Overview: This species, like _J. marlieri_, has a "habitat analogue", in this case _J. transcriptus_, which is the pure rock-dweller of the pair, while _ornatus_ is found where rocks meet sand. These smaller Julies are particularly noted for hugging the rocks with their bellies, swimming on their sides or even upside down to do so. They are also adept at swimming backwards out of tight crannies.

Native Range: East Africa: endemic to Lake Tanganyika. The base color exhibits some local variation, from almost white to ochre.

Maximum Length: 3.5 in (9 cm) TL.

Water: 75-82°F (24-28°C); pH: 7.5-9.0; hardness: 10-30°dGH.

Min. Tank Size: 25 gal | 24x16x16 in (95 L | 60x40x40 cm).

Feeding: Will take flake and granules, but live/frozen food better.

Behavior & Care: One pair of one Julie species per tank is again the rule, but the small species can also be mixed with other small Tanganyikans (rock- and shell-dwellers, cypricichlids) in a sparsely populated community. Water and rockwork as for _J. marlieri_.

Breeding: As for _J. marlieri_. As in all Julies, the sexes are similar but the male genital papilla is always visible, though usually pressed against a rock so it cannot be seen! Males are also eventually larger.

Labeotropheus fuelleborni Ahl, 1926
Fuelleborn's Cichlid (Fuelleborni)

Overview: _Labeotropheus_ belong to the so-called mbuna of Lake Malawi—a group of colorful but mainly very territorial rock-dwelling cichlids. There are just two species (the other is _L. trewavasae_), characterized by an underslung slit mouth and a bulbous nose which is used as a fulcrum to lever algae from rocks. Both species occur in geographical and sex-linked color morphs.
Native Range: East Africa: endemic to Lake Malawi, lake-wide.
Maximum Length: 6 in (15 cm) TL.
Water: 77–82°F (25–28°C); pH: 7.5–8.5; hardness: 5–20°dGH.
Minimum Tank Size: 65 gal | 48x18x18 in (240 L | 120x45x45 cm).
Feeding: In nature, algae and invertebrates. Feed live and frozen foods, chopped shrimp and mussel, and greens (e.g. spinach, lettuce); avoid beef heart and too much dry food which may cause "Bloat."
Behavior & Care: Keep in a crowded mbuna community packed with rockwork extending to the surface. Ideally, one male and two-plus females. Requires good quality, well-oxygenated water.
Breeding: Male and female are differently colored. Maternal mouthbrooder; the sexes pair only to spawn. Clutches are small (20–80). Females may need to be removed to brooding tanks.

Labeotropheus trewavasae, Trewavasae.

Melanochromis chipokae, female; male Chipokae have blue-black bands.

"Controlled crowding" is often used in mbuna aquaria to curtail aggression. A relatively large number of fishes are kept in a setup with no available territories and excellent filtration.

Labidochromis caeruleus Fryer, 1956
Yellow Labidochromis (Yellow Lab, Caeruleus)

Overview: *Labidochromis* are the nearest thing to peaceful mbuna, and ideal for the beginner with the group. They include algae-browsers and invertebrate-pickers. This one occurs in blue and white color forms as well as the yellow most commonly available.

Native Range: East Africa: endemic to Lake Malawi, north to central west and east coasts, in rocky habitats.

Maximum Length: 4 in (10 cm) TL.

Water: 77–82°F (25–28°C); pH: 7.5–8.5; hardness: 5–20°dGH.

Min. Tank Size: 25 gal | 24x16x16 in (95 L | 60x40x40 cm).

Feeding: Invertebrate-picker. Live/frozen foods, chopped shrimp and mussel. Beef heart and too much dry food may cause "Bloat."

Behavior & Care: Probably the only mbuna that can be kept in a small species tank, with more than one male present, without bloodshed. It can also be kept in a community of the less territorial mbuna. Lots of rockwork and good quality, well-oxygenated water.

Breeding: Sexes similar, but males usually have more eggspots and more black in the unpaired fins. Like all mbuna, a maternal mouth-brooder with a small clutch incubated for around 21 days. Females can brood in their permanent quarters without male harassment.

Lamprologus ocellatus (Steindachner, 1909)
Ocellatus

Overview: One of the Lake Tanganyika shell-dwellers, and one of the smallest cichlids known, but very courageous—it will attack a hand placed in its tank when breeding! There is also a gold form.

Native Range: East Africa: Lake Tanganyika, shell beds lakewide.

Maximum Length: 2.5 in (6 cm) TL.

Water: 77–82°F (25–28°C); pH: 7.5–9.0; hardness: 10–25°dGH.

Min. Tank Size: 10 gal | 18x12x12 in (40 L | 45x30x30 cm).

Feeding: Small live and frozen foods; will also take flake.

Behavior & Care: Can be kept in a small species tank (one pair) or in a larger community tank of small Tanganyikans. Must have spiral shells (escargot shells are ideal) and at least 2 in (5 cm) of fine sand so the chosen shells can be buried with their openings level with the surface of the substrate. Good quality, well-oxygenated water.

Breeding: Males are larger. The pair occupy a shell apiece but spawning takes place in the female's home, and care of eggs and larvae is by the female alone. The fry remain in the mother's shell for a long time, and, once they venture out, dash back when alarmed. Feed by squirting *Artemia* nauplii and microworm close to the shell (use a syringe with a long airline "nozzle") where they will find it.

Melanochromis auratus (Boulenger, 1897)
Auratus (Nyassa Golden Cichlid)

Overview: One of the longest-established, attractive, and popular of the mbuna, but one of the most difficult in terms of male harassment of females and best not tried by the mbuna novice. *M. johanni* and *M. joanjohnsonae* are better choices for beginners.

Native Range: East Africa: endemic to the south of Lake Malawi.

Maximum Length: 5 in (12.5 cm) TL.

Water: 77–82°F (25–28°C); pH: 7.5–8.5; hardness: 5–20°dGH.

Min. Tank Size: 65 gal | 48x18x18 in (240 L | 120x45x45 cm).

Feeding: *Melanochromis* are primarily carnivorous, so feed live and frozen foods: chopped shrimp, mussel, and fish, rather than greens.

Behavior & Care: No more than one *Melanochromis* male per tank as the stripe pattern triggers aggression. Multiple females to share the male's chasing—this is not aggression but simply that he thinks their proximity means willingness to spawn. Lots of rockwork extending to the surface, and surface refuges for females (plants, cork bark). Good quality, well-oxygenated water required.

Breeding: Maternal mouthbrooder. Sexes usually different in color; females sometimes assume the reversed, male, pattern but almost never have eggspots. Remove brooding females to separate quarters.

Mesonauta sp. 'Amazonas'
Festive Cichlid (Flag Cichlid, Festivum)

Overview: It is now known that there is a whole genus of festive cichlids and not just one species as once thought. Our long-established aquarium Festivum is almost certainly not *M. festivus,* but this undescribed species from the Manaus region, where the early hobby collections were made.

Native Range: South America: mainstream Amazon basin.

Maximum Length: 9 in (23 cm) TL.

Water: 75–82°F (24–28°C); pH: 6.5–8.0; hardness: 3–20°dGH.

Min. Tank Size: 65 gal | 48x18x18 in (240 L | 120x45x45 cm).

Feeding: Any of the usual aquarium fare; include vegetable foods.

Behavior & Care: One of a few large neotropical cichlids that can be kept in groups or with others of similar temperament, e.g. *Heros, Satanoperca*, Angels (*Pterophyllum scalare*). Aquarium strains are hardy, but soft, acid water is needed for breeding and for wild fish.

Breeding: Sexes virtually identical. The eggs are laid by preference off the bottom (e.g. on bogwood or a plant). In nature this species often lives and spawns on the underside of "floating islands" of vegetation, and leads its fry from below (from above in most cichlids), so they can forage from, and remain close to, the cover above.

Metriaclima estherae (Konings, 1995)
Red Zebra (Esther's Cichlid, Estherae)

Overview: Once thought to be a color morph of *M. zebra*, this mbuna species is now known to be distinct, as is *M. callainos*, the Cobalt Zebra. In nature there are brown and orange-blotched females as well as "red," and males are blue. A red aquarium strain of males has been created and the blue is now rarely seen, which is a pity, as "natural-strain" fry are color-sexable from first release.

Native Range: East Africa: endemic to Lake Malawi; rocky shore and reefs along a short stretch of the east coast.

Maximum Length: 5.5 in (14 cm) TL. Usually smaller.

Water: 77–82°F (25–28°C); pH: 7.5–8.5; hardness: 5–20°dGH.

Min. Tank Size: 38 gal | 36x16x16 in (140 L | 90x40x40 cm).

Feeding: Live/frozen foods, chopped shrimp/mussel, greens (e.g. lettuce, spinach); beef heart and too much dry food may cause "Bloat."

Behavior & Care: One of the more peaceful mbuna. Keep in a crowded community of mbuna of similar temperament (e.g. *Labidochromis*, *Iodotropheus*, small *Pseudotropheus*, most other *Metriaclima*), with lots of rocks and good quality, well-oxygenated water.

Breeding: Easily sexed by color, or the more numerous eggspots in red-strain males. Maternal mouthbrooder with small clutches.

Metriaclima zebra (Boulenger, 1899)
Zebra (Pseudotropheus Zebra)

Overview: The stripes in males look as if they have been painted on—a cichlid to equal any coral-reef fish. Females come in two color morphs: brownish, and orange with black blotches (OB). Some OB females are as stunning as males. "Marmalade Cats," a very rare OB male form (actually blue with blotches), are much sought-after. Lots of geographical variants of the Zebra are known and some may be separate species; avoid mixing them.

Native Range: East Africa: endemic to Lake Malawi; rocky shore.

Maximum Length: 6 in (15 cm) TL.

Water: 77–82°F (25–28°C); pH: 7.5–8.5; hardness: 5–20°dGH.

Min. Tank Size: 38 gal | 36x16x16 in (140 L | 90x40x40 cm).

Feeding: As for *M. estherae*. Can be greedy, even for a cichlid, and particularly prone to obesity and "Bloat" if fed unsuitable foods.

Behavior & Care: As for *M. estherae*. Males are 99% bluff—they will behave territorially but lose their stripes and head for cover if challenged. Rarely harasses females. An ideal beginner's mbuna.

Breeding: Easily sexed by color; subordinate or cowardly males may look like brown females but their eggspots give them away. Maternal mouthbrooder. Up to 80 fry brooded for 20–22 days.

The normal wild male *Metriaclima estherae* is blue, but the rare "red" male form has been line-bred and is now the standard aquarium form seen in most stores.

Metriaclima aurora is found on the east coast of Lake Malawi and at Likoma Island. This is a male, females are brownish. All of these species are still commonly sold under the incorrect genus name *Maylandia*.

Metriaclima lombardoi is a lot more "robust" in its behavior than other members of the genus. Here a pair from the species' main stronghold at the Mbenji Islands, Lake Malawi. Unusually the female is the blue fish.

Found on the east coast of Lake Malawi and in Lake Malombe, only the more northerly populations of *Metriaclima lanisticola* are small enough to use empty *Lanistes* shells as shelter.

Microgeophagus ramirezi (Myers & Harry, 1948)
Ram (South American Butterfly Cichlid, Ramirez's Cichlid)

Overview: A delightful little fish, deservedly popular, but difficult to keep alive and even harder to breed unless water conditions are just right—rarely the case in general communities. As a result, most stocks are farmed, and mass-production has led to poor quality so that aquarium strains are often washed-out imitations of their wild ancestors. There are captive-bred gold and long-finned strains.

Native Range: South America: Orinoco basin, streams and pools in the savannahs of Colombia and Venezuela.

Maximum Length: 2.5 in (6 cm) TL.

Water: 77–84°F (24–29°C); pH: 5.0–6.5; hardness: 0–5°dGH.

Min. Tank Size: 15 gal | 24x12x12 in (50 L | 60x30x30 cm).

Feeding: Does best on live and frozen foods, but will take flake.

Behavior & Care: Very soft, acid, very good quality, warm water; well-planted tank with caves and small peaceful tankmates that enjoy similar conditions. Peat filtration beneficial. If you cannot provide the right conditions, keep the more hardy and tolerant Bolivian Ram, _M. altispinosus_.

Breeding: Females have a rosy pink belly, males don't. Pair-forming substrate-spawner, quite easy to breed if conditions are right. The up to 300 tiny fry may require infusoria as first food.

Nannocara anomala Regan, 1905
Golden Dwarf Cichlid (Anomala)

Overview: A hardy dwarf cichlid, ideal for the beginner. Adults of both sexes are gorgeously colored in permanent quarters with décor, but rarely show their colors in the store. Do not be deterred!

Native Range: South America: Guyana, Surinam, and eastern Venezuela, in all types of water—clear, black, and white.

Maximum Length: 3 in (7.5 cm) TL.

Water: 75–82°F (24–28°C); pH: 6.0–7.5; hardness: 2–15°dGH.

Min. Tank Size: 15 gal | 24x12x12 in (50 L | 60x30x30 cm).

Feeding: Will take any aquarium fare of suitable size.

Behavior & Care: Keep a pair in a species tank or as part of a larger community of small fishes. Tankmates should be able to withstand occasional chasing in the lower part of the tank. Provide plenty of cover—plants, bogwood, caves—and fine gravel or sand substrate. Hardy as regards water chemistry, but quality should be good.

Breeding: Males are metallic green-blue with a golden sheen, females orange with a dark mid-lateral band. The pair usually spawn in a cave; clutch care is by the female, then both parents shepherd the fry. Broods can number up to 200 and can take *Artemia* nauplii and microworms as first foods, progressing quickly to crumbled flake.

Nanochromis parilus Roberts & Stewart, 1976
Parilus

Overview: One of a group of delightful dwarf cichlids that are trickier than many, so best left to the more experienced aquarist. This is the easiest. Often confused with *N. nudiceps*, which has no horizontal stripes in the upper tail in males.

Native Range: Central Africa: River Congo, in calm bank zones.

Maximum Length: 3.5 in (9 cm) TL.

Water: 77–82°F (25–28°C); pH: 6.0–7.5; hardness: 2–15°dGH.

Min. Tank Size: 38 gal | 36x16x16 in (140 L | 90x40x40 cm).

Feeding: Small live and frozen foods. Acclimated fish will also take flake and small granules, Cod roe, and other small foods.

Behavior & Care: Will tolerate harder, more alkaline conditions than other *Nanochromis*. Although these are small fish, the males may chase females relentlessly until they are ready to pair, so a relatively long tank is required, but this can be shared with other small fishes. Fine substrate, caves, bogwood, and plants as décor.

Breeding: Females are smaller, and very rounded in the belly, with the genital papilla visible, even when not ripe. Spawns in pairs in caves. Requires soft, slightly acid water for success. Courtship is initiated by the female, who also tends the eggs; both guard the fry.

Nanochromis transvestitus Roberts & Stewart, 1984
Transvestitus

Overview: One of the most attractive of all dwarf cichlids, but also one of the most difficult—not for the beginner! It requires highly specialized water conditions, and male behavior towards females makes many large Central American species look angelic.

Native Range: Central Africa: Lac Mai Ndombe, a large shallow lake in the Democratic Republic of Congo, south of the Congo.

Maximum Length: 2.5 in (6 cm) TL.

Water: 77–82°F (25–28°C); pH: 4.5–6.0; hardness: 0–5°dGH.

Min. Tank Size: 50 gal | 48x16x16 in (190 L | 120x40x40).

Feeding: Small live and frozen foods are best. Acclimated fish will also take flake and small granules, Cod roe, and other small foods.

Behavior & Care: Even cichlid experts have yet to find a definitive solution to the male-on-female aggression problem, which is the reason for such a large tank for this tiny fish. The most successful solution has proved to be a long tank, packed with hiding places (caves, plants, bogwood), several pairs competing, and other small fishes as additional distractions. Fine substrate.

Breeding: Females are more colorful. Cave-spawner like all *Nanochromis*. Male may kill female even after pairing and spawning.

Neolamprologus brichardi (Trewavas & Poll, 1952)
Bric (Fairy Cichlid, Princess of Burundi, Brichardi)

Overview: The best-known of a group of closely related species known as the lyre-tailed *Neolamprologus*. None is colorful, but they are incredibly graceful and often interesting in their behavior.

Native Range: East Africa: Lake Tanganyika, in rocky habitat.

Maximum Length: 4 in (10 cm) TL.

Water: 77–82°F (25–28°C); pH: 7.5–9.0; hardness: 10–25°dGH.

Min. Tank Size: 20 gal | 24x12x16 in (70 L | 60x30x40 cm).

Feeding: Small live/frozen foods, flake, Cod roe, other small foods.

Behavior & Care: Keep as a pair in a species tank, or in a larger, sparsely populated community tank of Tanganyikan crevice- and shell-dwellers. Lots of rocks; good quality, well-oxygenated water.

Breeding: Males are larger and have longer fins; most easily sexed at around 1 in (2.5 cm) when the white in male fin-edgings is bolder. Usually breeds in pairs, occasionally in harems, spawning in a crevice. Do not remove the fry until they measure around 1 in (2.5 cm), as the older fry guard their younger siblings while the parents relax! Can be difficult to start breeding; adding a "surrogate family" of .5-in (1-cm) Bric fry from another pair usually helps. Never remove all the fry or you will have to start all over again.

Neolamprologus leleupi Poll, 1956
Leleupi

Overview: One of the most colorful—and hence popular—Tanganyikan cichlids, but rather aggressive toward conspecifics because it lives solitary in the wild, except when breeding. Populations vary in color, from beige through yellow to deep orange.

Native Range: East Africa: Lake Tanganyika, in areas where rocks meet sand, at several disjunct locations around the lake.

Maximum Length: 4 in (10 cm) TL.

Water: 77–82°F (25–28°C); pH: 7.5–9.0; hardness: 10–25°dGH.

Min. Tank Size: 50 gal | 48x16x16 in (190 L | 120x40x40 cm).

Feeding: Invertebrate feeder. Small live and frozen foods. Will also take flake and small granules, and other small foods.

Behavior & Care: Keep as part of a community of small Tanganyika rock- and shell-dwellers in a long tank so that the pair can find space from one another. Lots of rockwork, and breaking this into separate piles with sand and shell-dwellers between may also help avoid trouble. Good quality, well-oxygenated water.

Breeding: Difficult to sex; adult males are larger. Starting with six youngsters should ensure a pair and reduce the aggression problem. A cave-brooder, with brood care by the female.

Neolamprologus multifasciatus (Boulenger, 1906)
Multifasciatus

Overview: A tiny, attractively colored shell-dweller, one of the smallest cichlids known but probably the most prolific digger in terms of size! It often lives in large colonies and digs pits (with shells at the bottom), apparently to trap the zooplankton on which it feeds. Shell-dwellers are often quite different in their habits, representing different evolutionary arrivals at the same type of home. Cf *Lamprologus ocellatus*—same abode, different behavior.

Native Range: East Africa: Lake Tanganyika, sand with shells in the Zambian coastal waters of the lake.

Maximum Length: 1.5 in (4 cm) TL.

Water: 77–82°F (25–28°C); pH: 7.5–9.0; hardness: 10–25°dGH.

Min. Tank Size: 15 gal | 24x12x12 in (50 L | 60x30x30 cm).

Feeding: Small live and frozen foods; will also take flake.

Behavior & Care: Very peaceful. Best kept in a colony in a reasonably sized species tank with lots of sand and shells, where it can dig to its heart's content. Good quality, well-oxygenated water.

Breeding: Males are slightly larger, but with a colony sexing doesn't matter. Spawns in the female's shell. Very easy to breed; the colony tends to grow rapidly and needs thinning out—or a larger tank!

Nimbochromis livingstonii (Günther, 1893)
Kaligono (Livingstonii)

Overview: *Nimbochromis* are piscivores that hunt small fishes by various forms of stealth. The native name Kaligono means "the sleeper," as this fish lies on its side on the sand to hunt. Small fish are attracted by anything white, including the patches on this fish, which suddenly "awakes" and grabs them!

Native Range: East Africa: endemic to Lake Malawi, lake-wide.

Maximum Length: 8 in (20 cm) TL.

Water: 77–82°F (25–28°C); pH: 7.5–8.5; hardness: 5–20°dGH.

Min. Tank Size: 65 gal | 48x18x18 in (240 L | 120x45x45 cm).

Feeding: Feed carnivore foods, including raw fish.

Behavior & Care: Fairly peaceful and easy to keep in a community of Malawi "haps" of similar size. Décor should be rocks and open substrate. Good quality, well-oxygenated water.

Breeding: A maternal mouthbrooder that breeds seasonally for short periods, as males don special (blue) breeding colors and cannot then hunt as normal. Outside the breeding period the sexes look the same. The male holds a territory near rocks, and spawning takes place on the substrate. The female broods the eggs and larvae for about three weeks, and guards the fry for 3–4 weeks after first release.

Nimbochromis polystigma Regan, 1921
Giraffe Cichlid (Polystigma)

Overview: This predator sometimes hunts in packs, but also uses its cryptic coloration to hunt alone by stealth. It rests upright on sand near plants or rocks, and seizes any small fish that comes near. *N. venustus* hunts in similar fashion on open sand, and its pattern is thought to resemble wave-rippled sand. *N. linni* has a similar coloration to *polystigma* but sits on rocks and uses its long, downward-pointing mouth to seize unwary small fish swimming below!

Native Range: East Africa: endemic to Lake Malawi, lake-wide.

Maximum Length: 10 in (25 cm) TL.

Water: 77–82°F (25–28°C); pH: 7.5–8.5; hardness: 5–20°dGH.

Min. Tank Size: 65 gal | 48x18x18 in (240 L | 120x45x45 cm).

Feeding: Piscivorous, so feed raw fish, shrimp, and other carnivore foods. Will take pellets, but avoid feeding too much dry food.

Behavior & Care: As for *N. livingstonii*. Note that the piscivorous behavior of *Nimbochromis* is not aggression, they are actually rather peaceful cichlids with any tankmates too large to eat.

Breeding: Like *N. livingstonii* (and all the genus), males hold territory and breed for short periods only, as otherwise they would starve without camouflage. Spawning and brood care as for *N. livingstonii*.

Oreochromis mossambicus (Peters, 1852)
Mozambique Mouthbrooder (Mozzie)

Overview: An easy cichlid with great character, but low popularity as it is destructive and produces lots of unsaleable fry. But so do the popular Oscar (*Astronotus ocellatus*) and many other neotropical cichlids! And, unlike Oscar & Co., Mozzies are peaceful. There are a number of man-made color forms. Introduced throughout the tropics as a tasty food fish, so if you tire of them…!

Native Range: East Africa: lower Zambezi drainage.

Maximum Length: 12 in (30 cm) TL.

Water: 70–86°F (21–30°C); pH: 6.0–9.0; hardness: 0–30°dGH.

Min. Tank Size: 65 gal | 48x18x18 in (240 L | 120x45x45 cm).

Feeding: Eats anything, eagerly. Include plenty of vegetable food.

Behavior & Care: Mozzies are very peaceful and virtually indestructible (check out the water parameters tolerated); but don't expect an attractive underwater scene as they dig enthusiastically. Efficient mechanical filtration required. Unfussy about décor; destroys plants.

Breeding: Males are slate-gray with a white chest and red fin margins; females plain olive. Sexable at about 2 in (5 cm). Pair-forming maternal mouthbrooder, quite different from the non-pairing "haps." Cannot be stopped from breeding. Useful producer of feeder fish!

367

Otopharynx lithobates Oliver in Eccles & Trewavas, 1989
Lithobates (Otopharynx 'Yellow Blaze', Red-top Aristochromis)

Overview: It is often said that if something remotely edible exists, a cichlid will have evolved to eat it. This one has a particularly unusual diet—it eats fish droppings, mainly those of herbivores. It is not necessary to provide this natural food in the aquarium!

Native Range: East Africa: endemic to Lake Malawi, in rocky habitat in a limited area of islands and mainland shore around Cape Maclear in the south. Some geographical variation.

Maximum Length: 6.5 in (16.5 cm) TL.

Water: 75–82°F (24–28°C); pH: 7.5–8.5; hardness: 5–20°dGH.

Min. Tank Size: 65 gal | 48x18x18 in (240 L | 120x45x45 cm).

Feeding: Will take any aquarium foods, but ensure a high vegetable content; avoid high-protein carnivore fare and too much dry food.

Behavior & Care: Keep in a community of other small Malawi haps—not with mbuna, as although it shares rocky habitat with them in the wild, it lives mainly in large caves, so is not in direct competition and is less robust. Lots of rocks, well-oxygenated water.

Breeding: Only males are colorful. Maternal mouthbrooder with no pair bond. Clutch size about 60 eggs. Females brood for 20–22 days, hiding in caves; they may take a little food while brooding.

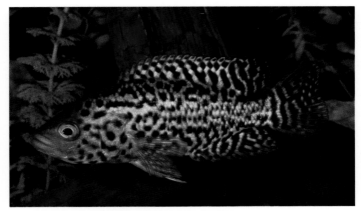

Parachromis managuensis (Günther, 1867)
Jaguar Cichlid (Mannie, Managuense, Managua Cichlid)

Overview: A real character, very popular with those who like their cichlids big and bad. In fact they aren't really bad, but, like most cichlid villains, misunderstood. Of course they will eat smaller fishes —they are piscivores! And yes, they dig—but that is the inevitable downside of breeding many cichlids—constructing nursery pits is part of their brood care. And who can blame them for attacking anything likely to eat their family?

Native Range: Central America: Atlantic slope drainages from Honduras to Costa Rica, including the Nicaraguan lakes.

Maximum Length: 24 in (60 cm) TL. Usually smaller in captivity.

Water: 75–82°F (24–28°C); pH: 7.0–8.5; hardness: 5–25°dGH.

Min. Tank Size: 65 gal | 48x18x18 in (240 L | 120x45x45 cm).

Feeding: Carnivore foods of suitable size, including raw fish.

Behavior & Care: Keep a pair in a species tank, or a "single" as an owner-responsive pet. Hardy and easy as long as its size and natural habits are taken into account. Needs very efficient filtration.

Breeding: Adult males are larger and much darker from around 6 in (15 cm) upwards. Lays 1000-plus eggs on a stone in the open. Pairs, once formed, remain harmonious for a long time, if not forever.

Paratilapia polleni Bleeker, 1868
Marakely (Polleni)

Overview: All Madagascar cichlids are endangered by habitat degradation and introduced tilapias, but this one has, fortunately, established a firm foothold in the hobby. The others are largely restricted to public aquariums. There are large- and small-spot forms, possibly separate species, so don't mix them. And don't buy this fish unless you intend to try to breed it—endangered species must be treated responsibly, not just as aquarium ornaments.

Native Range: Madagascar; widespread in various biotopes.

Maximum Length: 12 in (30 cm) TL.

Water: 75–82°F (24–28°C); pH: 7.0–8.5; hardness: 5–20°dGH.

Min. Tank Size: 65 gal | 48x18x18 in (240 L | 120x45x45 cm).

Feeding: Will take almost any carnivore and vegetarian foods.

Behavior & Care: Can be kept in pairs or (by experienced cichlid aquarists only, please!) with other relatively peaceful, large cichlids in a very large tank. Not difficult, but likes shady hiding places.

Breeding: Difficult to sex so best to start with six youngsters and grow them on to pair naturally. Lays large numbers of small eggs in a clump like a bunch of grapes, in a pit in the substrate. Parental care lasts several weeks. *Artemia* nauplii as first food.

Pelvicachromis pulcher (Boulenger, 1901)
Krib (Kribensis)

Overview: The best-known of a genus of fabulous dwarf cichlids. Attractive, small, easy to keep, sex, and breed, with dedicated brood care—arguably the best possible introduction to cichlids!

Native Range: West Central Africa: eastern Benin, Nigeria, and western Cameroon, in forest waters. Several geographical forms.

Maximum Length: 4 in (10 cm) TL.

Water: 75–82°F (24–28°C); pH: 6.0–8.0; hardness: 2–20°dGH.

Min. Tank Size: 15 gal | 24x12x12 in (50 L | 60x30x30 cm).

Feeding: Tank-breds will eat almost anything of suitable size. Wild fish may require small live and frozen foods, initially at least.

Behavior & Care: Species tank or community, but allow tankmates space of their own. Planted tank with caves (loves clay flowerpots). Wild fish require soft, slightly acid water. Avoid mixing forms.

Breeding: Sexes different in size, form, and finnage; in particular, males have pointed, females club-shaped, pelvic fins. The female initiates courtship and the pair then choose a spawning cave. The female tends the eggs; the male uses his body to block the entrance at night to keep out predators. Both parents shepherd the fry around the tank for many weeks, taking them back to the cave at night.

Placidochromis electra (Burgess, 1979)
Electra (Deepwater Hap, Haplochromis Jahni)

Overview: The name _Placidochromis_ means "peaceful (or placid) cichlid," and this attractive species is no trouble at all. But it won't show its best colors unless kept with similarly peaceful tankmates.

Native Range: East Africa: endemic to Lake Malawi; Likoma and part of the mainland east coast, over sand, sometimes near rocks.

Maximum Length: 7 in (17.5 cm) TL.

Water: 75–82°F (24–28°C); pH: 7.5–8.5; hardness: 5–20°dGH.

Min. Tank Size: 65 gal | 48x18x18 in (240 L | 120x45x45 cm).

Feeding: Omnivorous. Small live and frozen foods, chopped shrimp, and a ration of greens. No beef heart, and be sparing with dry food, to avoid "Bloat."

Behavior & Care: Keep in a community of other smallish, relatively peaceful, Malawi sand-dwellers (e.g. _Cyrtocara moorii_, _Aulonocara_, _Lethrinops_) and small open-water "haps" (e.g. _Copadichromis_). Never with the rock-dwelling mbuna. Rocky backdrop, open sand or gravel, good quality, well-oxygenated water.

Breeding: Males are larger and colorful; females silvery. No nest is constructed; spawning takes place on a rock or the substrate. Females are not harassed by males. Incubation period 20–22 days.

Placidochromis milomo (Oliver, 1984)
Super VC10 (Milomo, Labrosus)

Overview: A large but rather peaceful hap. The "rubber" lips in this fish (and several other Malawi cichlids) are used to create a seal against a rock or crack so anything living there can be sucked out. The lips require constant wear and tear of this kind to remain fully developed, and so tend to be smaller in the aquarium.

Native Range: East Africa: endemic to Lake Malawi, lake-wide.

Maximum Length: 10 in (25 cm) TL.

Water: 75–80°F (24–27°C); pH: 7.5–8.5; hardness: 5–20°dGH.

Min. Tank Size: 65 gal | 48x18x18 in (240 L | 120x45x45 cm).

Feeding: Small live and frozen foods, chopped shrimp, prawn, and mussel, Cod roe. Avoid warm-blood protein such as beef heart.

Behavior & Care: Best kept with other largish Malawi haps (e.g. _Nimbochromis_, _Protomelas_), but unlikely to harm smaller tankmates. Likely to be stressed if confined with thuggish mbuna. In the wild it can swim away! Rocks; good quality, well-oxygenated water.

Breeding: Maternal mouthbrooder. Sexes differently colored and males larger. Territorial only if more than one male present; otherwise, spawning takes place where the fish happen to be when the female is ripe. The fry are brooded for some time after first release.

Pseudocrenilabrus multicolor (Schoeller, 1903)
Egyptian Mouthbrooder

Overview: Before the boom in Malawis this fish was one of the very small number of mouthbrooders available, but it practically disappeared for a while in favor of its gaudier cousins. Luckily it has now experienced a revival. There are two other, slightly larger species, *Ps. philander* and *Ps. nicholsi*, in the genus.

Native Range: Africa; there are two subspecies, *Ps. m. multicolor* from the Nile drainage and *Ps. m. victoriae* from the Lake Victoria basin. Still and slow-flowing, vegetated waters.

Maximum Length: 3 in (8 cm) TL.

Water: 75–82°F (24–28°C); pH: 6.8–7.5; hardness: 2–15°dGH.

Min. Tank Size: 65 gal | 48x18x18 in (240 L | 120x45x45 cm).

Feeding: Will readily accept any small aquarium foods.

Behavior & Care: Males tend to pursue females assiduously, so best kept in a long tank with dense, tall planting for cover, and other small fishes as a distraction. Keep at least two females per male.

Breeding: Males are colorful and, even before they color-up fully, have an orange tip to the anal fin; females silvery olive. Spawning takes place in a small pit dug in the substrate. The fry are brooded by the female for 12–15 days, less than in most mouthbrooders.

Pseudotropheus crabro (Ribbink & Lewis, 1982)
Crabro (Hornet Cichlid, Wasp Cichlid, Chameleo)

Overview: One of the most interesting mbuna. It has a complex relationship with the Kampango catfish (*Bagrus meridionalis*), acting as both a cleanerfish and an egg-predator. Because the second activity is not welcomed by the Kampango(!), Crabro has evolved different coloration for each role, and the ability to change lightning-fast between them; hence its alternative name Chameleo.

Native Range: East Africa: endemic to Lake Malawi, except for the extreme north where replaced by the similar *Ps.* sp. 'Crabro Blue'.

Maximum Length: 6 in (15 cm) TL.

Water: 75–80°F (24–27°C); pH: 7.5–8.5; hardness: 5–20°dGH.

Min. Tank Size: 65 gal | 48x18x18 in (240 L | 120x45x45 cm).

Feeding: Small live and frozen foods, chopped shrimp and mussel, Cod roe. Beef heart and too much dry food may cause "Bloat."

Behavior & Care: One of the larger and more aggressive mbuna; keep in an mbuna community of similar species with masses of rockwork up to the surface. Good quality, well-oxygenated water.

Breeding: Breeding males are almost black; sex non-breeding males by larger size, more black in unpaired fins, and more eggspots than females. Mouthbrooding females best removed to separate quarters.

Pseudotropheus socolofi Johnson, 1974
Socolofi (Pindanni, Pindaani)

Overview: A very popular mbuna ever since its debut in the 1970s, because of its attractive sky-blue color and rather peaceful temperament—males rarely harass females. There are two forms, one with and one without a black dorsal-fin band; they apparently breed true but are considered the same species. The fry are gorgeous—like most mbuna fry they are miniatures of the parents, but with the color more vivid, and brilliant blue eyes.

Native Range: East Africa: endemic to Lake Malawi; a short stretch of the eastern (Mozambique) coast, where rocks meet sand.

Maximum Length: 4.5 in (11.5 cm) TL.

Water: 77–82°F (25–28°C); pH: 7.5–8.5; hardness: 5–20°dGH.

Min. Tank Size: 38 gal | 36x16x16 in (140 L | 90x40x40 cm).

Feeding: Small live/frozen foods, chopped shrimp/mussel, Cod roe, vegetable foods. Beef heart and excess dry food may cause "Bloat."

Behavior & Care: Keep in an mbuna community of the more peaceful species, though it can hold its own against the rougher types. One male and one or more females. Well-oxygenated water essential.

Breeding: Maternal mouthbrooder with 20–22 days incubation. Males larger, with more black in unpaired fins and more eggspots.

Pterophyllum scalare (Schultze, in Lichtenstein, 1823)
Angel (Angelfish, Freshwater Angelfish, Scalare)

Overview: Arguably the most widely kept cichlid, though its form is so unusual that many people don't realize it is a cichlid at all. Available in almost countless man-made color forms with finnage variants too. There are several similar species and the nominal range given probably includes different, undescribed species.

Native Range: South America: Ucayali and Amazon basin in Peru, Colombia, Brazil; rivers in French Guiana, and NW coastal Brazil.

Maximum Length: 6 in (15 cm) TL.

Water: 75–82°F (24–28°C); pH: 6.0–8.0; hardness: 2–20°dGH.

Min. Tank Size: 20 gal | 24x12x16 in (70 L | 60x30x40 cm).

Feeding: Any small aquarium foods; wild fish require live foods.

Behavior & Care: Aquarium-strain Angels will survive in almost any water in any community tank; wild ones require very soft, slightly acid water and more respectful treatment. Best kept in a group of six or more in a large, deep tank. May eat very small tankmates. Do not keep with fin-nippers!

Breeding: Virtually unsexable. Spawns off the bottom on anything available, including heaters if nothing better is provided! Aquarium strains tend to eat their eggs/larvae, necessitating artificial hatching.

Rocio octofasciata (Regan, 1903)
Jack Dempsey (Cichlasoma Octofasciatum)

Overview: The Jack Dempsey was named after a former world heavy-weight boxing champion because of its aggressive behavior, back when the hobby was in its infancy and only well-behaved fishes were known. In fact, it is rather peaceful compared to many cichlids we keep now without batting an eyelid. It's also a real eye-catcher, a bit of a character, and easy to keep and breed.

Native Range: Central America: Atlantic slope drainages from southern Mexico to Honduras.

Maximum Length: 8 in (20 cm) TL.

Water: 75–82°F (24–28°C); pH: 7.0–8.5; hardness: 5–25°dGH.

Min. Tank Size: 38 gal | 36x16x16 in (140 L | 90x40x40 cm).

Feeding: Carnivorous; will take any aquarium foods eagerly.

Behavior & Care: Keep as a pair in a species tank, with plenty of caves. Tends to dig quite a lot. Very hardy. Can be shy—if so, feed little and often so the fish learn to regard humans as benefactors!

Breeding: Males are larger, with longer fins, and tend to lose their stripe pattern. Lays several hundred eggs on a stone in the open. Often cannibalizes fry after 10–20 days, then produces a further brood. In the wild, the fry would have "left home" by this stage.

Satanoperca jurupari (Heckel, 1840)
Jurupari (Satan's Perch, Devil Fish)

Overview: If ever a fish was unjustly named it is this one. *Satanoperca* and its sister genus *Geophagus* are peaceful and sociable bottom-dwellers that live in groups and sift sandy bottoms for small particles of food. They are trustworthy even with small fishes that other cichlids of similar size would regard as snacks.

Native Range: South America: much of the Amazon drainage and rivers in eastern French Guiana and northwestern Brazil.

Maximum Length: 8 in (20 cm).

Water: 77–82°F (25–28°C); pH 6.0–7.5; hardness 2–10°dGH.

Min. Tank Size: 65 gal | 48x18x18 in (240 L | 120x45x45 cm).

Feeding: Small sinking carnivore and herbivore foods of any type.

Behavior & Care: Keep in a group of five-plus in a tank with a large bottom area. Plants, wood, and a large expanse of fine sand. Other peaceful, non-competing, off-the-bottom fishes as tankmates.

Breeding: Virtually unsexable; males ultimately larger. Pairs form with very little courtship visible, and spawn on wood or a stone. The female then picks up and mouthbroods the clutch. First release after about 10 days, before the yolk sac is absorbed. Feed fry on *Artemia* nauplii when the yolk is completely exhausted, a few days later.

Steatocranus casuarius Poll, 1939
Blockhead (Lumphead, Casuarius)

Overview: This fish is never going to win a beauty contest, but like all members of its genus it is interesting and has great charm. *Steatocranus* live on the bottom in rapids and have an atrophied swimbladder, as buoyancy would be a disadvantage in their habitat. They like to perch on rocks, and hop rather than swim, but will paddle to the surface to take food from your fingers.

Native Range: West Central Africa: rapids of the lower Congo.

Maximum Length: 6 in (15 cm) TL.

Water: 75–80°F (24–27°C); pH: 6.5–8.0; hardness: 2–15°dGH.

Min. Tank Size: 25 gal | 24x16x16 in (95 L | 60x40x40 cm).

Feeding: Any sinking or live foods of suitable size.

Behavior & Care: Very hardy and easy. Can be kept as a pair in a species biotope tank with water-worn rocks or with other rheophiles (rapids fishes) in a larger tank, but harmless in the general, planted community. Requires caves. The water should be well oxygenated, but not turbulent—rheophiles live beneath, not in, the rapids.

Breeding: Males have a more massive head and larger hump from an early age. Pair-bonding cave-brooder, with clutch care by the female. Eggs and fry are quite large, broods correspondingly small.

Symphysodon aequifasciatus Pellegrin, 1904
Discus (Pompadour Fish, King of the Aquarium)

Overview: More nonsense has been written about this cult fish than any other. They are "difficult" only when parboiled by over-high temperatures and reduced to nervous wrecks by being kept in bare tanks. They actually do very well and will even breed in a general community. Innumerable natural and man-made forms.

Native Range: South America: Amazon drainage in Peru and Brazil.

Maximum Length: 7 in (18 cm) TL.

Water: 75–82°F (24–28°C); pH: 6.5–8.0; hardness: 0–15°dGH.

Min. Tank Size: 65 gal | 48x18x18 in (240 L | 120x45x45 cm).

Feeding: Contented, unstressed discus will eat anything, including flake and small tetras! Don't feed heart, which is harmful to fishes.

Behavior & Care: Schooling fish—keep in a group of six-plus in a large aquarium with lots of hiding places (if they can hide, they feel secure and usually don't) and, ideally, very soft, slightly acid water. Wild Discus live in the same habitats as the easy, hardy Angel, _Pterophyllum scalare_! And do well kept in precisely the same way.

Breeding: Spawns off the bottom, in nature on the twigs and leaves of submerged bushes, during the floods. The fry feed on special body mucus secreted by the parents. Egg-eating is a problem in captivity.

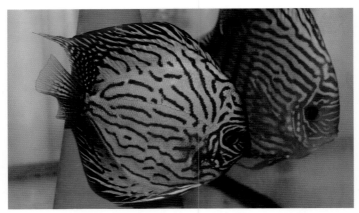

The coveted Brilliant Red Turquoise Discus is a cultivated form of *Symphysodon aequifasciatus*, representing years of selective breeding by discus enthusiasts. Terracotta clay cones are favored by some breeders as ideal spawning sites.

No two Discus are identical; there is a mind-boggling array of color forms in Discus, but the most important thing is healthy fish, always.

Teleogramma brichardi Poll, 1959
Brichard's Teleogramma

Overview: A strange snake-like little rapids-dwelling cichlid with a reduced swimbladder, which digs by burrowing head-first rather than the usual cichlid mouth-shovelling. Tricky, but rewarding.

Native Range: West Central Africa: Congo rapids near Kinshasa.

Maximum Length: 5 in (12.5 cm) TL.

Water: 75–80°F (24–27°C); pH: 6.5–7.5; hardness: 2–10°dGH.

Min. Tank Size: 20 gal | 30x12x12 in (65 L | 75x30x30 cm).

Feeding: Any sinking or live foods of suitable size.

Behavior & Care: Keep a pair in a species tank with water-worn (ideally) rocks, or with other rheophiles (rapids fishes) in a larger biotope tank. In species tanks, separate the pair with a divider until they have established territories, or murders may occur. Despite the reduced swimbladder, this fish can jump out of uncovered tanks or over dividers that don't reach the cover glass! Well oxygenated, but not turbulent water—rheophiles live beneath, not in, rapids.

Breeding: Easily sexed—females have a broad white marginal segment in the upper caudal lobe, males just a narrow white edging. Less easy to breed. Cave-spawner with small clutches of huge eggs, and fry that measure almost 1 in (2.5 cm) long on free-swimming.

Telmatochromis vittatus Boulenger, 1898
Vittatus

Overview: *Telmatochromis* fall roughly into two groups: the small ones with light and dark longitudinal bands, like *T. vittatus*; and the darker, grayish species (e.g. *T. temporalis*) with only barely discernible banding, if at all. The first group are rather peaceful little fishes, albeit sometimes scrappy among themselves, like most cichlids; the second can be thuggish towards tankmates, especially when breeding. You have been warned!

Native Range: East Africa: endemic to the southern half of Lake Tanganyika, in areas where rocks meet sand.

Maximum Length: 4 in (10 cm) TL.

Water: 77–82°F (25–28°C); pH: 7.5–9.0; hardness: 10–25°dGH.

Min. Tank Size: 25 gal | 24x16x16 in (95 L | 60x40x40 cm).

Feeding: Small live and frozen foods and greens; also takes flake, granules, chopped shrimp/mussel, and cod roe, once acclimated.

Behavior & Care: Can be kept in pairs, but better in a community of small Tanganyikan rock- and shell-dwellers. Lots of rockwork; good quality, well-oxygenated (but not turbulent) water.

Breeding: Unsexable except that males are larger. Crevice-spawner which has not often been bred in captivity, for reasons unknown.

Thorichthys meeki (Brind, 1918)
Firemouth

Overview: An evergreen cichlid, whose flamboyant mouth-to-mouth display is well known. When the gills are flared the head looks bigger and the black spots on the opercula look like the eyes of a much larger fish, to deter opponents and predators. But this is mostly bluff; Firemouths are not very aggressive fish. There are several other *Thorichthys* species, which can be treated similarly.

Native Range: Central America: Atlantic slope Mexico (including the *cenotes*, or sinkholes, of the Yucatan), Belize, and Guatemala.

Maximum Length: 6 in (15 cm) TL.

Water: 75–82°F (24–28°C); pH: 7.5–8.5; hardness: 5–25°dGH.

Min. Tank Size: 30 gal | 36x12x16 in (105 L | 90x30x40 cm).

Feeding: Any aquarium foods of suitable size. Earthworms!

Behavior & Care: Best in a species tank, but can share with other small "Centrals," (e.g. *Cryptoheros*). Keep two Firemouth pairs for ongoing spectacular boundary defense. Allow at least 24 in (60 cm) of tank length per cichlid pair. Digs nursery pits; requires caves.

Breeding: Difficult to sex—males have longer fins. Easy to breed. Usually spawns on a (near-) vertical surface, often beneath an overhang. Clutch care by female while male patrols boundaries.

Tilapia buttikoferi (Hubrecht, 1881)
Buttie (Buttikofer's Cichlid)

Overview: A very attractive cichlid that created a real stir when first imported and was on a lot of "wish lists" for a while, until it was realized that, unlike most tilapias, adult males can be real thugs, on a par with the "worst" Central American cichlids. Of course, this won the Buttie fans with those who like a challenge, and, like its trans-Atlantic cousins, it has great character as a pet.

Native Range: West Africa: Guinea, Sierra Leone, and Liberia, in larger rivers with rocky substrates.

Maximum Length: 16 in (40 cm) TL.

Water: 75–82°F (24–28°C); pH: 6.5–8.5; hardness: 5–30°dGH.

Min. Tank Size: 50 gal | 36x18x18 in (180 L | 90x45x45 cm).

Feeding: Unfussy, but requires vegetable food and will eat plants.

Behavior & Care: The tank size cited is for a one-fish species aquarium; pairs require larger tanks. No tankmates except perhaps an armored catfish with a Buttie-proof shelter. Bogwood and rocks as cover. Like most tilapiines, very hardy as regards water, lighting, etc.

Breeding: Males are larger with bolder colors. Separate the pair with a divider except when spawning, as males may kill unripe or even fry-guarding females. Produces huge broods.

Tropheus duboisi Marlier, 1959
Duboisi (Polka-dot Tropheus)

Overview: *Tropheus* are Lake Tanganyika analogues of the Malawi mbuna. There are several species, described and undescribed, and numerous geographical variants. Temperament is variable. *T. duboisi* is one of the more peaceful species. Though adults are not very colorful, the young are to die for, as they are black with white or yellowish spots, depending on the population.

Native Range: East Africa: endemic to Lake Tanganyika, rocky habitats in several areas in the north of the lake.

Maximum Length: 6 in (15 cm) TL.

Water: 75–82°F (24–28°C); pH: 7.5–9.0; hardness: 10–25°dGH.

Min. Tank Size: 65 gal | 48x18x18 in (240 L | 120x45x45 cm).

Feeding: Live/frozen foods, greens, chopped shrimp/mussel. Warm-blood meat (e.g. heart) and too much dry food can cause "Bloat."

Behavior & Care: Best kept in a small group, and can be kept with other *Tropheus* and mbuna. Don't mix these mouthbrooders with substrate spawners, as the latter will feel stressed by all the activity. Masses of rocks; good quality, well-oxygenated water.

Breeding: Hard to sex. First spawns often infertile. Small clutches of huge eggs brooded for about 35 days; new fry about 1 in (2.5 cm).

Tropheus sp 'Ikola'. 4.5 in (11.5 cm). An attractive Lake Tanganyika endemic found along the eastern shore from Isonga to Ikola.

Tropheus sp. 'Black' is an aggressive species found in the northern part of Lake Tanganyika, and has often been misidentified as *T. moorii*. This is the local variant from Pemba, perhaps the most attractive form.

Garden peas, crushed and the skins discarded, are a favorite food of *Tropheus*, and very good for them.

Tropheus sp. 'Cherry Spot' (or 'Kirschfleck') has a very limited distribution on the east coast of Lake Tanganyika.

The true *Tropheus moorii* is found only in the south of Lake Tanganyika and is a rather peaceful fish. A number of undescribed, more aggressive *Tropheus* species are often sold as *moorii*.

The more aggressive *Tropheus* are usually kept in large, "busy" groups (12+) to reduce one-on-one chasing and bullying.

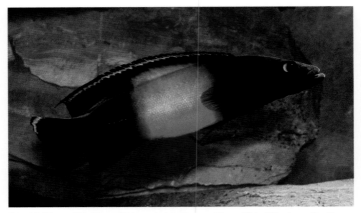

Crenicichla sp. 'Rio Xingu III' is probably the most beautiful of the large South American pike cichlids. Despite superficial similarities in pattern, they are only very distantly related to the Tanganyikan *Tropheus* spp. on preceeding pages.

Uaru amphicanthoides. Uaru are gentle giants (up to 18 in/45 cm), peaceful herbivores that will not prey on small tankmates, though aquarium plants are another matter!

Vieja synspila (Hubbs, 1935)
Quetzal Cichlid (Synspilum)

Overview: One of a group of closely related, large, rather peaceful cichlids with a similar color spectrum but different black markings. Do not mix these species as they hybridize readily.

Native Range: Central America: Atlantic slope drainages in Mexico, Belize, and Guatemala.

Maximum Length: 12 in (30 cm) TL.

Water: 75–82°F (24–28°C); pH: 7.0–8.5; hardness: 5–25°dGH.

Min. Tank Size: 65 gal | 48x18x18 in (240 L | 120x45x45 cm).

Feeding: Any foods of suitable size; plenty of vegetable matter.

Behavior & Care: Although this is a peaceful cichlid, with marital disputes almost unknown, its eventual size dictates a single-pair species tank. It can be grown on with other fishes, but may eat small tankmates. Provide hiding places in the form of well-founded rocks, large clay pipes, and/or bogwood. Good mechanical and biological filtration required, but avoid strong currents.

Breeding: Unsexable except when full grown, when males develop a hump. Grow on six youngsters to get a pair. Spawns more readily when young, but the eggs often fungus as males are not yet mature. In nature young females probably spawn with larger, mature males.

Periophthalmodon septemradiatus (Hamilton, 1822)
Ornate Mudskipper (Malaysian Mudskipper)

Overview: Mudskippers (*Periophthalmus* and *Periophthalmodon*) are members of the goby family that have evolved special features for life in tidal habitats. They can live both in water—often with their eyes protruding—and on/in wet mud when the tide goes out. They require a very special brackish aquarium, part water, part land—a paludarium. There are several species, all with similar requirements.

Native Range: Asia: India, Malaysia, Indonesia, in tidal waters.

Maximum Length: 4 in (10 cm) TL.

Water: 75–86°F (24–30°C); pH: 7.5–8.5; hardness: 10–25°dGH.

Min. Tank Size: 30 gal | 36x18x12 in (120 L | 90x45x30 cm).

Feeding: Best fed on live foods, including worms and small crickets.

Behavior & Care: The paludarium should have shallow water and a large land area of very fine sand, which must be kept moist. The décor (above and below water) should be primarily weathered or artificial wood that will not leach tannins. The air space should be kept humid and warm with a tight-fitting cover. In very large tanks it is possible to include a deep-water area and combine these fishes with other brackish species, (e.g. archerfishes, *Toxotes*).

Breeding: Breeds in mud tunnels, but not so far bred in captivity.

Anabas testudineus (Bloch, 1792)
Climbing Perch (Climbing Bass)

Overview: The Climbing Perch is so named because if its habitat dries up it can clamber out and migrate overland. It can also survive by burying itself in damp mud like a lungfish. It has a special accessory breathing organ (the labyrinth; fishes with this organ are called labyrinthfishes) that enables it to breathe air and thus survive in water with low oxygen. Very hardy, and hence one of the first ornamental fishes to survive the long sea voyage from Asia.

Native Range: Asia: India to the Wallace Line, including China.
Maximum Length: 10 in (25 cm) TL. Usually much smaller.
Water: 72–86°F (22–30°C); pH: 6.5–8.5; hardness: 5–25°dGH.
Min. Tank Size: 20 gal | 30x12x12 in (65 L | 75x30x30 cm).
Feeding: Live foods and vegetable foods, in variety.
Behavior & Care: Timid but aggressive, and best kept in a species tank. Fresh or brackish water—in the latter case plants and tankmates must be salt-tolerant. Provide hiding places and a layer of floating plants. Powerful jumper—tight-fitting cover required.
Breeding: The male has a longer anal fin. Mature at 4 in (10 cm). The eggs float and hatch in 24 hours. Infusoria as first food. No brood care, but the parents do not usually harm the fry.

Ctenopoma acutirostre Pellegrin, 1899
Spotted Climbing Perch (Spotted Ctenopoma, Spotted Bushfish)

Overview: *Ctenopoma* are the African cousins of *Anabas testudineus*, the Asian Climbing Perch, but unlike that species they do not leave the water; reports of them being found in trees relate to strandings after floods! But they do have a labyrinth and can breathe air. Some species breed like *Anabas*; others, including this one, build a nest of bubbles and the male guards the brood.

Native Range: Congo drainage, slow-moving smaller rivers.

Maximum Length: 6 in (15 cm) TL.

Water: 73–82°F (23–28°C); pH: 6.5–7.5; hardness: 0–10°dGH.

Min. Tank Size: 38 gal | 36x16x16 in (140 L | 90x40x40 cm).

Feeding: *Ctenopoma* are carnivores; live foods preferred.

Behavior & Care: Peaceful except when breeding, but may eat small tankmates. Unfussy about décor but should have hiding places and surface vegetation (tall, rooted, stemmed plants) for building a bubblenest. Best for a species tank or a community of larger fishes. Provide subdued lighting, and avoid strong currents.

Breeding: Males have spines on the body, females less spotted fins. The male "blows bubbles" to build the nest and guards the brood. Remove the female if she is continuously chased and attacked.

Ctenopoma maculatum, Climbing Perch. A larger climbing perch from Cameroon. Like *C. acutirostre* it is a bubblenest-builder, but it does not guard the nest.

Ctenopoma kingsleyae, Kingsley's Ctenopoma. Found in rivers from the Gambia to the Congo, this fish lays floating eggs like *Anabas testudineus,* with no brood care.

Belontia signata (Günther, 1861)
Combtail (Comb-tailed Paradise Fish, Ceylonese Combtail)

Overview: Not the sweetest-natured of fishes, the Combtail is an attractive-looking labyrinthfish but best left to aquarists used to dealing with aggression. Its relative *B. hasseltii*, from Malaysia and Indonesia, is larger but more peaceful—except when breeding.

Native Range: Sri Lanka, in standing or sluggish waters.

Maximum Length: 5 in (13 cm) TL.

Water: 75–82°F (24–28°C); pH: 7.0–8.0; hardness: 5–20°dGH.

Min. Tank Size: 38 gal | 36x16x16 in (140 L | 90x40x40 cm).

Feeding: Omnivorous, will take almost any aquarium foods.

Behavior & Care: Young specimens can be kept in a general community but adults are boisterous, aggressive, and tend to bite, so should be kept only with larger fishes. Can be kept with cichlids of similar size, whose antisocial behavior it often emulates! Requires plenty of cover, ideally dense planting, but also lots of swimming space. Avoid strong currents.

Breeding: Males have a longer dorsal fin. The eggs are laid on the underside of a plant leaf with a single large air bubble rather than a nest. The fry are free-swimming in around six days and can take *Artemia* nauplii as first food.

Betta splendens Regan, 1910
Siamese Fighting Fish (Siamese Fighter)

Overview: A cult labyrinthfish, known even to non-aquarists. Line-bred for pugnacity in its homeland, where bets are placed on fights, and then for finnage and color variants in the hobby, the aquarium "fighter" has come a long way from the original species. In fact, escapes of line-bred fish mean it is possible the original natural form no longer exists in the wild.

Native Range: Asia: Mekong basin, in still or sluggish waters.

Maximum Length: 3 in (7.5 cm) TL.

Water: 75–86°F (24–30°C); pH: 6.0–8.0; hardness: 5–25°dGH.

Min. Tank Size: 10 gal | 18x12x12 in (40 L | 45x30x30 cm).

Feeding: Any small carnivore and omnivore foods.

Behavior & Care: Peaceful towards other fishes. Well-planted tank with quiet tankmates and warm, clean water. No fin nippers. NEVER keep two males together—they will fight to the death.

Breeding: Only males have splendid finnage. Breeding tank with shallow (6 in/15 cm) water and surface vegetation. The male builds a bubblenest (see photo) among surface plants. No aeration or filtration (may destroy the nest). Brood care by the male; the female is best removed. Eggs hatch in 24 hours; fry require very tiny foods.

Betta pugnax (Cantor, 1850)
Penang Betta

Overview: The genus *Betta* contains far more species than the Siamese Fighter, and some are occasionally available to hobbyists. The genus includes not only bubblenest-builders but also male mouthbrooders, *B. pugnax* being one of the latter.

Native Range: Malaysia, Singapore, Indonesia, in flowing streams with vegetation.

Maximum Length: 4 in (10 cm) TL.

Water: 72–82°F (22–28°C); pH: 6.0–7.5; hardness: 0–10°dGH.

Min. Tank Size: 15 gal | 24x12x12 in (50 L | 60x30x30 cm).

Feeding: Small live and frozen foods. Sometimes takes flake.

Behavior & Care: This is actually a far better community fish than the Siamese Fighter as it hasn't been weakened by inbreeding, and males don't fight. Well-planted tank with bogwood, water current, quiet, peaceful tankmates. Avoid over-bright light.

Breeding: Males are more colorful with longer finnage. Best bred in a species tank if the fry are to be saved. The eggs are laid in batches which the male catches with his anal fin. The female then picks them up and spits them into his mouth. When released the fry require infusoria, followed by brine shrimp nauplii after about a week.

Betta splendens, Siamese Fighting Fish. Beauty is in the eye of the fishkeeper, and this species has myriad choices in pure or mixed colors.

Betta splendens, Siamese Fighting Fish (females). Although less dramatic in appearance than the males, female Fighters are not pugnacious and can be kept in groups. Two or three females per male makes for interesting interactions.

Betta channoides, the White Crescent Betta (or Snakehead Fighter), is best kept in a species tank with plants (Java Moss) and soft, acidic, and very clean water.

Betta macrostoma, Spotfin Betta. A lovely mouthbrooder from Borneo that is found in quiet pools as well as near waterfalls in swift currents. It is not commonly imported but can sometimes be found as contaminants in shipments of wild bettas from Malaysia.

Betta splendens. This fish is curious, alert, and very aware of its surroundings. Give it a proper home, no flower vases, and it will be a great pet!

Betta akarensis. The Akar Betta is unusual in the hobby, but can sometimes be found as contaminants in shipments of wild bettas. This is true of many of the genera of fishes shown in this book, so keep a sharp eye when fish shopping.

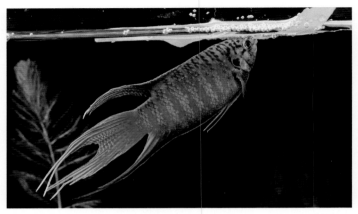

Macropodus opercularis, like the bettas, builds a bubblenest under a leaf. This anchors the bubbles that will hold the floating eggs while the father tends them.

The male Paradise Fish displays beautifully. Unfortunately this usually means he is getting ready to shred some fins if there is another male in the vicinity.

Macropodus opercularis (Linnaeus, 1758)
Paradisefish

Overview: Only the Goldfish has a longer history in the hobby than this colorful labyrinthfish; its tolerance of lower temperatures, poor water quality, and low oxygen meant it could be brought to Europe by ship back in the mid-1800s. Unfortunately its bright colors aren't matched by an equable temperament, and adult males will fight ferociously like *Betta splendens*. There are black and albino "man-made" forms.

Native Range: SE Asia, including China, Taiwan, and Vietnam.

Maximum Length: 4 in (10 cm) TL.

Water: 61–79°F (16–26°C); pH: 6.0–8.0; hardness: 5–20°dGH.

Min. Tank Size: 20 gal | 30x12x12 in (65 L | 75x30x30 cm).

Feeding: An omnivore that will take most standard aquarium fare.

Behavior & Care: Youngsters are peaceful but adult males are best not kept together. Well-planted tank with open swimming space. An adept jumper, so cover the tank tightly.

Breeding: Males brighter with longer fins. Builds a bubblenest on the underside of a large leaf. Trigger breeding by lowering water level and raising temperature. Brood care by male. Remove the female after spawning unless there is plenty of escape space.

Colisa lalia (Hamilton, 1822)
Dwarf Gourami

Overview: Gouramis are the most popular labyrinthfishes after *Betta splendens* and found only in Southeast Asia. The ventral fins are modified into long sensory "feelers" used to investigate the fish's environment, but are also irresistible to fin-nippers and many other fishes that snap up any potential food they see drift by! *Colisa* are small and peaceful, but susceptible to "Velvet" (*Piscinoodinium*).

Native Range: Asia: India, Pakistan, Bangladesh.

Maximum Length: 2 in (5 cm) TL.

Water: 72–82°F (22–28°C); pH: 6.5–7.5; hardness: 5–15°dGH.

Min. Tank Size: 15 gal | 24x12x12 in (50 L | 60x30x30 cm).

Feeding: An easy-to-feed omnivore that needs vegetable food.

Behavior & Care: A peaceful, shy little fish that requires similar tank-mates. Dense planting and floating plants. Water quality must be excellent, peat filtration beneficial. Be alert for signs of Velvet and use a proprietary treatment as soon as possible.

Breeding: Males are much more colorful. Shallow water—8 in (20 cm). The male builds a fairly robust bubblenest containing bits of plant and algae strands, and guards the eggs. Remove the female after spawning and the male after 2–3 days or he may eat the fry.

Colisa fasciata, Banded Gourami. This slightly larger cousin of the Dwarf Gourami comes from India, Bangladesh, Pakistan and is another excellent community fish.

Osphronemus goramy, Giant Gourami. Attractive when juvenile, but adults are large, gray, ugly fish that can top 24 in (60 cm)—too large for most domestic aquaria. The fish in the photo is a youngster.

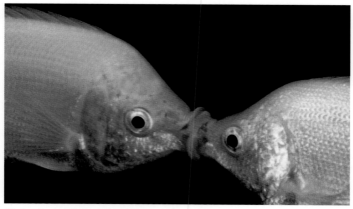

Helostoma temminckii Cuvier, 1829
Kissing Gourami

Overview: The Kissing Gourami is an old favorite that grows a lot larger than most people realize. It occurs in two natural morphs, the green from Thailand, rarely seen in the hobby, and the "pink kisser" from Java. The kissing is not affection but mouth-fighting, rather like in cichlids. It also kisses algae-covered surfaces to feed, and occasionally surprises tankmates with a gentle peck!

Native Range: SE Asia: Thailand and Java, in sluggish waters.

Maximum Length: 12 in (30 cm) TL.

Water: 75–82°F (24–28°C); pH: 6.5–8.5; hardness: 5–25°dGH.

Min. Tank Size: 65 gal | 48x18x18 in (240 L | 120x45x45 cm).

Feeding: Omnivorous, requiring ample vegetable food; eats algae.

Behavior & Care: A hardy, peaceful species for the community of larger fishes. Decorate the tank with rocks and Java Fern—soft-leaved plants will be eaten. May dig in the substrate.

Breeding: Virtually unsexable. Does not build a bubblenest but lays floating eggs like _Anabas testudineus_. Use a breeding tank and remove the parents after spawning. No brood care. The fry require infusoria, which can be produced "in-tank" by floating lettuce leaves on the surface where they slowly decompose.

Sphaerichthys osphronemoides Canestrini, 1860
Chocolate Gourami

Overview: Generally regarded as a real challenge even for experts, the Chocolate Gourami is best left in the shop unless you are prepared to put in all the special effort it requires.

Native Range: Malaysia, Sumatra, Borneo.

Maximum Length: 2.5 in (6 cm) TL.

Water: 75–86°F (24–30°C); pH: 4.0–6.0; hardness: 0–5°dGH.

Min. Tank Size: 20 gal | 30x12x12 in (65 L | 75x30x30 cm).

Feeding: Live foods in variety; may accept frozen and flake but live should form the bulk of the diet.

Behavior & Care: A peaceful, rather nervous fish that should be kept in pairs in a species tank or with quiet, non-boisterous tankmates. Well-planted tank. Water chemistry (soft, acid) is paramount, and water quality more so. Warm temperature required, peat filtration beneficial. Highly susceptible to bacterial and protozoan infections if conditions are not precisely to its liking.

Breeding: Males have a yellow border to tail and anal fin. Maternal mouthbrooder—the pair spawn on the bottom and the female then collects the eggs and broods them for around two weeks. The brood is small (up to 40) and on release the fry can take *Artemia* nauplii.

Trichogaster chuna (Hamilton, 1822)
Honey Gourami (Colisa Chuna, Colisa Sota)

Overview: *Trichogaster* are probably the most popular of the gouramis, with half a dozen species regular in the hobby and one in almost every community tank, but do not keep them with fishes that may nip the long ventral feelers. They are peaceful and offer a size range to suit most requirements. *T. chuna* is the smallest.

Native Range: Asia: northern India and Bangladesh, in ditches, pools, sluggish streams, and paddyfields.

Maximum Length: 2 in (5 cm) TL.

Water: 72–82°F (22–28°C); pH: 6.0–7.5; hardness: 0–15°dGH.

Min. Tank Size: 15 gal | 24x12x12 in (50 L | 60x30x30 cm).

Feeding: An obliging fish that will take most aquarium foods.

Behavior & Care: Keep with peaceful fishes of similar size in a heavily-planted tank with a layer of floating plants. Avoid excessive water movement.

Breeding: Sexes similar except when breeding, when they are quite different in coloration. The pair defend a small territory in which the male builds a bubblenest. Sometimes spawning precedes the construction work and the floating eggs are later collected by the male and blown into the nest. The fry require infusoria.

Trichogaster microlepis (Günther, 1861)
Moonlight Gourami

Overview: Sometimes subtle is just as beautiful as flashy colors, and the lovely Moonlight Gourami exemplifies this.

Native Range: Asia: Mekong and Chao Phraya basins in Cambodia and Vietnam, in still and slow-flowing waters.

Maximum Length: 6 in (15 cm) TL.

Water: 77–86°F (25–30°C); pH: 6.0–7.0; hardness: 0–10°dGH.

Min. Tank Size: 38 gal | 36x16x16 in (140 L | 90x40x40 cm).

Feeding: An omnivore. Feed live, frozen, prepared, and green foods.

Behavior & Care: A peaceful fish for the larger community. Plant heavily; this species may nibble fine-leaved species so use tougher growths like *Vallisneria* and Java Fern. This fish likes its water warm, and when dealing with air-breathers it is important that the air above the water is warm as well, especially with young fish. A good air space is essential—labyrinthfishes cannot get enough air via their gills and can literally drown without supplementary air!

Breeding: Pelvic fins orange to red in males, yellow in females. Bubblenester with male brood care. Lower the water level to about 8 in (20 cm) and raise the temperature by a degree or two. The eggs may number up to 1000 and the fry require infusoria.

Trichogaster trichopterus (Pallas, 1777)
Blue Gourami (Three-spot Gourami)

Overview: The hardiest of the smaller gouramis, and the one most frequent in aquaria. Like some other "bread and butter" fishes it has been kept and bred for so long that "sports" have occurred and been line-bred to produce man-made forms such as the "Cosby" and a pale orange semi-albino variety.

Native Range: Much of SE Asia, including the Mekong drainage, and parts of Indonesia, in sluggish, heavily vegetated waters.

Maximum Length: 6 in (15 cm) TL.

Water: 72–82°F (22–28°C); pH: 6.0–8.5; hardness: 0–25°dGH.

Min. Tank Size: 38 gal | 36x16x16 in (140 L | 90x40x40 cm).

Feeding: Will eat almost anything, including vegetable foods.

Behavior & Care: A hardy, peaceful, slow-moving fish. Prefers a well-planted tank but does well even with sparser décor. Easily bullied, even by smaller fishes, and may then hide; when adult can become timid after a change of tank or other major disturbance.

Breeding: Dorsal fin pointed in males. Builds a bubblenest, for which the breeding-tank water level should be lowered to around 6 in (15 cm). The male guards the nest and eggs, and may become aggressive towards the female, so remove her after spawning.

Trichogaster pectoralis, Snakeskin Gourami. At 8 in (20 cm) this is the largest member of its genus, but very peaceful for its size.

Trichogaster leeri, Pearl Gourami. Males of this hardy and easy species from Malaysia and Indonesia show more red than females.

Trichopsis vittata (Cuvier, 1831)
Croaking Gourami

Overview: Fishes are not always silent pets, and as its name suggests this gourami makes croaking sounds. Peaceful and fairly easy to maintain, it is trickier when it comes to breeding.

Native Range: Thailand to Vietnam and Indonesia (Java, Borneo, Sumatra), in shallow, sluggish, heavily vegetated waters.

Maximum Length: 2.5 in (6.5 cm) TL.

Water: 72–86°F (22–30°C); pH: 6.5–7.5; hardness: 3–15°dGH.

Min. Tank Size: 15 gal | 24x12x12 in (50 L | 60x30x30 cm).

Feeding: Enjoys small live, frozen, and prepared foods in variety.

Behavior & Care: An attractive, outgoing little fish as long as tank-mates are peaceful and do not dominate. Small barbs, characins, *Corydoras* catfishes and similar are ideal. The tank should be thickly planted with a layer of floating plants; wood and rocks can be included; but make sure there is plenty of open space for swimming. Both sexes make the strange croaking sounds.

Breeding: The male has a longer anal fin with a red edging. Use a breeding tank, lower the water to 4 in (10 cm), and raise the temperature to 86°F (30°C). Live food may help promote spawning. Bubblenest builder with paternal brood care. Broods are small.

Trichopsis pumila, Dwarf Croaking Gourami. This tiny 1.5-in (4 cm) gourami requires warm, soft, slightly acid water; despite its size it is aggressive when spawning.

Trichogaster trichopterus, Gold Gourami. A captive-bred variant of the Blue or Three-spot Gourami, this is a handsome fish, peaceful and an excellent choice for mid-size to large community aquariums.

Channa bleheri Vierke, 1991
Dwarf Snakehead (Bleher's Snakehead)

Overview: Snakeheads are found in Africa and southern Asia, and are grouped in two genera, *Channa* (Asian) and *Parachanna* (African). All are predators, and some grow to more than 3 feet (90 cm) long. A few measure "only" a foot or so (30 cm). The problem is, they are usually imported as "oddments" at small sizes and labeled simply "Snakehead", so you can't look up adult size. So beware! *C. bleheri*, however, is a delightful dwarf species.
Native Range: India.
Maximum Length: 8 in (20 cm) TL.
Water: 75–82°F (24–28°C); pH: 6.5–8.0; hardness: 5–25°dGH.
Min. Tank Size: 20 gal | 30x12x12 in (65 L | 75x30x30 cm).
Feeding: Small fishes, worms, pieces of fish, shrimp, prawn, etc.
Behavior & Care: Cannot be trusted with smaller fishes. Best kept in a species tank or perhaps with cichlids. Provide fine, soft substrate and hiding places (wood, rocks, clay pipes). Dense marginal planting and surface vegetation will make this fish feel at home.
Breeding: No details available. Some snakeheads are mouthbrooders, some produce floating eggs, others are bottom-spawners or nest-builders, with male brood care until free swimming.

Channa punctata (Bloch, 1793)
Spotted Snakehead

Overview: Like all snakeheads, this fish has an accessory respiratory organ that allows it to breathe air, a vital feature in its natural habitats, which are typically muddy and low in oxygen for at least part of the year. Snakeheads can also survive in wet mud, and reputedly wriggle overland to find water if their home dries up. This species is sometimes imported and is of aquarium size.

Native Range: Southern Asia, from Afghanistan to China, in pools, sluggish streams, ditches, and swamps.

Maximum Length: 14 in (35 cm) TL.

Water: 72–82 °F (22–28 °C); pH: 6.0–8.5; hardness: 0–25°dGH.

Min. Tank Size: 50 gal | 36x18x18 in (180 L | 90x45x45 cm).

Feeding: Carnivore: meaty foods, including feeder fish and worms.

Behavior & Care: Very aggressive towards its own kind and sometimes other fishes. Best kept singly in a species tank, or with robust fishes too large to eat or harass, in a spacious planted tank with plenty of room for all. Provide plenty of hiding-places of suitable shape and size—clay pipes are ideal.

Breeding: Sexing unknown and probably not bred. In the wild this species lays floating eggs among dense vegetation; no brood care.

Channa micropeltes (juv.), Giant Snakehead. At 55 in (140 cm) or more long, this Asian species is an excellent food fish but unsuitable for the aquarium.

Parachanna obscura, African Snakehead. A large (24 in | 60 cm) snakehead from West Africa, with male brood care.

Macrognathus zebrinus (Blyth, 1858)
Zebra Spiny Eel

Overview: Spiny eels are, as the name suggests, long eel-like fishes, and are found in Africa and Asia, in fresh and brackish water depending on the species. Some are very attractive, but many grow very large. Most are sold as small (4–6 in|10–15 cm) youngsters so it is important to resist these beauties till you have checked out eventual size. This one is feasible for a normal domestic aquarium.

Native Range: Asia: Burma and possibly Indonesia.

Maximum Length: 18 in (46 cm) TL. Usually smaller.

Water: 73–79°F (23–26°C); pH: 6.5–7.5; hardness: 5–15°dGH.

Min. Tank Size: 50 gal | 36x18x18 in (180 L | 90x45x45 cm).

Feeding: Live foods, including small fishes and worms.

Behavior & Care: Best kept singly in a species tank. Fairly unfussy and hardy. Will appreciate plants and eel-shaped hiding places such as large pieces of wood or clay drainpipes. As this fish spends most of its time on the bottom the substrate should be fine, soft sand to avoid abrasion to its underside. Like other spiny eels this fish can become very tame and hence a great pet.

Breeding: Virtually nothing is known about sexing and breeding.

Macrognathus maculatus, Frecklefin Eel. This modest-sized Asian species (11 in/ 28 cm) feeds on worms and bottom-dwelling insects and crustaceans.

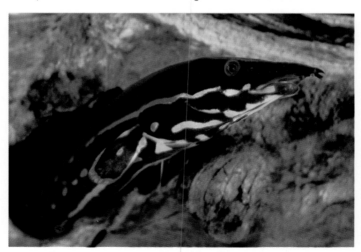

Mastacembelus erythrotaenia, Fire Eel. You will need a monster aquarium for this gorgeous spiny eel, which can grow to more than 3 feet (90 cm) long. Eye-catching and potentially huge, this eel is harvested both for the aquarium trade and human consumption.

Tetraodon miurus Boulenger, 1902
Congo Puffer (Spud)

Overview: Puffers are largely marine, but some are found in brackish and even completely fresh water. Most are not good aquarium fishes as they are aggressive towards tankmates, especially their own kind. Best left to the specialist!

Native Range: Africa: middle to lower Congo, sometimes in rapids.

Maximum Length: 6 in (15 cm) TL.

Water: 73–79°F (23–26°C); pH: 6.5–7.5; hardness: 0–10°dGH.

Min. Tank Size: 30 gal | 36x12x18 in (120 L | 90x30x45 cm).

Feeding: Puffers eat most foods, but shellfish form a major part of the natural diet. This wears down their teeth, which grow continuously to compensate. Insufficient wear in captivity can cause serious problems, so small shellfish, with shell, should be fed.

Behavior & Care: A freshwater species which needs ample space. Youngsters can be kept with larger fishes, but adults best kept alone. Provide a deep layer of soft sand as this fish likes to bury itself, to lie in wait for prey, with only its eyes (and mouth!) exposed. Doesn't eat plants; does eat small fishes. Well-oxygenated water preferred.

Breeding: Not known to have been bred in captivity. No external sex differences known.

Tetraodon nigroviridis Marion de Procé, 1822
Green Puffer (Tetraodon Fluviatilis)

Overview: Sold as attractive youngsters, this puffer grows to a fair size, is intolerant of its own kind, may eat smaller fishes (and bits—fins, scales—of larger ones), and plants. Like many puffers, it is poisonous if eaten; some members of the family contain tetraodotoxin, which causes paralysis and death through asphyxiation.

Native Range: Asia: Sri Lanka, Indonesia, China.

Maximum Length: 6.5 in (16.5 cm) TL.

Water: 75–82°F (24–28°C); pH: 7.5–8.5; hardness: 10–25°dGH.

Min. Tank Size: 30 gal | 36x12x16 in (105 L | 90x30x40 cm).

Feeding: Like *T. miurus* (qv) this fish must have shellfish, with shell, in its diet to wear down its teeth. It also requires green food.

Behavior & Care: Can be kept in brackish water but does well in fresh. Like most puffers this thug is best kept alone, and nothing is safe from its tough, shell-cracking teeth. It has even been known to bite into heater cables and airlines (some other puffers share this vice)! Heavily fortified aquarium with just substrate and rocks!

Breeding: Has been bred in brackish water. Substrate spawner with brood care by the male. No external sex differences. Puffers are rarely bred because it is so difficult to keep two together.

Carinotetraodon travancoricus, Malabar Pufferfish. 1.5 in (3.5 cm).

Tetraodon cochinchinensis, Fang's Pufferfish. 2.75 in (7 cm).

The freshwater Malabar Puffer from India is more suitable than most for aquarium maintenance, because of its small size. Slightly larger is Fang's Pufferfish from the Malay Peninsula and Indonesia.

Tetraodon lineatus Marion de Procé, 1822
Globe Fish

Overview: Puffers can make endearing, personable pets for those who buy them knowing their potential to grow, harass tankmates, destroy vegetation, and generally take bits out of everything in the aquascape. With their formidable dentition, they can make short work of most materials other than solid rock.

Native Range: Africa: Nile, Chad, Niger, Volta, Gambia, Senegal.

Maximum Length: 17 in (43 cm) TL.

Water: 75–82°F (24–28°C); pH: 7.5–8.5; hardness: 10–25°dGH.

Min. Tank Size: 90 gal | 48x18x24 in (320 L | 120x45x60 cm).

Feeding: In the wild, this species feeds heavily on mollusks, and, like all puffers, it must have shellfish, with shell, in its diet to wear down its teeth. It also requires green food.

Behavior & Care: Like most puffers, it will do best in brackish water. Because of its behavioral traits, it is a good choice to be kept singly and appreciated for its bold character. As with other large puffers, it is likely to bite anything put into the tank.

Breeding: No details of sexing or breeding available. Most puffers are unsexable. Rarely bred as it is so difficult to keep two together.

Tetraodon mbu, Giant Green Puffer, Max. Length: 26 in (67 cm).

Tetraodon fluviatilis, Green Pufferfish. Max. Length: 6.7 in (17 cm).

A suitable habitat for puffers would include rockwork and gravel, perhaps some sacrificial driftwood. Plants, even the plastic variety, will usually fall victim to the puffer's habitual biting.

Bailey, M. and P. Burgess. 1999. *The Tropical Fishlopedia*. Ringpress, UK.

Brichard, P. 1989. *Cichlids and all the other fishes of Lake Tanganyika*. T.F.H. Publications, Neptune City, NJ.

Evers, H.-G. and I. Seidel. 2005. *Catfish Atlas, Vol 1*. Baensch, Melle, Germany.

Froese, R. and D. Pauly. 2008. Editors. *FishBase*. World Wide Web electronic publication. www.fishbase.org, version (12/2008).

Fuller, I.A.M. 2001. *Breeding Corydoradine Catfishes*. IFE, Kidderminster, UK.

Fuller, I.A.M. and H.-G. Evers. 2005. *Identifying Corydoradinae Catfishes*. IFE, Kidderminster, UK.

Hawkins, A.D. 1981. *Aquarium Systems*. Academic Press, San Diego, CA.

Hieronimus, H. 1999. *Breathtaking Rainbows*. Aqualog, Rodgau, Germany.

Konings, A. 1998. *Tanganyika Cichlids in their Natural Habitat*. Cichlid Press, El Paso, TX.

Konings, A. 2007. *Malawi Cichlids in their Natural Habitat* (4th edition). Cichlid Press, El Paso, TX.

Kordera, H., Igarashi, T., Kuroiwa, N., Maeda, H., Mitani, S., Mori, F., and K. Yamazaki. 1994. *Jurassic Fishes*. T.F.H. Publications, Neptune, NJ.

Lamboj, A. 2004. *The Cichlid Fishes of Western Africa*. Schmettkamp Verlag, Germany.

Linke, H. and W. Staeck. 1994. *American Cichlids I, Dwarf Cichlids*. Tetra, Melle, Germany.

———————————— 1994. *African Cichlids I – Cichlids from West Africa*. Tetra, Melle, Germany.

Nelson, J. S. 1984. *Fishes of the World*. John Wiley & Sons, Inc., New York, NY.

Reis, R.E., Kullander, S.O. and C.J. Ferraris, Jr. (eds). 2003. *Check List of the Freshwater Fishes of South and Central America* (CLOFFSCA). EDIPUCRS, Porto Alegre, Brazil.

Riehl, R. and H. Baensch. 1982. *Aquarium Atlas, Vol. 1*. Baensch, Melle, Germany.

——————————— 1993. *Aquarium Atlas, Vol. 2*. Baensch, Melle, Germany.

——————————— 1996. *Aquarium Atlas, Vol. 3*. Baensch, Melle, Germany.

Römer, U. 2001/2. *Cichlid Atlas Vol. 1, South American Dwarf Cichlids.* Mergus, Melle, Germany.

Schäfer, F. 2005. *Brackish-Water Fishes – all about species, care and breeding*. Aqualog, Rodgau, Germany.

Scheel, J. 1968. *Rivulins of the Old World*. TFH Publications, Neptune City, NJ. USA.

Seegers, L. 1997. *Killifishes of the World: Old World Killis, Vol. 1*. Aqualog, Rodgau, Germany.

——————————— 1997. *Killifishes of the World: Old World Killis, Vol 2*. Aqualog, Rodgau, Germany.

——————————— 2000. *Killifishes of the World: New World Killis.* Aqualog, Rodgau, Germany.

——————————— 2008. *The Catfishes of Africa.* Aqualog, Rodgau, Germany.

Seidel, I. and H.-G. Evers. 2005. *Wels Atlas, Vol. 2*. Baensch, Melle, Germany.

Stawikowski, R. and U. Werner. 1998. *Die Buntbarche Amerikas, Vol.1*. Eugen Ulmer Verlag, Germany.

Sterba, G. 1962. *Freshwater Fishes of the World*. Odhams, London. UK.

Weidner, T. 2000. *Eartheaters*. Cichlid Press, El Paso, TX.

SPECIES INDEX

SPECIES INDEX

SPECIES INDEX

SPECIES INDEX

SPECIES INDEX

SPECIES INDEX

FURTHER READINGS

Microcosm/TFH Professional Series Titles

ADVENTUROUS AQUARIST GUIDE
The 101 Best Aquarium Plants
How to Choose & Keep Hardy, Vibrant,
Eye-catching Species That Will Thrive in
Your Home Aquarium
By Mary E. Sweeney

ADVENTUROUS AQUARIST GUIDE
The 101 Best Tropical Fishes
How to Choose & Keep Hardy, Brilliant,
Fascinating Species That Will Thrive in
Your Home Aquarium
By Kathleen Wood

ADVENTUROUS AQUARIST GUIDE
The 101 Best Saltwater Fishes
How to Choose & Keep Hardy, Brilliant,
Fascinating Species That Will Thrive in
Your Home Aquarium
By Scott W. Michael

Aquarium Corals
Selection, Husbandry & Natural History
By Eric H. Borneman

Aquarium Sharks & Rays
An Essential Guide to Their Selection,
Keeping & Natural History
By Scott W. Michael

Clownfishes
A Guide to Their Captive Care,
Breeding & Natural History
By Joyce D. Wilkerson

The Complete Illustrated Breeder's
Guide to Marine Aquarium Fishes
Mating, Spawning & Rearing Methods
for Over 90 Species
By Matthew L. Wittenrich

The Conscientious Marine Aquarist
A Commonsense Handbook
for Successful Saltwater Hobbyists
By Robert M. Fenner

The Marine Fish
Health & Feeding Handbook
The Essential Guide to Keeping
Saltwater Species Alive & Thriving
By Bob Goemans & Lance Ichinotsubo

Natural Reef Aquariums
Simplified Approaches to Creating
Living Saltwater Microcosms
By John H. Tullock

The New Marine Aquarium
Step-by-Step Setup & Stocking Guide
By Michael S. Paletta
PocketExpert Guide: Marine Fishes
500+ Essential-to-Know Species
By Scott W. Michael

POCKETEXPERT GUIDE
Marine Invertebrates
500+ Essential-to-Know Species
By Ronald L. Shimek, Ph.D.

POCKETEXPERT GUIDE
Reef Aquarium Fishes
500+ Essential-to-Know Species
By Scott W. Michael

Reef Fishes
A Guide to Their Identification, Behavior
& Captive Care
By Scott W. Michael

- Volume I:
  Moray Eels, Seahorses & Anthias
- Volume II:
  Basslets, Dottybacks & Hawkfishes
- Volume III:
  Angelfishes & Butterflyfishes
- Volume IV:
  Damselfishes & Anemonefishes
- Volume V: Wrasses & Parrotfishes
- Volume VI: Blennies & Dragonets
  (date TBA)
- Volume VII: Gobies & Dartfishes
  (date TBA)
- Volume VIII:
  Puffers, Triggers & Surgeonfishes
  (date TBA)
- **The Reef Fishes Encyclopedia**
  (date TBA)

MARY E. SWEENEY is the former editor of *Tropical Fish Hobbyist* magazine and a long-time book author and editor who worked for many years with the Axelrod family and T.F.H. Publications in Neptune City, New Jersey. She lives, writes, and keeps and breeds tropical fishes on the Jersey Shore with her husband and son.

MARY BAILEY has been keeping fishes for nearly 40 years. Cichlids are a particular passion, and she is known internationally as an expert on these fishes. She has previously co-authored six fishkeeping books and written innumerable articles for magazines in Europe and the USA. She is a member of the British Cichlid Association (since 1972), and has served in most of its committee posts, most recently as editor of its journal; she is also a member of the American Cichlid Association, the Catfish Study Group (UK), and the European Ichthyological Union. She lives and works in her 16th-century cottage in the wilds of Devon, UK, and enjoys horseriding, walking, and gardening.

AARON NORMAN is considered by many to be the dean of aquarium fish portrait photographers, having captured thousands of species images that exemplify natural settings, characteristic poses, accurate colors, and the behavioral traits of his subjects. As a lifelong ichthyophile, he is an inveterate tropical explorer. He lives and works in Manhattan.

Pterophyllum scalare, Black Lace Angelfish pair.